THE HOLY SEE
AND THE
EMERGENCE OF THE
MODERN
MIDDLE EAST

THE HOLY SEE AND THE EMERGENCE OF THE MODERN MIDDLE EAST

Benedict XV's Diplomacy in Greater Syria (1914–1922)

Agnes de Dreuzy

THE CATHOLIC UNIVERSITY OF AMERICA PRESS

Washington, D.C.

Library of Congress Cataloging-in-Publication Data

Names: Dreuzy, Agnes de, author.

Title: The Holy See and the emergence of the modern Middle East:
Benedict XV's diplomacy in Greater Syria (1914–1922) / Agnes de
Dreuzy. Description: Washington, D.C. : The Catholic University of
America Press, [2016] | Includes bibliographical references and index.
Identifiers: LCCN 2015039957 | ISBN 9780813228495 (cloth : alkaline
paper) Subjects: LCSH: Catholic Church—Foreign relations—Middle
East. | Middle East—Foreign relations—Catholic Church. | Church
and international organization—Catholic Church—History—
20th century. | World War, 1914–1918—Religious aspects—Catholic
Church. | World War, 1914–1918—Peace—History. | Benedict
XV, Pope, 1854–1922.Classification: LCC BX1617 .D74 2016 | DDC
327.456/34056—dc23 LC record available at
http://lccn.loc.gov/2015039957

In memory
of my grandmother
Augustine Beauvoir,
who witnessed
Benedict XV's pontificate
and suffered the horrors
of the Great War

CONTENTS

Acknowledgments, ix

Abbreviations, xi

Introduction:
Rethinking Benedict XV's Contribution
to International Relations, 1

PART 1. THE VATICAN AND CATHOLIC
INTERESTS IN PREWAR AND WARTIME
GREATER SYRIA, 1914–1917

1. Benedict XV, Pope of Peace, 15
2. Protection of Catholics in the Ottoman Empire, 37
3. Vatican Wartime Foreign Policy, 67
4. Protection of Catholic Clergy and Property, 107
5. Benedict XV's Humanitarian Assistance, 138

PART 2. POSTWAR PROTECTION OF CATHOLIC
INTERESTS, 1917–1922

6. The Holy See and the Postwar World Order, 167
7. The Holy See and Syria, 193
8. The Holy See and Palestine, 222

Conclusion, 259

Bibliography, 267
Index, 285

ACKNOWLEDGMENTS

I owe a particular debt of gratitude to Fr. Leo D. Lefebure, professor of theology and Matteo Ricci Chair at Georgetown University, without whom this book would have never been completed. In good health and bad, Fr. Lefebure has supported me as a friend and mentor who challenged me with his insights and encouraged me to always think further.

I am also very grateful to Fr. Joseph A. Komonchak, professor emeritus of the School of Theology and Religious Studies at the Catholic University of America, Fr. Mark Morozowich, SEOD, dean and associate professor of liturgical studies and sacramental theology in the School of Theology and Religious Studies at the Catholic University of America, Dr. Gretchen Reydams-Schils, professor and chair of the Program of Liberal Studies at Notre Dame University, and Dr. Donna Orsuto, professor at the Institute of Spirituality of the Pontifical Gregorian University in Rome. Without their unswerving guidance, care, and friendship, the completion of this book would have taken much longer. They remain trusted mentors, friends, and models of sound and demanding scholarship. I owe a special debt of gratitude to Donna Orsuto, who hosted me at the Lay Centre at Foyer Unitas in Rome, allowing me to write most of the manuscript in a heavenly environment.

This work was able to take shape by spending exciting weeks doing research in Rome in the Vatican Secret Archives, the archives of the Sacred Congregation "de Propaganda Fide," and those of the Congregation for Oriental Churches. I would like to thank especially Dr. Gianpaolo Rigotti for his patience with my broken Italian and his tremendous help in navigating through the Archives of the Congregation for the Oriental Churches.

I also would like to express my gratitude to Bishop Charles Morerod, OP, whose friendship, sharp wit, and kindness brightened my days in the Eternal City. While in Rome, it was also my privilege to meet with Fr. Carlo Pioppi, professor of church history at the Pontifical University of the Holy Cross, whose spiritual support was invaluable.

It is with great pleasure that I thank Trevor Lipscombe, director of the Catholic University of America Press, for his guidance and patience. Theresa Walker, managing editor at the CUA Press, and Aldene Fredenburg, my copy editor, also deserve my utmost gratitude.

"A friend is someone who knows the song in your heart and can sing it back to you when you have forgotten the words," wrote C. S. Lewis. During these years, I have been supported by Eugénie Cabot, Anne-Elisabeth Giuliani, Jill Kalinski, Ellen Kane, Solveig Loretz, Clare Wilde, and Fr. Thomas Longua. Without their kindness and huge sense of humor, the research and writing would have been far less enjoyable.

It is with great pride that I would like to thank my children, Olivia and Pierre, who as university students made very astute and refreshing comments on the manuscript. As for my husband, Philippe, he is my rock, a constant source of encouragement.

I dedicate this book to the late Jacques Gres-Gayer, who welcomed me with open arms when I arrived at the Catholic University of America and helped me discern my academic future. Rest in peace.

ABBREVIATIONS

ACCO	Archivio della Congregazione per le Chiese Orientali
AAS	*Acta Apostolicae Sedis*
AES	Affari Ecclesiastici Straordinari
AP, N.S	Archivio della S. Congregazione "de Propaganda Fide" Nuova Serie
Arch. Deleg.	Archivio Delegazioni Apostoliche
Arch. Nunz.	Archivio Nunziatura
ASS	*Acta Sanctae Sedis*
ASV	Archivio Segreto Vaticano (Vatican Secret Archives)
BEO	Babiâli Evrak Odas
BOA	Başbakanlik Osmanli Arşivleri, Stanbul
CRFJ	Centre de Recherche Français de Jérusalem
DH.EUM	Dahiliye Nezareti, Emniyet-I Umumiye Müdürlügü
FO	Foreign Office (G.B)
HHStA	Haus-, Hof-, und Staatsarchiv
HR.SYS	Hariciye Nezareti, Muhaberat-i
POI	Pontifical Oriental Institute
KCB	Knight Commander (Order of Bath)
KCMG	Knight Commander (Order of St. Michael and St. George)
NASB	New American Standard Bible
PA-AA	Politisches Archiv des Auswärtiges Amt (Federal Foreign Office)
PRO CAB	Public Record Office—Cabinet Papers
Segr. Stato	Segretaria di Stato

THE HOLY SEE
AND THE
EMERGENCE OF THE
MODERN
MIDDLE EAST

INTRODUCTION

Rethinking Benedict XV's Contribution to International Relations

If the successor of Gregory and Innocent is not to-day the
monarch of monarchs, the dispenser of crowns, the distrib-
utor of continents and oceans, he still personifies the great-
est moral force of the world.... If he is not a sovereign, for
lack of territory, he is still treated as a sovereign.... How-
ever, he does not have to make war.

—Alphonse Rivier, *Principes du droit des gens*

Had Pope Benedict XV read these lines, written in 1896 by the famed French professor of international law Alphonse Rivier, he would have approved. Indeed, the successor of Peter "does not have to make war" but may become involved in it as the church endures its hardships.[1]

Pope Benedict XV, elected to the throne of Peter on September 3, 1914, one month after the start of the First World War, was not the first pontiff to weather a war.[2] But this conflict was different. It was a total war that involved the world's great powers

---

1. Rivier, *Principes du droit des gens* (Paris: Arthur Rousseau, 1896), 1:120 (my trans).

2. After the assassination of Archduke Francis Ferdinand of Austria at Sarajevo on June 28, 1914, by Bosnian Serb nationalist Gavrilo Princip, Austria declared war on Serbia. European diplomacy failed to avert a generalized armed conflict that eventually engulfed most of Europe and saw the involvement of the Ottoman Empire, the United States, and Japan. World War I pitted the Central Powers (Germany, Austria-Hungary, the Ottoman Empire, and Bulgaria) against the Entente Powers (essentially Great Britain, France, Russia, Italy, and the United States). After four years of a "tragic and unnecessary conflict," Germany signed an armistice on November 11, 1918, ending military hostilities; John Keegan, *The First World War* (New York: Knopf, 1999), 3.

and empires.[3] It was fought on European and Ottoman soils as two different wars. One was a war of daily suffering for soldiers in the field and civilian populations under occupation, while the other was played in war cabinets where the future of empires and nations was settled.[4]

Although deprived from his de facto temporal sovereignty after the loss of the Papal States in 1870, Pope Benedict was actively involved at both levels, as two-thirds of the Catholics worldwide were directly affected by the war: 64 million living in Germany, Austria, and the other countries allied to them and 124 million on the Entente side.[5] The pontiff witnessed the sacrifice of a whole generation. He offered his personal wealth, sparing no energy to bring relief to the wounded soldiers fighting in the trenches as well as to the civilians suffering cruelties and deprivation. He also met with presidents, ministers, and ambassadors to ensure the protection of Catholic rights and interests in Europe and in the crumbling Ottoman Empire.

The Great War was to end all wars.[6] In the words of the historian David Fromkin, the Treaty of Versailles was akin to "A Peace to End All Peace."[7] In Europe, the Second World War with its cortege of atrocities was a direct outcome of the Great War. In the new emerging Middle East carved out of the vanquished Ottoman Empire, decisions were made whose consequences still

3. Total war implies "the breakdown of the distinction between organized combat and the societies, economies, and political systems that support it"; Roger Chickering and Stig Förster, eds., *The Shadows of Total War: Europe, East Asia, and the United States, 1919–1939* (Cambridge: Cambridge University Press; London: German Historical Institute, 2003), 3.

4. Martin Gilbert, *The First World War* (New York: Henry Holt, 1994), xv.

5. Hubert Jedin, *History of the Church*, vol. 10, *The Church in the Modern Age*, ed. Hubert Jedin, Konrad Repgen, and John Dolan (New York: Crossroad, 1981), 35.

6. The following terms are synonyms and will be used interchangeably: First World War, World War I (WWI), and the Great War.

7. David Fromkin, *A Peace to End All Peace* (New York: Henry Holt, 1989). The Treaty of Versailles, signed on June 28, 1919, by the Entente Powers and Germany, was a peace settlement imposing harsh terms and burdensome reparation payments on the defeated Germans.

hover over today's world politics. The opening of hostilities in August 1914 and the victory of the Entente Powers accelerated the disintegration of the "sick man of Europe."[8] Its alliance with Germany made it easy prey for partition among the victorious powers eager to reinforce their presence in this most strategic part of the world.

Benedict XV's pontificate coincides exactly with the reshaping of the Middle East from the beginning of the world conflict in August 1914 to the assignment of mandates in 1922 to France and Britain over Syria and Palestine. As John Pollard has demonstrated in his classic work *The Unknown Pope*, the pontiff and his reign have been unappreciated and largely overlooked, "fading into almost complete obscurity."[9] Carrying further the reappraisal of Pope Benedict's pontificate that Pollard started, this book seeks to explore whether the pontiff's leadership, often dismissed, was actually that of a geopolitical master well ahead of his time. Two tangible facts triggered this inquiry.

From an international perspective, one can notice "the rush of civil governments to the Vatican since the war."[10] In 1914, a dozen states were represented at the Vatican, with five nuncios and two internuncios abroad, while in 1921 twenty-five states had established ties with the Vatican and twenty-four nuncios and internuncios had been sent abroad. The demise of the Austro-Hungarian and the Ottoman Empires, which gave birth to new independent states, only partially explains this stunning increase. As described by a contemporary journalist, "the increase was in quantity as much as in quality. Governments formerly without relationships have established them. Governments which had

8. On the eve of the First World War, the Ottoman Empire was commonly referred to as the "sick man of Europe" because of the financial and territorial difficulties it was facing.

9. John F. Pollard, *The Unknown Pope: Benedict XV (1914–1922) and the Pursuit of Peace* (London: Geoffrey Chapman, 1999), xiii.

10. "The Procession to the Vatican," *Literary Digest*, Oct. 29, 1921, 30.

broken off relations have reestablished them and governments which had secondary relations have raised them to first-class."[11]

From a regional perspective, this study also recognizes the significance of the special tribute paid by Turkish Muslim, Jewish, and Christian rulers and notables to Benedict XV's reign. His love and respect for the Orient was acknowledged in their funding of a bronze statue of the pontiff that stands in the courtyard of the Cathedral of the Holy Spirit in Istanbul,[12] honoring him with the following words: "To the great pope of the world's tragic hour, Benedict XV, benefactor of the people, without discrimination of nationality or religion, a token of gratitude from the Orient, 1914–1919."[13] The closing sentence of an article published by the *New York Times* announcing the pontiff's death reinforces this observation. The author mentioned the arrival of two Franciscan friars from Constantinople, "bringing sacred images as tokens of the homage of the Catholics of the Orient. They had been a long time on the way, regarded their mission as compelling and were admitted to the Vatican."[14]

From this research, Benedict XV emerges as a statesman who anticipated the geopolitical revolution that would take place in the wake of the Great War and discerned the first tremors that precipitated the decolonization movement. His policy toward the crumbling Ottoman Empire and the newly emerging Middle East illustrates the depth and breadth of his vision and his shrewdness in choosing priorities. The pontiff designed a foreign policy tailored to answer the political trauma and the new

---

11. Ibid.

12. Constantinople became known as Istanbul (or Stamboul) after the city fell into Ottoman hands in 1453. In Europe, both names were used interchangeably until the creation of the Republic of Turkey in 1923, when Istanbul became the official name. This book covers the period preceding the birth of Turkey, and the primary sources (letters, newspapers, and journal articles) used in this study always mention Constantinople. Therefore, I will use the same terminology.

13. Rapporto, esemplare della lista di sottoscrizione, AP, N.S., vol. 658 (1920), rub. 126.

14. "Body of Pope Benedict XV Lies in State," *New York Times*, Jan. 23, 1922.

developments that had taken place in Europe and the Middle East. The abrogation of the French Catholic protectorate in the Ottoman Empire, the fall of the Russian Empire, the weakening of the Greek Orthodox churches, the increased sense of Muslim solidarity against the Christian population, the development of Zionists' ambitions, the British-Arab complicity, and the interest of Protestant America in the region were all new challenges to be faced as the Middle East was partitioned into different zones.

The original foundation of Benedict XV's Middle Eastern diplomacy resides in the combination of two approaches. The pontiff's main priority, in continuity with his predecessors, was to implement a diplomacy that not only ensured the protection of Catholic interests and the survival of Christians in the Middle East but also provided them with a dynamic ecclesiological structure. Pope Benedict completed and institutionalized the traditional ecclesiological approach in favor of unionism with the goal of strengthening the ecclesial structures of the Eastern Catholic churches and giving them a solid underpinning in the international legal sphere.[15] This ecclesiological approach was integrated in the pope's global geopolitical vision, which sought to emancipate the Catholic Church from the bondage of the European powers and prepare it for a new and prominent role in the world order that emerged following the end of the First World War.

The core of this book rests upon the evaluation of documents found in the Vatican Secret Archives (ASV), the Archives of the Congregation for the Oriental Churches (ACCO), and those of the Sacred Congregation for the Propagation of the Faith (AP, N.S.),[16] located in Rome, Italy. Its scope is limited to Greater Syria, the area also called geographical Syria, which encompassed

15. The traditional unionist ecclesiology was understood as a return of the separated brethren to the Catholic fold.

16. The Sacred Congregation for the Propagation of the Faith, commonly referred to as Propaganda Fide, was renamed in 1967 and is today known as the Congregation for the Evangelization of Peoples.

Palestine, Syria, and Lebanon. The work is divided chronologically into two parts: part 1 covers the period from the outbreak of war until British troops captured Jerusalem from the Ottomans (September 1914–December 1917); part 2 covers the postwar premandate era (December 1917–January 1922), closing with the untimely death of the pontiff on January 22, 1922.

Part 1 covers the different aspects of Benedict XV's wartime Eastern diplomacy in his protection of Catholic communities, his effort to arrange a positive environment for the rapprochement with the separated brethren, and his praised humanitarian assistance to all without discrimination of nationality or religion. An introduction depicts Giacomo Della Chiesa's background. It outlines the pope's policy and priorities in Europe, the main theatre of war, and provides the context within which the pontiff's Middle Eastern diplomacy unfolded. Dubbed the "Pope of Peace," Benedict XV crafted a foreign policy marked by its universality and peacemaking efforts, pursuing his own brand of realpolitik (chapter 1).

An overview of the historical and diplomatic background is necessary to understand the context in which Benedict's Eastern diplomacy unfolded. Chapter 2 explores the environment and conditions in which the Eastern and Latin Catholic communities existed in the Ottoman Empire, assessing their religious and legal status before the entry of the Porte into the war against France, Great Britain, and Russia on November 5, 1914.[17] The role granted to France was unique and must be emphasized, as it developed through the system of capitulations and the French Catholic protectorate over the Eastern and Latin Catholics in the empire. Along with the French protectorate, the competition of the unofficial Russian protectorate of the Orthodox churches deserves attention, as it affected both France and the Holy See

17. The Sublime Porte (or the Porte) is another name referring to the Ottoman government.

in their diplomatic endeavors with Constantinople. The unilateral abrogation of the capitulations by the Ottoman government on September 9, 1914, was received with shock by the European powers. It had multifold implications regarding the maintenance of the French protectorate in the Ottoman Empire and more particularly in the Holy Land. Only in this context can the originality of Benedict XV's foreign policy be fully appreciated (chapter 3). It resides in his integration of classic diplomatic functions of negotiation with an ecclesiastical policy that reflects the pontiff's Eastern ecclesiology. Benedict's foreign policy, which demanded high-level statesmanship, was meant to serve his unionist ecclesiology and ensure the protection of Catholic interests. At the geopolitical level, the pontiff crafted a diplomacy that answered a new situation, as the French protectorate had become ineffectual and the Ottoman government was pressuring the Holy See to establish direct diplomatic ties. Pope Benedict chose a strategy of patient observation, motivated by the uncertainty of the situation on the military front and the determination to avoid future confrontation with France. At the ecclesiological level, Benedict XV completed and institutionalized the traditional approach in favor of unionism previously implemented by Leo XIII, providing a theoretical and practical underpinning to his Eastern foreign policy.

While Pope Benedict was crafting his foreign policy in Rome, regional diplomacy in Greater Syria was handled by Msgr. Angelo Dolci, the apostolic delegate in Constantinople, and Msgr. Frediano Giannini, OFM, the apostolic delegate in Syria (chapter 4). Their daily struggle to prevent the confiscation of Catholic property and the persecution of Catholic clergy by the Ottoman government is well documented in the Vatican Secret Archives and the archives at Propaganda Fide. The daily correspondence between Rome and the apostolic delegates is arranged and safeguarded in the Roman archives and sheds light on the novel situation facing the Holy See. The discontinuation of the French protectorate and its consequences for the diplomatic Ottoman chessboard provided opportunities for the pontiff to engage in a direct dialogue with the Porte.

The protection of Catholic clergy and property went hand in hand with large-scale humanitarian assistance to the destitute population of Syria and Palestine, without racial or religious discrimination (chapter 5). Despite ample evidence that the Holy See's humanitarian endeavors were especially appreciated in the Ottoman Empire, the relief provided by the Vatican was rarely mentioned in the Western press and literature. This state of affairs was mostly the consequence of American Protestant competition and an attempt to control the philanthropic arena in the Ottoman Empire, a situation that eventually led to accusations of discrimination against the Catholic populations. This situation changed with the entry of the United States into the war in April 1917 on the side of the Entente Powers and the eviction of American citizens from Ottoman soil.

Part 2 begins after the capture of Jerusalem by British general Edmund Allenby in December 1917. With the subsequent assignment of mandates for Syria and Palestine to France and Britain, respectively, in July 1922, the Middle East entered a new era. During this period, shortened by the unexpected death of the pontiff on January 22, 1922, Pope Benedict had laid down the principles upon which the postwar pontifical foreign policy would be based. His regional diplomacy in Syria and Palestine are case studies that mirror his foreign policy worldwide.

Three principles underpinned Pope Benedict's vision of the new world order (chapter 6). The pontiff, who had acquired a new moral authority and political prestige with the close of the war, initiated a policy that shifted away from its past Eurocentric vision of the world. This approach was combined with an anticipation of the decolonization era and self-determination of national minorities. Pope Benedict completed these guiding principles with a policy of emancipation of the missionary world from colonial powers, preparing the Catholic Church for an active and independent role in the postwar world.

These principles were the crux of Benedict XV's diplomacy in the short period that preceded the official assignment of the French and British mandates on Syria and Palestine.

In Syria and Greater Lebanon (chapter 7), the pontiff navigated between the pressure of French imperialism and Prince Faisal's Arab nationalism. Two significant studies published in 2004 and 2006 by the French historian Gérard Khoury serve as main sources of information. One is a compilation of letters and official reports written by Robert de Caix with additional comments from Khoury.[18] The other study compares the political visions of Robert de Caix and Louis Massignon.[19] Both men were highly influential in crafting the new French foreign policy in Syria and Lebanon. Pope Benedict's guiding principles in forging his diplomacy in Syria were attuned to Massignon's global vision of the Arab world, a vision that resented nationalist tendencies. Massignon, like Pope Benedict, was thinking in the long term and emphasized the interdependence between the spiritual and political worlds. This approach was opposed by Robert de Caix, who was a forceful advocate of the establishment of a French mandate as a colonial device. Most members of the higher clergy supported de Caix's vision, as they were anxious to ensure immediate protection of Catholic minorities living in a Muslim world plunged into turmoil.

In Palestine (chapter 8), the political context was dominated

18. Gérard Khoury, *Une tutelle coloniale: Le mandat français en Syrie et au Liban; Écrits politiques de Robert de Caix* (Paris: Belin, 2006).

19. Gérard Khoury, "Robert de Caix et Louis Massignon: Deux visions de la politique française au Levant en 1920," in *The British and French Mandates in Comparative Perspectives: Les mandats français et anglais dans une perspective comparative,* ed. Nadine Méouchy and Peter Sluglett, 165–84 (Leiden: Brill, 2004).

by the tension between Britain and France regarding the continuation of the French protectorate over the Holy Places, the implementation of a Jewish national homeland, and the aggressive proselytizing of the Protestant missions. The foundational question revolved around the control of Palestine by the British and how they would satisfy the Holy See's claims over the Holy Places. Pope Benedict, to the dismay of many Catholic officials, endorsed the British mandate willingly, as it represented a unique opportunity for the Holy See to gain its emancipation from France in this region of the world. British rule meant the advance of the Zionist and Protestant causes in Palestine. This was well understood by the pontiff. In contrast with Sergio Minerbi's conclusion in *The Vatican and Zionism* that Benedict XV's pontificate maintained an anti-Zionist stance,[20] this study contends that thorough analysis of archival documents, if situated in a long-term geopolitical context, supports the thesis that Benedict's policy was sympathetic to Zionist ambitions, hence breaking with his predecessors.

The Protestant threat was also well evaluated by Benedict XV, as the solution to confront this danger had been at the core of Pope Benedict's pontificate from the first day. In order to survive and thrive as minorities, the Latin and Eastern Catholics, already strengthened by the ecclesial structure provided by the Congregation for the Oriental Church[21] and the guidance offered by Pope Benedict in his encyclical on missions, *Maximum Illud*,[22] needed to present a common front, therefore reestablishing harmony among Catholics.

Benedict XV reigned during the decade that witnessed the emergence of the new Middle East and brought the long nine-

---

20. Sergio I. Minerbi, *The Vatican and Zionism: Conflict in the Holy Land, 1895–1925* (Oxford: Oxford University Press, 1990).

21. Benedict XV, "Motu Proprio *Dei Providentis* [May 1, 1917]," *AAS* 9 I (1917): 529–31.

22. Benedict XV, "Apostolic Letter *Maximum Illud* [Nov. 30, 1919]," *AAS* 11 (1919): 440–55.

teenth century to a close. The pontiff responded to new stakes with new perspectives and equipped the church for its future, following a twofold goal. One was to ensure the immediate and long-term protection of Eastern Catholics in the Middle East by strengthening their ecclesial structure and preparing the church for an expected rapprochement with the Orthodox churches. Benedict's second ambition was universal, as he foresaw the major geopolitical shifts of the mid-twentieth century and how they would affect the universal church. He freed it from the shackles of imperialism and restored the prestige and moral authority of the papacy, hence guaranteeing its independence in the new emerging world order.

Benedict XV's pontificate inspired his successors in their discernment of the role of the church in the modern world. The pontiff embraced the new democratic nation-states that issued from the collapse of the Austro-Hungarian, Russian, and Ottoman Empires, initiating the development of a new dynamic toward democratic nations. The internationalization of the church, supported by the signing of numerous concordats, was pushed forward under Benedict's successor, Pius XI, who developed most of Benedict's initiatives.

Fifty years after his election, Pope Benedict's vision of the role of the church in the modern world was vindicated. Two documents are foundational in this matter. One is Pope John XXIII's last encyclical, *Pacem in Terris*, which set human rights as a major factor in international diplomacy.[23] The second document is the Pastoral Constitution *Gaudium et Spes*, on the church in the modern world, promulgated by Pope Paul VI in December 1965 during the fourth and last session of the Second Vatican Council.[24]

---

23. John XXIII, "Encyclical *Pacem in Terris* [Apr. 11, 1963]," *AAS* 55 (1963): 257–304.

24. Second Vatican Council, "Constitutio pastoralis de Ecclesia in mundo huius tempris" [Pastoral Constitution on the Church in the Modern World] (*Gaudium et Spes*) [Dec. 7, 1965]," *AAS* 58 (1966): 1025–1120.

It must be read and interpreted under the light of *Pacem in Terris*. The church must reflect its new globalized identity in its governance. This has to be done through its missionaries and must be founded on the equality of all peoples,[25] a theme central to Benedict XV's understanding of the dialogue between the church and the modern world.

25. Francesca Aran Murphy, "Globalization from Benedict XV to Benedict XVI: The 'Astonishing Optimism' of *Gaudium Spes* in a Missionary Context," *Nova et Vetera*, English edition 8, no. 2 (Spring 2010): 395–424.

1

THE VATICAN AND CATHOLIC INTERESTS IN PREWAR AND WARTIME GREATER SYRIA, 1914-1917

1

BENEDICT XV, POPE

OF PEACE

On January 22, 1922, the Catholic world entered into mourning. Pope Benedict XV had passed away in the early morning, after falling ill with pneumonia. The *New York Times* immediately noticed that "for the first time in the history of relations between the Italian government and the Vatican the Italian government ordered that the flags be half-masted on all government offices in honor of the death of the pontiff."[1] It was an unprecedented sign of the respect and prestige enjoyed by the pontiff and his function in the years following the close of the Great War.

Yet Benedict's short reign of seven years, four months, and nineteen days, although manifesting "his roving intelligence [and] his vivid penetration,"[2] failed to impress his contemporaries and observers of Vatican politics. Laboring under the hardships of World War I, he was dubbed the "Pope of Peace," a pope with idealistic views and unrealistic expectations. The harsh judgment his person and his reign patiently endured during his lifetime compels a rereading of his pontificate with the retrospect of history under the light of information gathered from Roman archives, sources unavailable to his early detrac-

1. "Body of Pope Benedict Lies in State," *New York Times*, Jan. 23, 1922.
2. Anne O'Hare McCormick, *Vatican Journal, 1921–1954* (New York: Farrar, Straus, and Cudahy, 1957), 19.

tors. Benedict XV eventually emerges as a gifted statesman pursuing his own brand of realpolitik.

THE ROAD TO THE CHAIR OF PETER

In November 1917, in a confidential memorandum to the London Foreign Office, J. D. Gregory, secretary at the British mission to the Holy See, described Pope Benedict XV as "a very decided mediocrity" with "the mentality of a little official, the inexperience of a parochial Italian who has hardly traveled at all, and a tortuous method of conducting affairs that arises from years of office work connected with a fifth-rate diplomacy."[3] Francis MacNutt, papal chamberlain under Pius X, more charitable in his verdict, recognized that Benedict XV was "esteemed a great diplomat" but added that he impressed him more "as a meticulous, accomplished bureaucrat; a conscientious, painstaking understudy of Cardinal Rampolla, under whom he had served some sixteen years, and whom he honoured and venerated."[4]

Giacomo Giambattista Della Chiesa was well equipped for the diplomatic service of the Holy See. Born on November 21, 1854, to a noble Genoese family, he was ordained a priest in 1878, graduated doctor of theology cum laude in 1879, and received a doctorate in canon law in 1880. He became a student at the Academy of Noble Ecclesiastics, the school training future Vatican diplomats, where he met Msgr. Mariano Rampolla del Tindaro in 1881, an encounter that shaped his future and interest in Oriental matters.[5] The latter was won over by Della Chiesa's diligence, his logical and insightful mind, and his power of objec-

3. J. D. Gregory to the London Foreign Office, FO/371/3086, Confidential Memorandum, Nov. 30, 1917, quoted in *Great Britain Legation: Anglo-Vatican Relations, 1914–1939; Confidential Annual Reports of the British Ministers to the Holy See, London, England*, ed. Thomas E. Hachey (Boston: G. K. Hall, 1972), xx.

4. Francis Augustus MacNutt, *A Papal Chamberlain: The Personal Chronicle of Francis Augustus MacNutt* (London: Longmans, 1936), 312.

5. Mariano Rampolla (1843–1913) became secretary of the Sacred Congregation of the Propagation of the Faith for Matters of Oriental Rite in 1877.

tive analysis, a critical skill in diplomatic matters. Della Chiesa's first significant assignment, at the age of twenty-nine, was to the nunciature of Madrid, Spain. He was appointed secretary to the new nuncio, his mentor Rampolla, under whom he served from 1883 to 1887. When in 1887 Pope Leo XIII called Rampolla to be his secretary of state, the newly appointed cardinal named Della Chiesa his secretary, then his *sostituto* in 1901.[6] On the retirement of his long-time friend, following the election in 1903 of Pius X, Della Chiesa continued to hold office at the Curia under the new secretary of state, Rafael Cardinal Merry del Val, before being "exiled" to the see of Bologna in 1907.[7] This move was interpreted as a covert dismissal of a prelate whose views did not align with those of the new pontiff and his secretary of state. Pius X named Della Chiesa cardinal in May 1914, barely three months before he entered the conclave to elect the pope who was to succeed Pius, who breathed his last on August 20, 1914.

The conclave met at an inauspicious time—from August 31 to September 3, 1914—a month after the opening of hostilities. The odds of succeeding Pius X did not seem to favor Giacomo Della Chiesa. Many were puzzled by his election, as he was not known outside "his Bolognese exile."[8] His first biographer, Walter Peters, recounts that American cardinal Gibbons, archbishop of Baltimore, "when told that Della Chiesa was the new pope, innocently asked...'Who's he?'"[9]

The newly elected pope was viewed as the Rampolla candidate with diplomatic views in line with those of his patron. Mariano Cardinal Rampolla, a Sicilian aristocrat, had been Leo XIII's brilliant secretary of state. His pro-French positions and

6. After the secretary of state, the *sostituto*—or papal undersecretary of state—is usually the most influential official at the Curia.

7. Bologna was the fourth-largest diocese in Italy.

8. John F. Pollard, *The Unknown Pope: Benedict XV (1914–1922) and the Pursuit of Peace* (London: Geoffrey Chapman, 1999), xiii.

9. Walter H. Peters, *The Life of Benedict XV* (Milwaukee, Wisc.: Bruce, 1959), 75.

his alleged Russian sympathies had cost him the throne of Peter in the conclave of 1903. The election of Rampolla, who had received the most votes in the first rounds, was vetoed by Emperor Franz Josef of Austria-Hungary. Jan Cardinal Puzina of Krakow, exercising for the very last time this ancient privilege on behalf of the emperor, sanctioned Rampolla's pro-French positions, which offended the Central Empires and his presumed Russian sympathies, which were greatly despised by the Polish Church.

According to John Pollard, the most recent biographer of Benedict XV, Cardinal Piffl, the archbishop of Vienna, affirmed in his diary that the five Austro-Hungarian cardinals supported Della Chiesa despite their government's objections.[10] They were not convinced by the objections of Cardinal Hartmann of Cologne, who claimed that electing Della Chiesa would be an insult to the memory of Pius X.[11] On the tenth ballot of the third day, Giacomo Della Chiesa was elected 258th successor of Peter.

Although the political situation had suffered a dramatic turn since Leo XIII's pontificate (1878–1903), Della Chiesa's election was immediately understood as a return to the policies of Pope Leo and those of his secretary of state, Cardinal Rampolla. He assumed the name of Benedict in honor of Prospero Lambertini (Benedict XIV), the pope who had been archbishop of Bologna until his elevation to the throne of Peter in 1740, and as a special devotion to St. Benedict of Nursia, patron saint of Europe.

Benedict appointed Pietro Cardinal Gasparri as his secretary of state, succeeding Cardinal Ferrata, who had died unexpectedly on October 10, 1914. Pietro Gasparri, nicknamed *il contadino*,[12] was recognized for his intelligence, his sense of humor, and his diplomatic ability.[13] After almost twenty years spent as professor of canon law at the Institut Catholique in Paris and apostolic

---

10. Pollard, *Unknown Pope*, 64.   11. Ibid., 60.

12. Italian word meaning "the farmer."

13. Alec Randall, *Vatican Assignment* (London: Heinemann, 1956), 61.

delegate in South America, Gasparri was called back to Rome by Pius X in 1904 to lead the project of a new code of canon law. He was made a cardinal in 1907.

In his diary, Baron Carlo Monti, Della Chiesa's childhood friend and director of the office for administrating ecclesial funds in the Italian government, asserts that the pontiff was sole architect of the Holy See's foreign policy. The reason, first and foremost, is that Cardinal Gasparri was absorbed in the compilation of the code of canon law until its promulgation on the Feast of Pentecost in 1917.[14] In addition, although Gasparri was a great mind—sometimes compared to the gifted secretary of state of Pius VII (1800–1823), Ercole Consalvi—he lacked the sophistication and diplomatic tact appropriate for the task.[15] Count de Salis, in a report on the British mission to the Holy See, corroborated Monti's depiction of Gasparri, describing him as "careless in dress and impatient of formalism."[16] Rennell Rodd, British ambassador to the Italian court, predicted that Gasparri would be an "active assistant" rather than a "counselor or guide" in foreign affairs, since Pope Benedict had solid diplomatic skills inherited from the school of Leo XIII and Cardinal Rampolla.[17] Peters makes the interesting point that Benedict XV's choice of Gasparri as secretary of state broke a long tradition, since the latter "had never attended the Academy of Noble Ecclesiastics.... It was unthinkable [he wrote] that one should rise to the highest office in the specialized field of Vatican diplomacy without the training of that school,"[18] especially in wartime.

14. Corresponds to May 27, 1917.

15. Antonio Scotta, La conciliazione ufficiosa: Diario del barone Carlo Monti "incarito d'affari" del governo italiano presso la Santa Sede (1914–1922) (Città del Vaticano: Libreria Editrice Vaticana, 1997), 1:45.

16. Hachey, ed., Great Britain Legation, 15.

17. Rodd to Grey, disp. 355, Sept. 6, 1914, FO/371/2006, quoted in William A. Renzi, "The Entente and the Vatican during the Period of Italian Neutrality, August 1914–May 1915," Historical Journal 13 (Sept. 1970): 491.

18. W. H. Peters, Life of Benedict XV, 90.

19

BENEDICT XV, THE UNIVERSAL POPE

It was the fate of this "little man, awkward, tired, sallow, one shoulder slightly higher than the other, with no eloquence, no radiance, no personal charm,"[19] to bear the heavy burden of laboring during a war he repeatedly called "the suicide of civilized Europe."[20] Although Pope Benedict did not have physical attributes that stir people, expectations ran high after his election. His young age—he was only sixty years old—and his training in the realm of ecclesiastical diplomacy were significant assets in wartime. A skilled politician and a moral leader, he was expected to be an active player on the war scene, taking sides and judging governments in the name of the long-accepted just-war theory.[21]

He was indeed an active participant, but as a transnational actor whose sovereignty transcends legal frontiers.[22] In a world driven by hatred of neighbors, he sought peace for all through reconciliation, knowing well that he was sacrificing moral prestige for the sake of evangelical and charitable considerations, laboring for peace against powerful nationalistic forces. On August 24, 1918, a few months before the guns fell silent, the *Journal*

19. McCormick, *Vatican Journal*, 17.

20. Benedict XV, "Lenten Letter to Cardinal-Vicar Pompilj, *Al Tremendo Conflitto* [Mar. 4, 1916]," *AAS* 8 (1916): 59.

21. The just-war doctrine was first articulated by St. Ambrose and later developed by St. Augustine and St. Thomas Aquinas. According to this theory, all governments are obliged to avoid war. However, in some specific circumstances, it is the right and duty of leaders to wage war in order to obtain justice. The act must be morally justifiable. It must be a last resort, be done with the right intention, and be proportional to the offense.

22. Ivan Vallier, "The Roman Catholic Church: A Transnational Actor," in *Transnational Relations*, ed. Robert O. Keohane and Joseph S. Nye, 129–52 (Cambridge, Mass.: Harvard University Press, 1972). In a famous essay written in 1970, Vallier defined the role of the Catholic Church as a transnational actor. A few years later, J. Bryan Hehir also described the Holy See as a transnational actor, based in one place but whose presence is felt in several states. It "possesses a trained corps of personnel, a single guiding philosophy, and a sophisticated communications system"; Hehir, "The Catholic Church and the Middle East, Policy and Diplomacy," in *The Vatican, Islam, and the Middle East*, ed. Kail C. Ellis, 109–24 (Syracuse, N.Y.: Syracuse University Press, 1987), 110.

de Genève encapsulated in a few sentences the crux of the situation facing Benedict XV's pontificate.

In summary, to assess in fairness the policy of the Holy See, one must comprehend its underlying motives. Powerless to be...the supreme judge and the arbitrator of humanity—that his most ferocious adversaries, the anti-clericals, accuse him not to be—the pontiff became everywhere the protector of Catholic communities. Once the retrospect of history enables us to appreciate all of the complexities of this war, it is likely that our descendants will be less severe towards Benedict XV.[23]

Pope Benedict did not take side during the conflict. He was vilified for this choice by both sides and by governments, lay people, and clergymen alike. He was accused of concealing his true leanings. The Entente suspected pro-German tendencies, while the Central Powers called him the *Französische Papst*. The protestations of Count de Salis, the British minister to the Holy See, that Benedict was "genuinely neutral,"[24] and those of de Salis's secretary, J. D. Gregory, who was "convinced that he [was] not either temperamentally or politically pro-German,"[25] did not prevail. The British government was certain that the Holy See favored the Central Powers. Lord Cecil, the British undersecretary of state for foreign affairs, remarked that "the moral failure of the papacy in this crisis is a blow to all forms of Christianity."[26]

In the universal church there were many who expressed their disappointment at the pontiff. The future French cardinal Bau-

23. "En résumé, pour apprécier avec équité la politique du Saint-Siège, il faut en comprendre la raison profonde. Ne pouvant aspirer, en plein vingtième siècle, à être le juge suprême et l'arbitre de l'humanité—que ses adversaires les plus résolus, les anticléricaux, lui reprochent...de ne pas être—le Pape s'est fait partout le protecteur des catholiques, individus et collectivités. Lorsque le recul de l'histoire permettra d'apprécier toutes les complexités infinies de cette guerre, il est probable que nos descendants seront moins sévères pour Benoît XV"; Hachey, ed., *Great Britain Legation*, 6 (my translation).

24. V. H. Rothwell, *British War Aims and Peace Diplomacy, 1914–1918* (Oxford: Clarendon Press, 1971), 103.

25. Hachey, ed., *Great Britain Legation*, xx.

26. Minutes on a letter from Roderick Jones to Lord Cecil, Feb. 26, 1917, Lloyd George MSS.F/62/3/3, quoted in Rothwell, *British War Aims*, 103.

21

drillart was representative of the prevalent mood, complaining about Benedict's lack of courage. He warned him that being gentle was not an option in wartime and would have a most negative consequence with the transfer of moral authority and prestige to the still-neutral Protestant president of the United States.[27] Baudrillart begged the pontiff to promulgate "a simple encyclical on Christian laws of war [that] would be a relief for conscience."[28]

Courage the pontiff did not lack: courage to stay firm throughout the storm raging against his impartial position. With time, Baudrillart softened his stance, recognizing Benedict XV's obligation to protect Catholics on both sides of the war, but like most of his contemporaries he regretted the pontiff's lack of charisma. In a letter to his friend Father Vogt, sent after his meeting with Gasparri and Pope Benedict on September 10, 1915, Baudrillart wrote:

The pope is not a *Boche déguisé*; he believes in the final victory of Germany....He is convinced that the duration of the war will worsen the Allies' situation. This consideration, the fear of a revolution in Italy, and a profound sentiment of humanity that makes war atrocities despicable to him, explain his attitude. Unfortunately, neither he, nor his secretary of state has the *grande manière* to say or make things known.[29]

Could the pope's stance have been different? Would Leo XIII (1878–1903) or Pius X (1903–14) have followed a different policy? These were persistent questions pondered during and after Benedict XV's pontificate. Both popes would likely have acted differ-

---

27. Alfred Baudrillart, *Les carnets du Cardinal Baudrillart, 1er août 1914–31 décembre 1918* (Paris: Editions du Cerf, 1994), 86.

28. Baudrillart, *Carnets*, 112 (my translation).

29. "Le pape n'est pas un *Boche déguisé*; il croit à la victoire finale de l'Allemagne....Il est persuadé que la durée de la guerre aggravera la situation des Alliés. Cette considération, la crainte de la révolution en Italie, et un très profond sentiment d'humanité qui lui rend odieuses les atrocités de la guerre, expliquent toute son attitude. Malheureusement, ni lui, ni son Secrétaire d'État n'ont la *grande manière* pour dire ou pour faire entendre les choses"; Baudrillart, *Carnets*, 258 (my translation).

ently, if for only one reason: their widely different characters. Leo XIII, with his well-known Francophile tendencies, would almost certainly have condemned the Central Powers for leaving their Catholic populations in a perilous situation. As for Pius X, he may have been tempted to side with the Catholic Austrian Empire.[30]

"The prudent but not inactive silence of Benedict XV"[31] and his impartial stance were the most effective position to adopt. To side with one or the other party would have put the Holy See in a dangerous quandary and would have denied the pope the opportunity to offer widespread relief through humanitarian assistance. The pontiff chose silence and faced without budging the accusations of moral bankruptcy of the papacy. He foresaw that a temporary loss of prestige was the price to pay to protect the integrity of the church and its relationship with the world. Benedict XV was a man ahead of his time, laboring relentlessly against the current. Beyond the practical constraints bearing on his wartime diplomacy, his line of policy in foreign affairs was guided by two main postulates. He had a modern sense of the role of the church in the world, a world in which the church had lost its temporal power. He had the sense of a church not above the world but actively guiding it through the "precept of mutual charity."[32] He understood the transnationality of the institution as a means to reach beyond all borders and devise peace for all for the sake of Christian unity. The foundation of this universal role was found in the Gospel, stressing charity over justice. As Vicar of Christ, the pontiff believed that the universal church's greatest duty was to promote a spirit of unity, love, and concord.

---

30. George F. La Piana, "From Leo XIII to Benedict XV," *American Journal of Theology* 21 (Apr. 1917): 188.

31. Ibid., 190.

32. "Nothing was so often and so carefully inculcated on His disciple by Jesus Christ as this precept of mutual charity as the one which contains all others.... 'Let us love one another for charity is God'"; Benedict XV, "Encyclical Letter *Pacem, Dei Munus Pulcherrimum* [May 23, 1920]," *AAS* 12 (1920): 211.

It is in this context that Benedict's condemnation of the war must be appreciated. The pontiff was genuinely appalled by the "useless slaughter."[33] There was no "just" or "unjust" war in his eyes, which by no means meant that he intended to modify the church's doctrine on warfare, which since St. Augustine had justified the recourse to arms in case of just war. To preserve the integrity of the church and stop the carnage that was leading to the destruction of Europe, Benedict relinquished his moral prestige for the sake of peace. He resisted the temptation to point fingers in a world crippled by the raging fires of nationalism.

BENEDICT XV, THE PEACEMAKER

On September 8, 1914, a few days after his election, Benedict issued an exhortation to the Catholic world.

We hold it a duty imposed on us by the Good Shepherd...to embrace with fatherly affection all the lambs and sheep of His flock. After His example, We must be, and indeed We are, ready to give Our life for their salvation, and therefore We are firmly resolved to leave nothing undone to hasten the end of this calamity.[34]

On his deathbed the pontiff repeated this statement, uttering that he was willingly laying down his life for the peace of the world.

His first encyclical *Ad Beatissimi*, promulgated on November 1, 1914, was given a cold reception.[35] It was dismissed as a weak document, emphasizing love and charity above justice and authority, an ineffective address to a vindictive world. The further

33. Benedict XV, "Apostolic Exhortation *Dès le début* [Aug. 1, 1917]," *AAS* 9 (1917): 423. It is also known as the Peace Note of August 1, 1917.

34. "Nous avons reçu de Jésus-Christ, Bon Pasteur...le devoir d'embrasser dans un amour paternel tous ceux qui sont des agneaux et des brebis de son troupeau. Puisque donc, à l'exemple du Seigneur lui-même, Nous devons être prêts, ainsi que Nous le sommes, à donner même Notre vie pour leur salut à tous, Nous avons fermement décidé de ne rien négliger de ce qui sera en Notre pouvoir pour hâter la fin d'une si grande calamité"; Benedict XV, *Actes de Benoît XV* (Paris: Bonne Presse, 1924), 1:15 (my translation).

35. Benedict XV, "Encyclical Letter *Ad Beatissimi Apostolorum Principis* [Nov. 1, 1914]," *AAS* 6 (1914): 585–99.

publication of the details of a day of prayer to be held all over the world, on January 10, 1915, was also ignored.[36] The most outspoken, like Benito Mussolini in Italy, criticized "the ridiculous prayers for peace even among the fighting soldiers."[37] A few influential bishops, in Belgium especially, refused to read the pontiff's text.

Benedict XV's efforts to secure the neutrality of Italy also ended in failure. The entry of Italy into the war on May 24, 1915, on the side of the Entente, compelled the Holy See to devise a new line of European foreign policy. Its fragile enclave position on Italian soil justified this move. As a direct consequence of these new diplomatic difficulties, the Holy Father published, on July 28, 1915, an apostolic exhortation *To the Belligerent Peoples and their Rulers*, which marked a turning point in the development of the Holy See's foreign policy.[38] From a diplomatic line limited to general principles and localized actions, Benedict XV turned

36. The prayer is as follows: "Dismayed by the horrors of a war which is bringing ruin to peoples and nations, we turn, O Jesus, to Thy most loving Heart as to our last hope. O God of Mercy, with tears we invoke Thee to end this fearful scourge; O King of Peace, we humbly implore the peace for which we long. From Thy Sacred Heart Thou didst shed forth over the world divine Charity, so that discord might end and love alone might reign among men. During Thy life on earth Thy Heart beat with tender compassion for the sorrows of men; in this hour made terrible with burning hate, with bloodshed and with slaughter, once more may Thy divine Heart be moved to pity. Pity the countless mothers in anguish for the fate of their sons; pity the numberless families now bereaved of their fathers; pity Europe over which broods such havoc and disaster. Do Thou inspire rulers and peoples with counsels of meekness, do Thou heal the discords that tear the nations asunder; Thou Who didst shed Thy Precious Blood that they might live as brothers, bring men together once more in loving harmony. And as once before to the very of the Apostle Peter: *Save us, Lord, we perish.* Thou didst answer with words of mercy and didst still the raging waves, so now deign to hear our trustful prayer, and give back to the world peace and tranquility. And do thou, O most holy Virgin, as in other times of sore distress, be now our help, our protection and our safeguard. Amen"; official translation in *Ecclesiastical Review* 58 (Feb. 1918): 204; original translated text in Benedict XV, "Prayer for Peace Prescribed by Pope Benedict XV, to be said 21 March," Ecclesiastical Review 52 (Mar. 1915): 353. The Latin text is found in Benedict XV, "*Decretum Preces Pro Pace Certis Diebus Dicendae Praescribuntur* [Jan. 10, 1915]," *AAS* 7 (1915): 13–14.

37. W. H. Peters, *Life of Benedict XV*, 123.

38. Benedict XV, "Apostolic Exhortation *To the Belligerent Peoples and Their Rulers* [July 28, 1915]," *AAS* 7 (1915): 365–68.

to realpolitik, to a full-blown active diplomacy.[39] After the failure of his pacifist approaches, the pontiff entered into a peace offensive. Secret diplomatic efforts to bring the belligerents to the negotiating table collapsed. His famous Peace Note of August 1, 1917, to the warring powers was received with contempt and swiftly discarded.[40]

The papal Peace Note of August 1, 1917, suggested a return to the status quo *ante bellum*. If the impact of nationalism was the immediate danger facing the Holy See, the collapse of the existing balance of powers was a long-term danger that could affect the authority and integrity of the church. A status quo *ante bellum* would avoid two great dangers. A German victory would mean a Protestant victory, but, even worse for the Holy See, a victory of the Entente could mean the collapse and disintegration of the Austro-Hungarian Empire. The fall of the Habsburg Empire was anticipated with apprehension by the pontiff, not so much because it was the only remaining Catholic bastion but because of its role as a bulwark against Russian Orthodoxy and an element of stabilization in a region in turmoil.

Benedict's offer to the belligerents was met with disdain. Germany informed the pope that "the Imperial Government [would], in this peace respect, support every proposal which is compatible with the vital interests of the German Empire and people."[41] On the Entente side, the long overdue reply was officially forwarded to the pope by the American president, Woodrow Wilson, in the name of the Allies. If Great Britain had politely acknowledged the note stating that no definitive answer could be formulated until Germany had made clear her inten-

39. See Francis Latour, *La papauté et les problèmes de la paix pendant la première guerre mondiale* (Paris: L'Harmattan, 1996); Nathalie Renoton-Beine, *La colombe et les tranchées: Les tentatives de paix de Benoît XV pendant la Grande Guerre* (Paris: Editions du Cerf, 2004).

40. Benedict XV, *Dès le début*, 417–20.

41. [London] *Times*, *The History of the Times: The 150th Anniversary and Beyond, 1912–1947* (London: Times Printing House Square, 1952), 332.

tions regarding the future of Belgium, Italy was furious at the allegation that the Entente Powers were fighting in a "useless slaughter,"[42] implying that Italy and its allies were engaged in an immoral war. The papal appeal was understood partly as a maneuver to derail the fighting spirit of the troops, but above all as a strategy to increase the Holy See's international prestige and eventually participate in the future peace negotiations. France simply dismissed the note.

Initially, Paris and London advised Washington to ignore the pope's message. A different recommendation was given to President Wilson by his adviser Colonel House, who asked him "to take the peace negotiations out of the hands of the pope and hold them in [his] own."[43] Wilson's reply reached Benedict XV on August 29, 1917. It was a carefully worded text stating, "we cannot take the word of the present rulers of Germany as a guarantee of anything that is to endure."[44] It was a polite but firm *fin de non-recevoir* and a complete political defeat for the pope.

BENEDICT XV, THE REALIST DIPLOMAT

The Roman Question, a church-and-state conflict between the Holy See and the Italian Republic lingering since 1870, contributed significantly to the Holy See's diplomatic retreat in Europe prior to the First World War. The political state of affairs between Italian forces in way of unification and the Holy See had been deteriorating since 1848.[45] The unstable situation reached its climax on September 20, 1870, when royal Italian troops stormed Rome, annexed the city, and forced the pontiff to abandon the re-

---

42. Benedict XV, *Dès le début*, 420.

43. Charles Seymour, *Intimate Papers of Colonel House* (New York: Houghton Mifflin, 1928), 3:156.

44. Arno J. Mayer, *Political Origins of the New Diplomacy, 1917–1918* (New Haven: Yale University Press, 1959), 235.

45. Following the revolutionary upheaval of 1848 and the storming of the papal residence fomented by Italian Republicans, Pope Pius IX fled Rome and took refuge in Gaeta in November 1848. He returned in 1850 after the fall of the ephemeral Roman Republic.

maining Papal States. Pope Pius IX (1846–78) retreated to his last bastion, the Vatican. A final and viable settlement was reached in 1929 under Pius XI's pontificate (1922–39).[46] Until then, each of Pius IX's successors dubbed himself "the prisoner in the Vatican." The Holy See's loss of the Papal States meant the loss of its temporal sovereignty. The question arose immediately about its new international legal status. Anticlerical forces and political theorists implied that, with the loss of temporal power, the Holy See had also lost its privileges as an international juridical subject. Against this allegation, the papacy opposed its unparalleled spiritual sovereignty as the foundation of its international juridical personality. From 1870 onward the papacy asserted that its sovereignty, and therefore its international juridical status, had never been founded on its temporal power and the possession of territories but on its spiritual and divine sovereignty, which nobody ever contested. Without temporal sovereignty the Holy See subsisted as a sui generis power that had the right to enter into diplomatic relations with individual states and be, therefore, an active participant on the international diplomatic chessboard. This right was derived from its spiritual sovereignty and was never granted to the government of the church by other nations on the basis of the possession or not of an independent territory, which was "an external, though entirely accidental, expression of sovereignty."[47]

The Holy See had been invited to participate in the Con-

46. The Lateran Treaties were signed by Benito Mussolini, minister president of Italy, and the Holy See's secretary of state, Pietro Cardinal Gasparri, in February 1929. They include three documents: a financial compensation offered by Italy to the Holy See for the loss of the Papal States; a concordat defining the rights and liberties of the Catholic Church in Italy; and a treaty in which the Holy See recognizes the state of Italy, with Rome as its capital, while Italy recognizes papal sovereignty over a new state, the Vatican City State, a guarantee of the pope's complete independence.

47. Edward Heston, "Papal Diplomacy: Its Organization and Way of Acting," in *The Catholic Church in World Affairs*, ed. Waldemar Gurian and Matthew A. Fitzsimons, 38 (Notre Dame, Ind.: University of Notre Dame Press, 1954).

gress of Vienna in 1815.[48] On this occasion, its role and status as a subject of international law were clearly stated and its prestige enhanced. The apostolic nuncio, as a permanent diplomatic representative of the Holy See, was named dean of the entire diplomatic corps. Yet, it was the papal court's first and last significant diplomatic involvement with the Concert of Europe until World War I. Pius IX did not take part in the Congress of Paris in 1856, even though some important issues at stake were religious.[49] The Holy See was also excluded from the 1899 and 1907 Hague peace conferences convened to revise the laws and customs on warfare.

The loss of temporal power stimulated a redesigning of papal international relations. Reigning over an institution whose mission had become essentially spiritual, the pontiffs started to exert a diplomatic influence that did not rest upon classic weapons such as military power but on the moral prestige and religious authority of the papacy.[50]

The spiritual nature of the government of the church suggests a diplomacy anchored in idealism more than realism. This has

48. After the fall of Napoleon Bonaparte, the Congress of Vienna met to draw the new map of Europe, ensuring a balance of powers among European nations in order to prevent future conflicts.

49. The Crimean War (1853–56), fought by Russia against France, Great Britain, and the Ottoman Empire, finds its immediate origin in the Franco-Russian dispute over the Holy Places of Palestine. Russian attempts to secure a protectorate over the Orthodox population collided with the French Catholic protectorate and the country's political and religious interests in the region.

50. See Robert Heinl Jr., *Dictionary of Military and Naval Quotations* (Annapolis, Md.: United States Naval Institute, 1966), 88, quoted in Paul Gordon Lauren, "Theories of Bargaining with Threats of Force: Deterrence and Coercive Diplomacy," in *Diplomacy: New Approaches in History, Theory, and Policy*, ed. Paul Gordon Lauren, 184 (New York: Free Press, 1979). "Diplomacy without arms is music without instruments," once uttered Frederick the Great. Echoing this well-accepted realist theory, many political scientists stress the ineffectiveness as a policy instrument of diplomatic persuasion without the ability to threatening to use force. The respected diplomatic historian René Albrecht-Carrié noted more than fifty years ago that "if diplomacy stresses negotiations, these have no meaning divorced from the background of power"; Albrecht-Carrié, *A Diplomatic History of Europe since the Congress of Vienna* (London: Harper and Row, 1958), 4.

always been true but only to a certain extent. The pontifical line of foreign policy, pragmatic and prudent, is entrenched in realism and pays attention to designing a balanced policy that takes into account the power of national forces at work in each state and the need to protect the rights and interests of Catholic communities. The Holy See's main challenge has always been to adapt to changing situations while maintaining the church's tradition and transnationality through a prudent and moderate diplomacy rooted in continuity and seeking to promote justice and charity as ultimate norms of the international order.[51] Such a delicate crafting became a true challenge to Pope Benedict during the Great War. His pontificate attests that the Holy See's role in the international order is of a "moral and humanitarian nature."[52]

With the outbreak of the Great War in August 1914, the European diplomatic scene underwent a Copernican change, shaking the foundations of international relations and the methods of conducting diplomacy.[53] "Whether just or unjust, war is the supreme disaster, a disaster for which nothing can compensate."[54] War implies a rupture. For the Catholic Church, the First World War meant a dangerous disruption of unity and loyalty to the Holy See. The main source of dissension was the power of patriotic discourse in belligerent countries and the intensification of nationalistic trends.

The disruption of unity was as destabilizing as the difficulty of keeping long-term diplomatic goals at a time of complete reshuffling of the geopolitical and social scene. In wartime, foreign policy and war policy become one. For military powers, it

51. A. C. F. Beales, *The Catholic Church and International Order* (Harmondsworth, UK: Penguin, 1941), 66.

52. John R. Quinn, "From a Moral Voice Raised in the International Dialogue," *Origins* 13 (May 3, 1984): 571.

53. See John Duncan Gregory, *On the Edge of Diplomacy: Rambles and Reflections, 1902–1928* (London: Hutchinson, 1929), 34.

54. D. A. Binchy, "The Vatican and International Diplomacy," *International Affairs* 22 (Jan. 1946): 50.

means that immediate military demands often take precedence over long-term political objectives.[55] For the Holy See, it implies a prudent diplomacy that is partly dependent upon military successes of belligerent countries. To attain long-term and steadfast goals, the Holy See must be ready to consider new interlocutors and reassess the importance of historical ties without sacrificing deep-rooted diplomatic continuity.

At the opening of hostilities, the Great Powers' political and military alliances were such that a diplomatic inconsistency was immediately noticeable at the Vatican. On the Entente side, France, Great Britain, and Russia were allies of the first hour. Italy joined them in 1915 and the United States in 1917.[56] The diplomatic presence of the Allies at the Vatican was an embarrassment to themselves and shortsighted, considering the 124 million Catholics living on this side of the war theater.[57] Catholic but anticlerical France had cut ties with the Holy See in 1904 and had thus no official legation at Rome at the outbreak of war. Imperial Orthodox Russia had a chargé d'affaires, Dimitri Nelidov, but his influence was hampered by the Tsar's religious policies in Russian Poland. Protestant Great Britain had had no envoy since the sixteenth century. As for Italy, the Roman Question prohibited any diplomatic ties. Only Belgium was represented at the papal court by Maximilian d'Erp, who was suffering poor health. The situation of the Central Powers, dominated by "a principle of authority, traditions of hierarchy and discipline to

55. Roberta Warman, "The Erosion of Foreign Office Influence in the Making of Foreign Policy, 1916–1918," *Historical Journal* 15 (Mar. 1972): 134.

56. The United States, a newcomer on the European political scene, had no diplomatic ties with the Holy See. Other countries joined the war on the Entente side, but none of these powers was as politically or militarily influential as Great Britain, France, Russia, or even Italy. None had an established diplomatic presence at the Vatican at the outbreak of the war.

57. Jean-Marie Mayeur, "Les Églises et les relations internationales: L'Église catholique," in *Histoire du Christianisme des origines à nos jours*, vol. 12, *Guerres mondiales et totalitarismes (1914–1958)*, ed. Jean-Marie Mayeur, Charles Pietri, André Vauchez, and Marc Venard, 305 (Paris: Desclée, 1990).

which the Catholic Church had always shown predilection,"[58] was much more enjoyable. More than 64 million Catholics were living in Catholic Bavaria, Protestant Germany, and the Catholic Austrian Empire. A small minority was scattered in the Muslim Ottoman Empire. The Central Powers' diplomatic missions were of high quality. Three distinguished diplomats enjoyed much prestige at the Curia. The Austro-Hungarian envoy, Prince Johann Schönburg-Hartenstein, was the Catholic ambassador par excellence. The Bavarian minister, Baron Otto von Ritter, and the Prussian minister, Otto von Mühlberg, were most commendable representatives of the German interests at the Holy See.

Great Britain was the first and only Entente ally to realize the importance and immediate necessity to enter into diplomatic intercourse with the Holy See. During the first months of the conflict, Cardinal Gasquet, the only British cardinal resident in Rome, was alone to defend the Entente's conduct of the war and explain the reasons that had motivated the opening of hostilities.[59] Still, he convinced the British government to be proactive and send an envoy to the papal court. London followed the cardinal's advice and dispatched an official diplomatic mission to the Holy See.

Two main reasons justified this pertinent choice. Millions of Catholics on each side of the war theater could prove a powerful and influential force. Some form of diplomatic relations was then necessary to counterbalance the assumed leaning of the Holy See in favor of the Central Powers. On arrival in Rome for the conclave that elected Benedict XV, the English cardinals had already noticed strong pro-German influences.[60] Therefore, after centuries of "evasions and subterfuges,"[61] the British gov-

58. Maurice Pernot, *Le Saint-Siège, l'Église catholique et la politique mondiale* (Paris: Armand Colin, 1924), 28 (my translation).

59. Renzi, "Entente and the Vatican," 497.

60. Shane Leslie, *Cardinal Gasquet* (London: Burns and Oates, 1953), 213.

61. Robert Graham, *Vatican Diplomacy: A Study of Church and State on the International Plane* (Princeton, N.J.: Princeton University Press, 1959), 70.

ernment, in a most pragmatic move, appointed an envoy to the Holy See. On December 12, 1914, the London *Times* announced that "the king has been pleased to approve the appointment of Sir Henry Howard, KCB, KCMG, as Envoy Extraordinary and Minister Plenipotentiary, with a view to his proceeding on a special mission to His Holiness the Pope. He will be accompanied by Mr. J. D. Gregory, of the Foreign Office, as secretary of the Mission."[62] Both men were Roman Catholics. In October 1916, Count de Salis replaced Sir Henry.

The British mission was initially conceived as a temporary wartime expedient. Controversy over the need to maintain it after the end of the hostilities led the British government to officially declare that millions of Roman Catholic subjects throughout the British Empire would be offended if the mission were closed. It was thus given the status of legation and became permanent in 1926. Britain might well be mostly Anglican, but its empire was not so.[63]

The official reason for sending an envoy was to explain to the Holy See the motivations behind the war and convert the pope to the British view, with the hope that he would eventually take sides in favor of the Entente. The instructions issued to Sir Henry by Sir Edward Grey, the British secretary for foreign affairs, were to present the pope with "the motives which compelled His Majesty's government to intervene in the War, and to inform him of the British attitude towards the various questions arising therefrom."[64] The British government was hoping to benefit from the moral authority of Pope Benedict if he came to embrace the Al-

---

62. Editorial, "British Mission to the Pope: Sir H. Howard's Appointment," (London) *Times*, Dec. 12, 1914, 9.

63. "'Really with all the Catholic interests in the Empire, it seems absurd that there should be no official means of communication between the British government and the Pope,' wrote Cardinal Gasquet to Lord Grey on November 20, 1914"; Leslie, *Cardinal Gasquet*, 214.

64. Hachey, ed., *Great Britain Legation*, viii.

lies' side. It was also hoped that the mission would have access to the wealth of information that the Holy See had the reputation to collect. Ecclesiastical and political information inundated the Holy See's secretariat of state with data sent by nuncios, missionaries, and Catholic laymen from all over the world.

The British government tried to persuade the French to resume diplomatic relations with the Holy See. It was opposed by Foreign Minister Théophile Delcassé, who feared that a ferocious anticlerical reaction could endanger the *union sacrée*.[65] He eventually sent an unofficial delegate in 1915, the writer Charles Loiseau, who was a good observer of Roman politics. The presence of British and French envoys, official or not, did allow a more fruitful diplomatic intercourse between the Allies and the Holy See.

As for Italy, its government was adamant about ostracizing the Holy See in the diplomatic scene in order to avoid a much-feared internationalization of the Roman Question. The personality of the Italian foreign minister, Sidney Sonnino, and his anticlericalism and Protestantism were obstacles to good will and understanding with the Holy See. Italy entered the war on the Entente side in May 1915, on one express condition stated in the secret Treaty of London signed between Italy and the Entente Powers on April 26, 1915. Article 15 of the treaty concerned the status of the Vatican and stipulated, "France, Great Britain and Russia pledge themselves to support Italy in not allowing the representatives of the Holy See to undertake any diplomatic steps having for their object the conclusion of peace or the settlement of questions connected with the present war."[66] Baron Sonnino's insistence on inserting the article prohibiting the Holy

65. Renzi, "Entente and the Vatican," 500.

66. J. A. S. Grenville, ed., *The Major International Treaties, 1914–1973: A History and Guide with Texts* (London: Methuen, 1974), 26, quoted in Robert John Araujo and John A. Lucal, *Papal Diplomacy and the Quest for Peace: The Vatican and International Organizations from the Early Years to the League of Nations* (Ann Arbor, Mich.: Sapientia Press of Ave Maria University, 2004), 104.

See from sitting at the peace table was a direct response to Pope Benedict's clear intention to raise the Roman Question at the future Peace Congress. In his first encyclical, *Ad Beatissimi*, the pontiff had expressed his wish.

For a long time past, the Church has not enjoyed that full freedom which it needs. And so while earnestly desiring that peace should soon be concluded amongst the nations, it is also Our desire that there should be an end to the abnormal position of the Head of the Church, a position in many ways very harmful to the very peace of nations. We hereby renew, and for the same reasons, the many protests Our Predecessors have made against such a state of things, moved thereto not by human interest, but by the sacredness of our office, in order to defend the rights and dignity of the Apostolic See.[67]

Despite the many protests, once the terms of the secret treaty were leaked to the Holy See by the end of 1915, the Allies remained firm. In December 1914, the apostolic nuncio in Madrid, Msgr. Ragonesi, had informed the pontiff that Italy would not allow the Holy See to participate in the future peace conference. In late 1915, Cardinal Gasparri tried to enroll the help of the apostolic delegates in Canada, Australia, and United States. All replied that there was nothing they could do.[68] Therefore, the Holy See did not officially participate in the peace negotiations.

Italy's decision to enter the war on the Entente side raised another diplomatic difficulty for the Holy See. The status of the representatives accredited to the Holy See by the Central Powers became a delicate issue that was resolved by their being expelled from the Italian territory and finding refuge in Lugano, Switzerland. Although the lines of communication remained open between the Holy See and both camps, diplomatic inter-

---

67. Benedict XV, *Ad Beatissimi*, art. 31.

68. Ragonesi to Gasparri, Dec. 16 and 23, 1914, ASV, Segr. Stato, Guerra (1914–18), fasc. 84. See also the letter sent by the apostolic delegate in Canada to Cardinal Gasparri in which he laments that it was extremely difficult to obtain Protestant support: "Con quei signori noi non abbiamo, si puo dire, alcuna relazione"; Pellegrino Stagni to Gasparri, Nov. 19, 1915, ASV, Segr. Stato, Guerra (1914–18), fasc. 84.

course between the Vatican and the Central Powers went under special scrutiny by the Italian government. Eventually, the war years went rather smoothly between the Vatican and the Quirinal. Baron Carlo Monti, the director of the office for administering ecclesial funds, deserves credit for his unrelenting good will and thoughtfulness in his facilitating unofficial diplomatic intercourse between the Holy See and the Italian government.

It is within this European diplomatic context that Pope Benedict assessed the significance of the many issues raised by the vulnerability of Catholic communities in the Ottoman Empire. The volatile diplomatic situation on the Ottoman battlefield, although secondary to the European war scene, remained high on Benedict's foreign policy list of priorities. The Holy See's distinctive interest for the fate of Catholic communities in the Ottoman Empire was informed by two circumstances. First, it has always been the Holy See's policy to protect Catholics and preserve Catholic interests wherever they are in the world. This unswerving commitment throughout the centuries was given additional impetus under Benedict XV's pontificate. Dubbed the "Pope of Peace," Benedict should also be remembered as "the pope who so loved the East."[69] As such, he initiated a new model of proactive and integrated diplomacy that intertwined classic diplomatic functions of negotiation with an ecclesiastical diplomacy that reflected his Eastern ecclesiology.

69. In a talk given to the Congregation for the Oriental Churches, on June 9, 2007, Pope Benedict XVI stressed that he took the name "of a pope who dearly loved the East"; Benedict XVI, "Visit of His Holiness Benedict XVI to the Congregation for the Oriental Churches, 9 June 2007," http://www.vatican.va/holy_father/benedict_xvi/speeches/2007/june/documents/hf_ben-xvi_spe_20070609_congr-orientchurch_en.html.

2

PROTECTION OF CATHOLICS IN
THE OTTOMAN EMPIRE

STATUS AND ORGANIZATION OF
EASTERN CHRISTIANS IN MUSLIM LANDS
Islamic Law and Christian Rights: *Dhimmitude*
and the *Millet* System

Islam moved from Arabia to Syria in the seventh century. Jerusalem and Damascus became holy cities, second only to Mecca and Medina. The region, the cradle of Christianity, eventually became predominantly Muslim.[1] With the Ottoman invasion of Syria in August 1516, the newly subjugated country became part of the Ottoman Empire. As such, it was integrated into the Ottoman fabric united by a common language, Arabic, and a common religion, Islam. "A mosaic of religious and other minori-

---

1. "They [The Christians] of the population were by far the majority [in 732] in the former Roman provinces, in the three so called Oriental Patriarchates of Alexandria, Antioch, and Jerusalem...perhaps 50 percent of the world's confessing Christian from the mid-seventh to the end of the eleventh centuries found themselves living under Muslim rule." But "by then [the times of the Crusades] the indigenous Christians living among the Muslims had begun their long slide into that demographic insignificance in the Middle East that is the fate of their communities in modern times"; Sidney H. Griffith, *The Church in the Shadow of the Mosque: Christians and Muslims in the World of Islam* (Princeton, N.J.: Princeton University Press, 2008), 11 and 13; see also Michelle U. Campos, *Ottoman Brothers: Muslims, Christians, and Jews in Early Twentieth-Century Palestine* (Stanford, Calif.: Stanford University Press, 2011), 9. Campos notes, "by the sixteenth century, the split between the Muslim population and the non-Muslim population in the empire had flipped to approximately 60–40."

ties,"[2] Jewish and Christian for the most part, strove to survive and develop in this Muslim environment.[3]

Ottoman rulers developed a sophisticated system of Islamic law, differentiating between their Muslim majority and non-Muslim minority subjects. Islamic law, which established a "pattern of stratification among the Christian and Muslim inhabitants,"[4] was enforced at both the personal and communal levels. To the rights and duties of the *dhimmis* as individuals corresponded the rights and duties of the *millet* as a communal religious community.[5]

Regarded as "People of the Book" by Muslims,[6] Christians were considered as *dhimmis* or *rayas* and were tolerated and protected, but their status was inferior to the status of Muslims and they suffered from many restrictions. *Dhimmis* could not serve in the civil service or in the army. Other restrictions were imposed regarding the clothes they might wear or their places of worship. Churches could not be higher than mosques, and no new churches could be built. They were subject to discrimination and at times even persecution, but they were not forced to convert.[7] According to the renowned Arabic and Syriac Christian-

2. A. L. Tibawi, *A Modern History of Syria, Including Lebanon and Palestine* (London: Macmillan, 1969), 20.

3. See Youssef Courbage and Philippe Fargues, *Chrétiens et juifs dans l'Islam arabe et turc* (Paris: Fayard, 1992).

4. Kemal H. Karpat, *Studies on Ottoman Social and Political History* (Leiden: Brill, 2002), 29.

5. Recep Senturk, "Minority Rights in Islam," in *Islam and Human Rights: Advancing a U.S.–Muslim Dialogue*, ed. Shireen T. Hunter and Huma Malik, 71 (Washington, D.C.: Center for Strategic and International Studies Press, 2005).

6. The "People of the Book" are those who possess a monotheistic religion based on revelation. Islam recognizes Christianity as an incomplete form of Islam itself. Jews are also considered "People of the Book."

7. Bat Ye'Or points out that "either the individual or the tribe would convert to Islam, thus submitting to the Prophet's authority, or conversion was replaced by payment of a tribute to the Prophet…principles directly mentioned by Muhammad in the letters he sent to the Christian leaders and governors. He gave them the choice between conversion or tribute, failing which war was declared"; Bat Ye'Or, *Islam and Dhimmitude: Where Civilizations Collide* (Madison, N.J.: Fairleigh Dickinson University Press, 2002), 41. See

ity scholar Sidney Griffith, it is this life in *dhimmitude* as second-class citizens that "shaped their enduring ecclesial identities, both culturally and intellectually, within the context of several local determining circumstances: their encounter with the Muslims, their adoption of the Arabic language, and their isolation from other Christian communities outside of the Islamic world."[8]

For centuries, in the absence of nationalistic movements, religion was given a determinant role in the establishment of corporate identities in the Ottoman Empire. The line of demarcation between communities was not along racial or geographical lines but along religious ones. This distinctiveness was associated with the *millet* system.[9] Braude and Lewis described this system as "a series of *ad hoc* arrangements made over the years" and offered by the Ottoman government to the major religious communities in the form of legal autonomy.[10] "They mix but do not combine," they added, pointing out a fundamental weakness of the empire.[11] The *millet* system was originally conceived to institutionalize the status of the Orthodox Christians, granting them autonomy in religious and cultural affairs. The first *millets* were the Greek Orthodox (1453), Armenian Orthodox (1461), and Jewish (end of fifteenth century) *millets*. They had their own religious edifices, schools, hospitals, and ecclesiastical courts. The chief of a *millet* reported directly to the Ottoman sultan.

In the mid-nineteenth century, during the Tanzimat period, a generalized effort by the Ottoman government to recognize and empower new Christian *millets* was launched under the pressure of European powers. The Tanzimat period was an era of reforms

also Antoine Fattal's excellent study on the legal status of *dhimmis* in Muslim lands, re-edited in 1995: Fattal, *Le statut légal des non-musulmans en pays d'Islam* (Beirut: Imprimerie catholique, 1958).

8. Griffith, *Church in the Shadow*, 130.

9. A. L. Macfie, *The End of the Ottoman Empire, 1908–1923* (London: Longman, 1998), 7.

10. Benjamin Braude and Bernard Lewis, eds., *Christians and Jews in the Ottoman Empire: The Functioning of a Plural Society* (New York: Holmes and Meier, 1982), 12.

11. Ibid., 1.

and Westernization that followed the Russian military defeat in the Crimean War and the acknowledgment of French and British political and military ascendancy in the empire. This expansion from the three original *millets* to nine and then later eleven transformed the essence of the *millet* from a religious community into an "ethno-religious and national congregation."[12] The majority of the new *millets* were Eastern rite Catholic *millets* that parted from their original Orthodox community.

Except for the Maronites of Lebanon, who claim to have always been Catholic in communion with Rome, the Eastern rite Catholic churches stem from an Orthodox dissident body. All of them accept the spiritual and legal authority of the pope. They are autonomous and retain their distinctive liturgical rites and canonical traditions and are headed by their own patriarch. At the outbreak of the war, the main Eastern Catholic *millets* in Greater Syria were the Melkite or Greek Catholic *millet* of Byzantine rite (recognized in 1848), the Armenian (1831), and the Syrian (1830) *millets*. The Maronite Christians of Lebanon, who had been part of the Armenian *millet*, were granted autonomy in 1860–61. The Maronites and Melkites were the most numerous in Lebanon and Syria. A vestige of Christianity in the heart of Islam, the Eastern rite Catholics of the Ottoman Empire were like many "frail branches united to the trunk of the Universal Church. Eastern Catholics were...Arab but not Moslem, Eastern but not schismatic, Catholics but not Latin."[13] A minority among a large Latin Catholicity, they also remained a minority in a predominantly Orthodox Eastern Christianity.

12. Kemal H. Karpat, "Ottoman Views and Policies towards the Orthodox Christian Church," in *Orthodox Christians and Muslims*, ed. N. M. Vaporis, 151 (Brookline, Mass.: Holy Cross Orthodox Press, 1986); also published in *Greek Orthodox Theological Review* 31 (1986): 151.

13. Neophytos Edelby, "Our Vocation as Eastern Christians," *Proche-Orient Chrétien* 3 (1953): 201–17, quoted in Maximos IV Sayegh, ed., *The Eastern Churches and Catholic Unity* (New York: Herder and Herder, 1963), 25.

As for the Latin Catholics, foreign non-Muslim subjects, they were never identified as members of a *millet*. They were essentially members of the numerous religious orders that covered the Ottoman Empire with a net of missions and, as such, were under foreign diplomatic protection. French and Italian religious orders were the most visible.[14]

From *Dhimmitude* to Civil Equality

In the mid-nineteenth century, France and Great Britain made good use of their dominant position and sought improved welfare for the Christian populations of the empire, requesting from the sultan measures of equality between *dhimmis* and Muslims. The Sublime Porte bowed to the Franco-British petition, proclaiming in the most solemn manner new rights for the *dhimmis*. On February 18, 1856, the sultan announced in the *Hatt-i Humayun*, an imperial reform edict, reforms that would protect property and persons and ensure the equality of all his subjects before the law, without discrimination of religion. In December 1876 the first constitution in Ottoman history was promulgated, stressing that "all Osmali are equal before the law...without distinction as to religion."[15] Although the principle of equality had become official policy, real equality never prevailed. The Constitution of 1876 was suspended in 1878 and restored in 1908 after the Young Turk Revolution.[16]

Aspiring to transform the Ottoman Empire into a modern nation-state on the model of European nations, the reformist

14. See Vartan Artinian, "The Formation of Catholic and Protestant Millets in the Ottoman Empire," *Armenian Review* 28, no. 1 (Spring 1975): 3–15.

15. *Das Staatsarchiv*, XXXI (1877), no. 5948, quoted in Roderic H. Davison, "Turkish Attitudes Concerning Christian-Muslim Equality in the Nineteenth Century," *American Historical Review* 59 (July 1954): 848.

16. The Young Turk Revolution of 1908, led by Enver, Talat, and Djemal Pasha, was opposed to the regime of Sultan Abdul-Hamid II. It allowed the establishment of a second constitutional and parliamentary regime, the foundation of the modern Turkish state that emerged from the partition of the defeated Ottoman Empire.

Young Turks aimed to resist European encroachment and to counter nationalist and separatist tendencies at work in some of the Christian *millets*. Resting on the principle of equality, the new Ottoman citizenship obtained by the *dhimmis* should have logically signaled the termination of the *millet* system. In effect, the *millets* were not abolished but their essence changed. A religious *millet* consciousness was succeeded by a national *millet* consciousness, but an Ottoman consciousness was never able to take shape.[17]

Christians in a Muslim Land: A Symbolic Presence

It is nearly impossible to provide reliable statistics regarding the size of the Christian communities in the Ottoman Empire, even less to single out their Catholic population. Estimates offered by Western sources often conflict with Ottoman censuses.[18] According to Western sources, by 1914, the Christian population of Greater Syria represented almost a third of the overall population, reaching a peak after a steady increase that began in the second half of the nineteenth century. Christians made up around 60 percent of the population in Lebanon, 11 percent in Palestine, and 10 percent in Syria.[19] These statistics, which do not differentiate between Catholic and other Christian denominations, should be treated with circumspection. According

17. According to Senturk, "this project of integrating all religious communities under one national identity failed...as ethnic groups rose as minorities with distinct secular identities"; Senturk, "Minority Rights," 87–88.

18. Wagstaff, in agreement with Kemal H. Karpat, argues that "the Ottoman censuses of 1828/29–1831, 1881/82–1893 and 1906/07...are far more reliable than the statistics presented by most foreign 'experts' and local community leaders"; J. M. Wagstaff, "A Note on Some Nineteenth-Century Population Statistics for Lebanon," *British Society for Middle Eastern Studies* 13 (1986): 27.

19. Philippe Fargues, "The Arab Christians of the Middle East: A Demographic Perspective," in *Christian Communities in the Arab Middle East: The Challenge of the Future*, ed. Andrea Pacini, 48–66 (Oxford: Oxford University Press, 1998); see also Justin McCarthy, *The Population of Palestine: Population History and Statistics of the Late Ottoman Period and the Mandate* (New York: Columbia University Press, 1990).

to Ottoman statistics for Lebanon, in 1914, the Christians represented only 30 percent of the total population, with 17 percent recognizing themselves as Maronite or Catholic.[20]

The discrepancy between estimates, although noteworthy, did not mask the Christians' marginal position in an overwhelmingly Muslim environment. In the late nineteenth century, Syrian economic emigration to Europe and the New World and Muslim immigration from the European territories lost to the Ottoman Empire accelerated the existing trend. The Ottoman defeat in the 1877 war against Russia had resulted in the loss of lands populated by over a million Muslim Turkish people. This massive immigration to the empire's remaining territories destroyed the fragile balance between Christians and Muslims, favoring the Muslim population, which became the overwhelming majority, therefore defeating the purpose of a multinational state based on common citizenship.[21]

Yet, the Christians' religious, cultural, and political significance in Greater Syria transcend all numbers. Descendants of the first Christians, they have a symbolic role especially in the Holy Land. Because of their education in European missionary schools, they also have facilitated the Westernization of the region. They have been the linchpin between Christian Europe and the Muslim Ottoman Empire, with a strong influence on the decision-making process of the Holy See and the great European powers.

CHRISTIANS UNDER RELIGIOUS PROTECTORATES

Capitulations and French Catholic Protectorate

For centuries, the protection of the Latin and Eastern rite Catholic churches in the Middle East has not rested on the Holy

---

20. Wagstaff, "Note on Statistics," 33. According to the same sources, the Muslims represented 70 percent of the total Lebanese population and the Greek Orthodox 15 percent.

21. Karpat, "The Transformation of the Ottoman State, 1789–1908," *International Journal of Middle East Studies* 3 (July 1972): 272.

See, which had no diplomatic ties with the Ottoman government, but on France's privileged relationship with Constantinople. The Holy See was represented by an apostolic delegate with no official diplomatic status and therefore no official power to interact with the Porte.

The foundation of its cultural and economic influence in the region, the exclusive relationship of France with Constantinople, went back to 1536, when Suleiman the Magnificent, the Ottoman sultan, granted to King Francis I of France concessions in order to facilitate trade. These extraterritorial commercial and juridical conventions became known as capitulations. They allowed French diplomats accredited to the Porte to protect French interests. French subjects gained commercial rights and fiscal immunity. They answered to French law only, since foreigners had no juridical status in Ottoman Muslim lands.[22] The privileged status enjoyed by France was later extended by the sultans to other nations—Britain in 1583, Holland in 1613, and Austria in 1615—but the French ambassador always held preeminence over representatives from other European courts.

The Sublime Porte developed a balanced legal system differentiating between Ottoman and non-Ottoman Christian subjects. Christian Ottoman subjects, as *dhimmis*, were members of different *millets* benefiting from their special jurisdiction. Except for the Maronites, the majority of them were Orthodox Christians, all under Ottoman rule. Non-Ottoman Christians were originally merchants navigating under French pavilion who were protected by the King of France in their commercial activities. In 1604 new capitulations broadened this French protectorate to European pilgrims to the Holy Land. The French protectorate had become religious.

22. Hussein I. El-Mudarris and Olivier Salmon, eds., *Le Consulat de France à Alep au XVIIe siècle: Journal de Louis Gédoyn, vie de François Picquet, mémoires de Laurent d'Arvieux* (Alep: Ray, 2009), 11–12.

In 1740, the Porte granted new capitulations to France, converting two hundred years of tradition into an international legal document. According to this detailed text, France could invoke a French Catholic protectorate over all Latin rite Catholics, thus becoming the official representative of the pope in a predominantly Muslim empire. Latin Catholics living in the empire, Catholic missionaries, and papal apostolic delegates, regardless of their country of origin, were under French diplomatic protection.[23] The Latin Catholic protectorate was later extended to the Eastern rite Catholics, although this never became official. The de facto protection of Eastern Catholics, who were Ottoman subjects, was not mentioned in the capitulations of 1740 and as such represented an abuse of law. The establishment of new Eastern Catholic *millets* in the nineteenth century created a novel situation in which members of the *millet* had a double allegiance to the sultan as Ottoman subjects and to the pope as Catholics. As Catholics living under the limitations imposed by the Islamic law, it became therefore natural for those communities to seek the protection of France. Although accepted as a customary right, the protectorate over Eastern Catholic Ottoman subjects became an object of tension between the French government and the Porte. In the nineteenth century, in some instances, Eastern Catholics reinterpreted the traditional protectorate of France in the Orient, transforming its essence from a spiritual and religious protective device into an abusive use of consular prerogatives.[24]

In the absence of diplomatic relations between the Holy See and the Ottoman Empire, France had become the sole representative of the Holy See before the Sublime Porte. On August 20,

---

23. El-Mudarris et al., *Consulat de France*, 18. The Franciscans had been present in the Holy Land since the Crusades, under the protection of French consuls, but were not considered missionaries. The first missionaries were the Jesuits, followed by the Capuchins in 1625.

24. Nadine Picaudou, *La décennie qui ébranla le Moyen-Orient, 1914–1923* (Paris: Editions Complexe, 1992), 22.

1898, in a letter addressed to Cardinal Langénieux, Pope Leo XIII officially recognized the French protectorate as

a special mission [in the Orient] entrusted to (her) [France] by Divine Providence; a noble mission consecrated not only by a centuries-old practice, but also by international treaties, as recently acknowledged by our Congregation of Propaganda in its deliberation of 22 May 1888. The Holy See, in fact, does not wish to interfere with the glorious patrimony which France has received from its ancestors and which it, without a doubt, deserves to retain, always proving itself to be up to its mission.[25]

The capitulations, "a relic of the medieval system of international law,"[26] had signaled the beginning of French preeminence in the Ottoman Empire, a supremacy that was not seriously challenged until the late nineteenth century when British influence began to supplant that of France.[27] France's prestige was dependent upon a vast array of religious and educational institutions and on its financial and cultural influence in many sections of the population. Its *mission civilisatrice* had become the arm of French colonial expansion meant to export her civilization to the world.[28]

Tradition and interest had justified France's jealous defense

---

25. "La Francia ha in Oriente una missione speciale, affidatale dalla divina Provvidenza; nobile missione, consacrata non soltanto da una pratica secolare, ma altresì da trattati internazionali, come lo ha riconosciuto in questi giorni la Nostra Congregazione della Propaganda colla sua dichiarazione del 22 maggio 1898. La S. Sede, infatti, non vuole toccar nulla del glorioso patrimonio che la Francia ha ricevuto dai suoi antenati, e ch'essa intende senza alcun dubbio meritarsi di conservare, mostrandosi sempre all' altezza della sua missione"; Leo XIII, "Apostolic Letter *Maximo cum Animi* [Aug. 20, 1898]," *ASS* 31 (1898–99): 193–95 (my translation).

26. Hans Kohn, *Nationalism and Imperialism in the Hither East* (London: Routledge, 1932), 69.

27. "In 1831 Mehemet Ali, pasha of Egypt, inflicted disastrous defeats on the sultan, whose empire was saved from imminent destruction only by British intervention in 1840. From that day British influence began to supplant that of France in the Near East"; Henry H. Cumming, *Franco-British Rivalry in the Post-War Near East: the Decline of French Influence* (London: Oxford University Press, 1938), 6.

28. Matthew Burrows, "'Mission Civilisatrice': French Cultural Policy in the Middle East, 1860–1914," *Historical Journal* 29 (1986): 109. Nevakivi also claims that "the total prewar number of Syrian students attending French schools amounted to 50,000 while the total number of students attending the schools of other nationalities was 23,000"; Jukka Nevakivi, *Britain, France, and the Arab Middle East, 1914–1920* (London: Athlone, 1969), 5.

of her privilege over the centuries, with the protectorate having proven a crucial weapon in the battle of influence among the Great Powers in the Near East, satisfying France's imperialistic designs on the Ottoman Empire and, above all, in Syria. In the volatile nineteenth century, it became an object of power and attack in the great diplomatic game opposing European nations on the Ottoman theatre. After 1900, France narrowed and focused its religious and cultural interests on Greater Syria.[29] Its international position became insecure as the severing of diplomatic ties with the Holy See in 1904 harmed the legitimacy of maintaining the French protectorate. Although future Prime Minister Clemenceau was quick to claim that "anticlericalism is not an article for export,"[30] France's position was attacked domestically and internationally.

Domestically, anticlerical republican forces questioned the Catholic exclusivity implied by the protectorate, alienating not only the Muslim population but also, most importantly, the Orthodox communities, which needed help against Muslim harassment.[31] While some diplomats of the old school, such as Paul Cambon, the ambassador to Great Britain, and Camille Barrère, the ambassador to Italy, regretted the slow vanishing of the centuries-old protectorate, others, such as the ambassador in Constantinople, Maurice Bompard, were in favor of its dying out, arguing that economic and financial tactics should be the instrument of modern imperialism.[32]

Internationally, the attacks were more substantial. In 1913, a decisive study was presented to the French government that con-

29. Philip S. Khoury, *Syria and the French Mandate: The Politics of Arab Nationalism, 1920–1945* (Princeton, N.J.: Princeton University Press, 1987), 27.

30. Howard Sachar, *The Emergence of the Middle East, 1914–1924* (New York: Knopf, 1969), 162.

31. Joseph Hajjar, *Le Vatican, la France et le catholicisme oriental (1878–1914)* (Paris: Beauchesne, 1979), 278.

32. Catherine Nicault, "The End of the French Religious Protectorate in Jerusalem (1918–1924)," *Bulletin du CRFJ* 4 (Spring 1999): 80.

sidered the different factors weakening France's position in the Levant as well as its protectorate.[33] The severing of diplomatic ties with the Holy See had had the most damaging effect. In the missions, after the closure of Catholic seminaries and the expulsion of religious orders from France, Italian and German priests replaced French missionaries. Italian was spreading quickly, replacing French as the privileged language. The author noted that at the Curia, Germany was influencing the pope to abolish the French protectorate in favor of Italy. Italy itself was powerful at Propaganda Fide, in charge of organizing all the missionary activities of the church. In 1906, under papal pressure, France relinquished part of its protectorate, enabling Italian missionaries to seek protection directly from their native consulates in Syria, effectively reducing the protectorate to the Franciscan Custody of the Holy Land and the Latin patriarchate.[34] Although theoretically an international and transnational institution, the Custody was ruled by Ottoman law.[35]

The French protectorate was a double-edged sword for the Holy See. On one hand, it had efficiently ensured the protection of Catholics in the Ottoman Empire since the 1500s. On the other hand, it had limited the direct influence of the Holy See on Catholic missions active in the Ottoman Empire, since many of their missionaries were of French nationality, therefore directly dependent upon the policy of France in the region. Because of the association of the French protectorate with Western missionary activities, it also "raised cultural and political barriers between Frenchmen...and the Muslim majority."[36] It was also

33. Archives du Quai d'Orsay, Paris, le 30 Avril 1913, Protectorat et Saint Siège; Saint Siège, protectorat, dossier général, X (37), fol. 34-35, quoted in Hajjar, *Vatican*, 310.

34. For a detailed description and history of the Custody of the Holy Land and the Latin patriarchate, see Roberto Mazza, "Church at War: The Impact of the First World War on the Christian Institutions of Jerusalem, 1914-20," *Middle Eastern Studies* 45, no. 2 (Mar. 2009): 207-27.

35. Mazza, *Jerusalem: From the Ottomans to the British* (London: I. B. Tauris, 2009), 63.

36. Philip S. Khoury, *Syria and French Mandate*, 27.

true of other Christian Europeans in their relationship with the Muslim population.

Anticlerical France slowly reoriented its centuries-long policy of protecting exclusively Christian populations. Paris chose to limit its zone of intervention to Greater Syria but to provide culturally and economically to the entire population. This new policy of deconfessionalization directly hurt the Holy See's interests in Syria.[37]

Hence, although the Holy See had no direct diplomatic ties with the Ottoman Empire and needed the mediation of one of the Great Powers, the question was raised of the legitimacy of the French protectorate and the resolution of the Holy See to maintain it. In 1904, Gasparri, a canon lawyer, had written a study reviewing the legal aspects of the French protectorate and its limits. According to the future secretary of state, the protectorate had been established to protect the church's interests at a time when the Ottoman government was hostile to the papacy. But in the case of a "non-barbarous government," as the Ottoman Empire had become in the early twentieth century, the French protectorate had no reason to remain.[38] The future cardinal's position was a clear reminder that, from a Vatican perspective, the French protectorate was the result of a non-legally binding preferential treatment granted to France by the Holy See.

Nevertheless, on the eve of the unanticipated abrogation of the capitulations by the Porte in September 1914, the French protectorate was alive although weakened, resting on three main pillars that enhanced the prestige of France: the capitulations; the order given by the Holy See to all religious communities of Latin rite, regardless of their country of origin, to seek consular protection with France—with exceptions allowed for the Italians;

---

37. Vincent Cloarec, *La France et la question de la Syrie, 1914–1918* (Paris: CNRS, 1998), 39.
38. Pietro Gasparri, *Il Protettorato cattolico della Francia nell'Oriente e nell'estremo Oriente: Studio storico giuridoco di un prelate Romano* (n.p.: 1904).

and the liturgical honors granted to French officials,[39] a customary prerogative that had never been binding on the Holy See.[40]

France was not the only nation with a tradition of protecting Christians in the Ottoman Empire. In 1774, the capitulations had been extended to Russia, a novel development in Russo-Ottoman relationships. Claiming a protectorate over the Greek Orthodox population of the empire on the model of the French protectorate, Russia never officially obtained this privilege but could allege a manifest de facto role in the protection of the Orthodox population and, to the Holy See's greatest concern, in the active proselytizing religious policy led by Russian missionaries and envoys.

Competition of the
Russian Orthodox Protectorate

From the eighteenth century the Holy See had entertained a deep apprehension about Russian Orthodoxy and its expansionist policy in the Ottoman Empire.[41] These fears were justified. In 1774, the Peace Treaty of Kutchuk-Kainardji was signed between Empress Catherine II and the Ottoman sultan Abdul-Hamid marking the end of the first Russo-Turkish War. Many diplomats of the time considered that treaty as the first step toward the dissolution of the Ottoman Empire and its partitioning among the Great Powers. Article 11 extended the privilege of

---

39. The liturgical honors were granted by Propaganda Fide in *Règlement de la S.C. de la Propagande de 1742, sur les honneurs à rendre aux consuls de France dans le Levant*. "On y établit qu'à l'entrée en charge du consul, on chanterait un Te Deum solennel dans l'Eglise de la Mission; que dans l'Eglise il y aurait une place réservée au consul; que le Préfet de la Mission devrait envoyer un serviteur avertir le Consul de l'heure de la Messe"; ASV, Arch. Nunz. Parigi, b. 392, fasc. 304, Affari politici e religiosi Questione d'Oriente.

40. Gasparri to Denys Cochin, June 26, 1917, in response to Denys Cochin to Gasparri, June 4, 1917, ASV, AES Francia, 1917, pos. 1295–96, fasc. 686. Denys Cochin was the undersecretary at the ministry of foreign affairs in Paris, France.

41. The Orthodox Church of Russia became autocephalous in 1589. In 1721, Tsar Peter the Great abolished the Russian patriarchate and created a Holy Synod to govern the national church.

the capitulations to Russia, and Article 3, vague in its wording, constituted the foundation for a Russian protectorate over the Orthodox communities in the Ottoman Empire. The immediate consequence was the beginning of Russian interference in the empire's internal affairs, especially in the Holy Land, and the dependency of the Greek Orthodox Church on the Russian Orthodox Church.

In the nineteenth century, in a determined pan-Slavic and pan-Orthodox effort, Moscow, which dubbed itself the "Third Rome,"[42] sought to supersede the ecumenical patriarchate of Constantinople by first taking foot in the Holy Land. The goal was to hold the smaller patriarchate of Jerusalem in order to justify a future takeover of the powerful patriarchate of Constantinople. The visit of General Alexis Neidhart in 1893 to Jerusalem comforted the Holy See and the Great Powers in their fear that Russia was trying "to establish complete control over the Church of the Holy Sepulchre...in order to confirm her pretensions to the protection of the Greek Orthodox Christians, and ultimately to her rule over the Holy Land."[43]

Russia was responding to French Catholic progress in Greater Syria. The tsarist government had noticed with worry that the Orthodox community in Palestine had been plummeting, while the Catholic population had risen from 3,000 to 13,000 between 1840 and 1880. The Orthodox, which represented 90 percent of the Christian population of Palestine in 1840, had decreased

42. See Marshall Poe, "Moscow, the Third Rome: The Origins and Transformations of a 'Pivotal Moment,'" *Jahrbücher für Geschichte Osteuropas* 49, no. 3 (2001): 412–29. The "Third Rome" is a reference relative to Rome and Byzantium, which are considered the first and second Rome, respectively. In the nineteenth century, the old Russian expansionist and messianic doctrine became a reflection of imperial ideology, claiming to resurrect the Eastern Empire and represent the true Christian faith.

43. Confidential dispatch No. 63 from Consul J. Dickson, Jerusalem, to Sir F. Clare-Ford, Constantinople, October 12, 1893, regarding the visit to Jerusalem of General Alexis Neidhart, chief of the chancery of the Emperor of Russia [FO195/1806], quoted in *Minorities in the Middle East: Religious Communities in Jerusalem, 1843–1974, and Minorities in Israel*, ed. B. Destani, 1:259 (Chippenham, UK: Archive Editions, 2005).

to 67 percent in 1880.[44] In 1882, to counteract this preoccupying dwindling, Tsar Alexander III extended his support to the foundation of the Imperial Orthodox Palestine Society with the intention of reinforcing the Orthodox communities under Russian protection and eventually conquering Palestine and Syria. The Palestine Society came after the Russian launch in 1858 of a permanent ecclesiastic mission in Jerusalem whose goal was not only to counter Catholic and Protestant proselytizing, but also to maintain a political presence in the region. The Russian institution, accused of deception and greed, showed little interest in church matters, comforting the French assumption that its only goal was to muster political gains in the region.[45]

The religious and military conquest of Jerusalem would have given Russia much prestige. Not only it would have provided a much-needed homogeneity to the Russian Orthodox fabric, but most importantly, the tsar would have acquired a moral authority equal to the pope's with the utmost advantage of possessing Jerusalem while the Roman pontiff was a "prisoner in the Vatican."[46]

The Holy See was disturbed by those Russian efforts that could eventually affect the stability of the Eastern rite Catholic churches. These Catholic communities were under constant proselytizing from both their mother church and the recently established Protestant missions. Some Eastern rite Catholics were attracted by their Orthodox original church at a time when Rome had engaged in a much resented effort of Latinization of the Eastern rites, especially under Pius IX (1846–78).

In this unstable context, the abolition of the capitulations by the Ottoman government on September 9, 1914, came as a

44. Derek Hopwood, *The Russian Presence in Syria and Palestine, 1843–1914: Church and Politics in the Near East* (Oxford: Clarendon Press, 1969), 99.

45. Ibid., 121.

46. Negib Azoury, *Le réveil de la nation arabe dans l'Asie turque* (Paris: Plon, 1905), 54–55.

thunderbolt to the Great Powers. The first consequence of this unilateral act was the collapse of the foundations on which the protection of Christians—Catholic, Orthodox, and Protestant— had rested. To the Holy See, it meant a complete reappraisal of its religious policy in the Ottoman Empire and, by the same token, a questioning of the role of France as privileged protector of Latin and Eastern Catholics in the Empire. Pope Benedict was left facing an array of new diplomatic challenges, but also new opportunities never encountered by the Holy See in the past.

THE ABOLITION OF CAPITULATIONS AND
THE FUTURE OF A FRENCH PROTECTORATE
A View from the Apostolic Delegation
in Constantinople

After secret negotiations with Germany, which had been an influential political, economic, and military presence in Constantinople since the beginning of the reign of Emperor Wilhelm II (1888–1918), the Ottoman government, under the rule of the Young Turks Enver Pasha, Mehmed Talat, and Djemal Pasha,[47] ranged itself with the Central Powers on August 2, 1914. It was a deeply anchored fear of Russian expansionism that eventually led the Ottoman Empire into German arms.[48] It took another couple of months after the signing of the secret treaty for Constantinople to enter the war against the Entente.[49]

---

47. They were leaders of the Committee of Union and Progress (CUP) that had taken control of the Ottoman government in 1908. Enver Pasha was pro-German, Mehmed Talat was not afraid of Russia, and Djemal Pasha was known as a Francophile; see also footnote 16 in this chapter.

48. For a detailed analysis of this issue, see Lucien J. Frary and Mara Kozelsky, eds., *Russian-Ottoman Borderlands: The Eastern Question Reconsidered* (Madison: University of Wisconsin Press, 2014); see also Michael A. Reynolds, *Shattering Empires: The Clash and Collapse of the Ottoman and Russian Empires, 1908–1918* (Cambridge: Cambridge University Press, 2011).

49. See Kristian Coates Ulrichsen, *The First World War in the Middle East* (London:

Taking advantage of the situation created by the outbreak of the war in Europe, the Ottoman government abolished the capitulations on September 9, 1914, the new law taking effect on October 1, 1914. At this time, Constantinople was still maintaining its neutrality in the European conflict. The abrogation was the first tangible result of the secret alliance treaty signed between Germany and the Ottoman Empire in August 1914. It amounted to a call to further emancipation following the restoration of the Constitution in 1908 and an official denunciation of all protectorates.

Although it should not have come as a complete surprise to the Great Powers, since the Porte had already officially complained in an 1869 memo about the abusive use of the capitulations by Christian Ottomans, this unilateral act was received with shock and anger by all nations concerned, Germany included.[50] In a most unusual move, countries at war forgot their belligerence for a moment and joined to protest to the Porte. They reminded Constantinople that the capitulations were international binding treaties whose unilateral abrogation was therefore not juridically valid. As the belligerent countries never recognized the legal validity of the abolition, the capitulations remained officially in effect until the signature of the Treaty of Lausanne of 1923,

---

Hurst, 2014); Mustafa Aksakal, *The Ottoman Road to War in 1914: The Ottoman Empire and the First World War* (Cambridge: Cambridge University Press, 2010); Eugene Rogan, *The Fall of the Ottomans: The Great War in the Middle East* (London: Basic Books, 2015).

50. "Les capitulations ayant été consacrées par les traités postérieurement conclus entre la Sublime-Porte et les puissances étrangères, doivent... être scrupuleusement respectées au même titre que ces traités. Il est toutefois connu que, dans la pratique, on leur donne une élasticité qu'elles ne comportent pas, et qu'à côté des privilèges déjà exceptionnels accordés par ces actes, il existe des abus manifestes qui occasionnent des difficultés incessantes.... C'est pourquoi la Sublime-Porte, en ordonnant aux autorités impériales d'observer strictement et en toute loyauté les dispositions contenues dans les capitulations, ne saurait trop leur recommander en même temps de repousser toute prétention qui dépasserait les limites des privilèges consacrés par ces actes et qui porterait atteinte aux droits souverains et imprescriptibles de sa Majesté Impériale le Sultan"; Gérard Pélissié du Rausas, *Le régime des capitulations dans l'empire ottoman* (Paris: Arthur Rousseau, 1902), 1:222.

which brought an end to the war between Turkey and the Allies and recognized the frontiers of the new state of Turkey under the leadership of Mustafa Kemal.

The Ottoman decree abolishing privileges enjoyed through the capitulations also caused grave concern at the Vatican. In an article published in the *New York Times* a few days after the promulgation of the decree on September 14, the author synthesized with some emotional exaggeration the issues at stake:

It [the Ottoman decree] not only sweeps away the famous French protectorate over Christian affairs in the Orient, but also utterly destroys the liberty of public worship and the rights of semi-religious institutions, such as schools and hospitals, which Christianity, in virtue of a portion of the capitulations, has enjoyed throughout the Ottoman Empire since the age of the Crusaders.... The Holy See is entering a lively protest because it foresees that so revolutionary a change must deprive it of all binding force in administrative matters, while the resultant disendowment means financial ruin.[51]

In a long report addressed to Eugenio Pacelli, secretary for extraordinary ecclesiastical affairs, on September 10, 1914, Msgr. Vincenzo Sardi, the apostolic delegate in Constantinople, offered a balanced analysis of the new situation, stressing the same points of concern.[52] The question of freedom of worship was not a source of worry to him. He emphasized the financial consequences of the abrogation of the capitulations, pondered the future independence of Catholic schools, and argued that the cessation of the French protectorate would not be harmful to the Holy See and the Catholic communities in the Ottoman Empire.

Regarding the freedom of worship, unlike the writer from the *New York Times*, Sardi did not anticipate any negative repercussion on the free exercise of the Catholic cults in the Ottoman

51. "Vatican Will Oppose the Ottoman Decree," *New York Times*, Sept. 14, 1914, 4.

52. Sardi to Pacelli, Sept. 19, 1914, ASV, Segr. Stato, 1915, rubr. 257, fasc. 1. Sardi was apostolic delegate from 1908 to November 1914. He was then replaced by Angelo Dolci.

Empire. He added that the hatred demonstrated in the past by Muslims against "the Christian dogs" was quickly receding and stressed that, although the Young Turks manifested an attachment to religious indifference, the majority of the population was very religious. There was therefore no risk in seeing the Ottoman government choose an antireligious or areligious course. To the risk of potential Christian persecutions, Sardi opposed the good relations between the Ottoman government and the Catholic Church.[53] The risk of a return to *dhimmitude* was almost nonexistent due to the Young Turks' latest efforts to modernize the empire and modify the judicial status of foreign subjects. The abrogation of the capitulations was therefore more a cry for complete sovereignty than an attack against Christians.

On the other hand, the financial repercussions resulting from the abolition of the capitulations were a source of concern to the apostolic delegate. The loss of capitulatory privileges meant the loss of tax exemption enjoyed until then by all religious establishments, seminaries, schools, and other properties that were listed by France as being under French protection, decreasing the funds otherwise available to these institutions. The Ottoman government in the Treaty of Mytilene of 1901 had officially recognized this list of establishments. A new agreement was signed in 1913 in which the rights and privileges of the Catholic communities in the Holy Land were recognized.

The apostolic delegate explained that the abrogation would subject the majority of the religious institutions, but not all establishments, to the common tax law. Those intended for worship, like churches and chapels, would certainly benefit from the same rights that were granted to the mosques, as required by the Qu'ran. In addition to new taxes, religious establishments would also be subjected to new customs duties. Until then, churches

53. Ibid.

had been able to obtain goods directly from abroad and were thereby exempted from customs. The Catholic churches benefited greatly from the tax exemption. Sardi concluded that the new measure was not unjustified, being in part a response to the abusive behavior of European residents who were taking advantage of this privilege.

As regards the independence of the Catholic schools, the apostolic delegate noted that most students were Ottoman subjects (Turkish, Greek, Armenian, or Jewish). Therefore, the abolition of the capitulations would not affect them. The only change would be the right of the government to inspect the schools and to order the Turkish language to be taught.[54]

As long as the Ottoman Empire maintained neutrality in the war, the Holy See did not perceive maintaining the French protectorate as a major problem. In the same relation, Sardi noted that the French protectorate was the result of two kinds of agreements. One, ratified by international treaties, dealt with the privileges accorded by the Ottoman Empire to France. This agreement was questionably revoked by the unilateral abrogation of the capitulations by Constantinople. The other agreement was between the Holy See and France. It was a privilege recognized by the Holy See but was not binding, contrary to what a French minister had uttered in 1905: that "this protectorate over the Orient did not stem from the pontiff's benevolence, but from international treaties."[55]

In the absence of diplomatic ties with France since 1904 and in a context of declining influence of the French protectorate since the beginning of the century, the Holy See had the diplomatic power to question the future of the protectorate and consider other alternatives, among them transferring the protectorate to

54. Ibid.
55. Gasparri to French ambassador, no date, ASV, Arch. Nunz. Parigi, b. 392, fasc. 304 (my translation).

another Catholic power or entering into direct diplomatic ties with the Ottoman government. Sardi made no mystery of the fact that France was not interested in religion per se but that the French government continued to protect Catholic establishments, not because they were Catholic but rather because they were, in their immense majority, French. The French zeal to respect their commitment was, according to Sardi, visible in only two fields: the liturgical honors and the diplomatic representation of the Holy See to the Porte. Dismissing the issue raised by the maintaining of the liturgical honors as incidental, he noted with some irritation that "the ostentatious tutelage of the apostolic delegate, who, according to the [French] embassy, should not make a move without being taken by the Ambassador's hand," had become even more exigent since the diplomatic break.[56]

A few weeks later, Cardinal Gasparri echoed Sardi's frustration and irritation when he wrote—although the letter was never sent—to the new apostolic delegate in Constantinople, Msgr. Angelo Dolci,[57] and instructed him to

end the dependence of the apostolic delegation on France in matters regarding visit to the sultan as it does not fall under the obligations of the protectorate and is extremely unseemly for the papal representative. . . . If the ambassador calls upon history or tradition, Msgr Dolci [will] reply that the apostolic delegation cannot, without it being at the expense of its dignity, be subjected to the continuation of a humiliating tutelage, devoid of any legal foundation and much less understandable now that France ignores the Holy See.[58]

56. "La tutela ostentata del Delegato Apostolico, il quale, secondo le idee dell'Ambasciata, non dovrebbe muoversi se non condotto a mano dall'Ambasciatore"; Sardi to Pacelli, Sept. 19, 1914, ASV, Segr. Stato, 1915, rubr. 257, fasc. 1 (my translation).

57. Angelo Dolci (1867–1939) was appointed apostolic delegate in Ecuador, Bolivia, and Peru in 1906 before being transferred to Constantinople. He officially became the apostolic delegate of Constantinople on November 13, 1914. In 1922, he was appointed nuncio to Belgium before being sent to Romania.

58. "Cessare la dipendenza della Delegazione Apostolica dall'Ambasciata di Francia nelle visite al Sultano sia perche essa non rientra affatto nel Protettorato sia perche e in

Sardi concluded his relation by predicting that the cessation of the French protectorate after the abrogation of the capitulations would not hurt the Holy See's interests.

A View from the Apostolic Delegation in Syria and Palestine

From Beirut, a few hundred miles away from Constantinople, the apostolic delegate to Syria (and Palestine), Msgr. Frediano Giannini, shed a different light on the impact that the abrogation of the capitulations would have on the Catholic presence in the Holy Land. Since 1906, when Italian missionaries were granted the Holy See's authorization to seek protection from the Italian consulates, the French protectorate in the Holy Land had been reduced, aside from French institutions, to the Latin patriarchate and was weakened in the Franciscan Custody, his members being essentially Italians.[59] Unlike Sardi—and later Dolci—who were at the center of the international diplomatic game in Constantinople, Giannini had a more concrete approach, aware of the daily vicissitudes of the Custody and the Latin patriarchate. He saw the situation as extremely serious.[60]

The Holy Places of Palestine had always been at the core of the Holy See's diplomacy in the Middle East. After his closing speech at the Council of Clermont in 1095, thousands of Latin Catholics had answered Pope Urban II's call to wage war against Islam and deliver from Muslim hands those most sacred places venerated by Christians, thereby launching the First Crusade. Jerusalem

---

sommo grado indecorosa per il rappresentante Pontificio....Se l'ambasciatore appellasse alla tradizione o consuetudine, Mons. Dolci risponda che la Delegazione Apostolica non puo senza scapito della sua dignita assoggettarsi alla continuazione di una cosa umiliante tutela, priva di qualsiasi fondamento giuridico e tanto meno comprensibile ora che la Francia ignora la S. Sede"; Instructions for Msgr. Dolci, Oct. 1, 1914, ASV, Segr. Stato, Guerra (1914–18), fasc.1 (my translation).

59. Catherine Nicault, "End of the French Religious Protectorate," 80.

60. Giannini to Gotti, Oct. 15, 1914, ASV, Arch. Nunz. Libano, Registry Propaganda Fide, 68 (1913–16), 162–63.

fell into Christian hands in July 1099. The establishment of the Christian kingdom of Jerusalem soon followed. Latin Catholics established themselves in Palestine and peacefully cohabitated with Eastern rites Christians already present in the Holy Land. The first Latin clergymen were Franciscan friars. They were authorized by the sultan to take care of the Church of the Holy Sepulchre in 1219. After the departure of the crusaders, they became guardians of the site. In 1342, with the bull *Gratias Agimus*, Pope Clement VI officially handed over the Holy Places to the Franciscans, giving birth to the Franciscan Custody.[61] Their custody of these sacred sites was not to be threatened by the military victory of the Ottoman sultan, Selim I, who led his armies into Palestine and conquered Jerusalem in December 1516.[62]

Throughout centuries, the small Latin Catholic community, heir of the crusaders, faced two opponents. The Ottoman Muslims, who had taken control of the Holy Land, treated the Christians with some tolerance but as *dhimmis*. They were respectful of the Franciscan Custody. The question of the Holy Places was essentially a problem affecting different Christian denominations and their conflicting claims of ownership over them. Although the Franciscans asserted that their authority over the Holy Places was going back to the fourteenth century, the Orthodox churches alleged their own rights as sole owners of the same sites since the fourth century. The dispute over conflicting rights eventually became a political issue that greatly influenced the state of affairs in Europe.

Sole official owners of the Holy Places, the Franciscans had allowed the Greek Orthodox to enjoy free exercise of their devotions. Still, the relationship was factious. Over the centuries, the Greek patriarchs of Jerusalem were able to secure *firmans* giving

---

61. See Mazza, "Church at War," 207–27.

62. Charles Frazee, *Catholics and Sultans: The Church and the Ottoman Empire, 1453–1923* (New York: Cambridge University Press, 1983), 59.

them possession of different sites. These mandates decreed by the sultan signified the end of the Franciscan supremacy over the Holy Land and the beginning of open conflict between European countries interested in strengthening their presence in Palestine through the diplomatic protection of their Christian subjects. The Holy See, whose interests and rights in Palestine preceded those of European powers, could only rely on the goodwill of France in its enforcing of the capitulations and defending the popes' rights through the protection of the Latin rite churches and missions.

France had the opportunity to manifest its good intentions to the papacy when, in 1676, a new *firman* was secured by the Greek Orthodox patriarch of Jerusalem, giving him sole ownership of the Church of the Holy Sepulchre. After France complained, a famous *firman* was issued in 1690 that reversed the decree of 1676 and declared the Franciscans legitimate owners of the Holy Places.[63] The situation was unstable. The Franciscans needed French help to fight the religious battle against the Greek Orthodox Church, even though they resented France's protection. They did not trust France, whose *raison d'état* could result, at any time, in an alliance with the Ottomans against another Catholic European country. Most of the Franciscans involved in the custody were Italian (with a few Spaniards) and were reluctant to accept French diplomatic protection, favoring the patronage of Spain, Piedmont-Sardinia, or Austria.[64]

The atypical relations between Paris and the Holy See, a consequence of the protectorate, had ambiguous effects on the successive popes' attempts to ensure the protection of the Holy Places. No concrete action was possible without French diplomatic inter-

63. Hajjar, *Le christianisme en Orient* (Beirut: Librairie du Liban, 1971), 7.

64. Henry Laurens, "Le Vatican et la question de la Palestine," in *Nations et Saint-Siège au XXe siècle*, Colloque sous la direction d'Hélène Carrère d'Encausse et de Philippe Levillain (Paris: Fayard, 2003), 305.

vention, which didn't swerve over the centuries. This dependency restricted the Holy See's efforts to find common ground with the Orthodox Church, efforts that would have implied a friendly relationship between France and Russia, the Greek Orthodox Church's protector.

The question of the Holy Places eventually became a political battle between France and the Russian Empire. While the Holy See's rights to protect the sacred sites of Palestine depended on the French Catholic protectorate, the Orthodox Church's fortune in the same places was directly contingent upon the state of its relations with Orthodox Russia. The political friendship or animosity between the sultan and the tsar was consequently of crucial importance to the Holy See, as well as the quality of the diplomatic relations between France and Russia.

In the context of an alliance between Paris and Constantinople through the capitulations, the tension between Latin Catholics and Greek Orthodox put a strain on Russian-Ottoman relationship. The *firman* of 1690 acknowledged this state of affairs and made French protection official. The capitulations of 1740 solemnly confirmed the rights of France, especially over the Church of the Holy Sepulchre and the Church of the Nativity in Bethlehem. In 1767, merely twenty years later, the Latin Catholics were expelled from Bethlehem and the sultan placed the Church of the Holy Sepulchre and several other sanctuaries under the protection of the Greek Orthodox.

Geostrategic reasons motivated political alliances and added to the difficulties of the Holy See ensuring the protection of the Holy Places. Starting in the nineteenth century, France, Russia, and the Holy See could not do without the British, to whom Palestine had become a strategic buffer to Egypt. London was extremely protective of its dominion over Egypt and later over the Suez Canal. When the Suez Canal was opened in November 1869, the British route to India shifted from Constantinople and the Bosphorus to Egypt. In an era of imperialistic appetites, the Ottoman Empire became the receptacle of all rivalries and changing alliances among the Great Powers. The Eastern question—that is, the issue of the decay of the Ottoman Empire and its consequences for greedy European powers—became intricately linked to the question of the Holy Places of Palestine.

With the first half of the nineteenth century came multiple causes for concern to the papacy. Pope Pius IX expressed his apprehension to the French government on the occasion of the establishment in Jerusalem of an Anglo-Prussian bishopric in 1841 and the constitution of a Russian ecclesiastical mission in 1847. Facing French reticence and fear that a Latin patriarchate could weaken the Catholic protectorate by creating a new, overlapping jurisdiction, Pius IX nevertheless reestablished it with the apostolic letter *Nulla Celebrior* of July 23, 1847, after a hiatus of more than five hundred years.[65]

The revival of the Latin patriarchate created new tensions between the patriarch and the Custos but did not lessen the wide influence of the Franciscan Custody, under the ecclesiastic authority and jurisdiction of the patriarchate. Interreligious tension reached its peak in 1852, when France intended to reassert the sole rights of the Latin rite churches over the Holy Places, as granted by the *firman* of 1690. Saint Petersburg's reply was immediate and threatening. Russia impressed upon a weak Ottoman Empire its claim as protector of the fifteen million Ottoman subjects of Orthodox obedience. The *firman* of 1852 declared that the status quo, the arrangement officially enforced since 1767 in favor of the Greek Orthodox, was to be maintained. The Crimean War ensued, leading to Russia's defeat. The treaty of peace,

---

65. There had been no Latin Patriarchate of Jerusalem since 1291, after the last crusading stronghold had fallen; see Pius IX, "Apostolic Letter *Nulla Celebrior* [July 23, 1847]," *Acta Pius IX*, vol.1.

signed in Paris in 1856, designed a specific law regarding the Holy Places of Palestine. A few years later, the Treaty of Berlin of 1878, in its famous article 62, recognized

the right of official protection by the Diplomatic and Consular Agents of the Powers in Turkey...both as regards the above-mentioned persons [ecclesiastics, pilgrims, and monks of all nationalities] and their religious, charitable, and other establishments in the Holy Places and elsewhere. The rights possessed by France are expressly reserved, and it is well understood that no alterations can be made in the *status quo* in the Holy Places. The monks of Mount Athos, of whatever country they may be natives, shall be maintained in their former possessions and advantages, and shall enjoy, without any exception, complete equality of rights and prerogatives.[66]

Under Leo XIII's papacy, the situation became more intricate. In Pope Leo's Great Design to re-Christianize the world, Russia was a key piece. Thus, he favored the Franco-Russian alliance of the late nineteenth century, which had implications for the Holy Places. The French and Russian governments were eager to transpose their good relationship on the continent to the Holy Land, which had a positive impact on the cohabitation between Latin Catholics and Greek Orthodox in the region. But it also had the unwelcome consequence of giving Russia and France legitimate reasons to gain control over Palestine under the pretext of protecting the Holy Places.

In this historically unstable context, the abrogation of the capitulations came as a shock to both the European powers and the Holy See. On October 14, 1914, the general governor of Beirut issued instructions stipulating that

The religious and personal protectorate resulting from ancient treaties that the French government and other foreign powers enjoyed over foreign Catholics was abolished. The right to a protectorate that...France had over religious of French nationality and foreign establishments of Latin rite was also abrogated. Consequently, the intervention of

---

66. "The Treaty of Berlin," (London) *Times*, July 17, 1878, 10, col. A.

consuls will be forbidden in the Ottoman Empire and especially in the Holy Places.... The status quo in the Holy Places remains as it was before.[67]

On the same day, Auguste Boppe, adviser to the French embassy at Constantinople, echoed the concern expressed by Giannini regarding the future of the Holy Places. In a note addressed to René Viviani, president of the council, the diplomat questioned the validity of the decree of abrogation of the capitulations as regards their impact on the status of Jerusalem and the Holy Places. He stressed the international dimension of the issue and its earlier resolution by Article 62 of the Treaty of Berlin of 1878. In a detailed report, he explained that, according to the Ottoman government, the suppression of the religious protectorate over the Holy Places was a direct consequence of the abrogation of the capitulations, concluding

It [the protectorate] has been...sanctioned...by the Treaty of Berlin that bears the signature of Turkey along with that of the six European Great Powers.... It is a serious question that is raised with incredible thoughtlessness by the Ottoman government, that the conflagration of Europe has rendered foolish.[68]

France and the Holy See were aware that since the Congress of Paris of 1856, when the Ottoman Empire was admitted for the first time into the family of nations, the Porte was eager to abol-

---

67. "A été aboli le protectorat religieux et personnel résultant des traités anciens qu'avaient le gouvernement français et les autres puissances étrangères sur les catholiques étrangers. A été aboli aussi le droit de protectorat... que la France avait sur les religieux de nationalité française et sur les établissements étrangers du rite latin. En conséquence on n'acceptera plus l'intervention des consuls en pays ottoman et spécialement dans les Lieux Saints.... Le status quo dans les Lieux Saints demeure comme auparavant"; Gotti to Gasparri, Oct. 29, 1914 (Inserto : Communicato del Governatorato Generale di Beirut, 15 Octobre 1914), ASV, AES, Austria, 1913–15, pos. 1047, fasc. 445 (my translation).

68. "Il a...été consacré...par le traité de Berlin qui porte la signature de la Turquie à côté de celle des six autres grandes Puissances de l'Europe.... C'est une bien grave question qui se trouve ainsi posée avec une incroyable légèreté par le gouvernement ottoman, que la conflagration de l'Europe a littéralement frappé de vertige"; Hajjar, *L'Europe et les destinées du Proche-Orient* (Damas: Dar Tlass, 1998), 5:43 (my translation).

ish the capitulations, which it saw as a serious infringement of its sovereignty and rights. The Young Turks were in the process of reforming their whole judicial system when the war broke out.[69] Therefore, the apparent surprise of the French government as well as the reaction of the Holy See and other powers were disingenuous and indicated how little political credibility the Ottoman government had been left with. This fact had a noticeable impact on the Holy See's choice of diplomatic course during the war in its interaction with the Porte.

The entry of the Ottoman Empire in the war as an ally of the Central Powers on November 5, 1914, caused another Copernican revolution on the Ottoman diplomatic scene. The recriminations of the Entente Powers that the abrogation of the capitulations and the ending of the protectorates were unlawful were lost in the tumult that ensued once the Ottoman Empire became engulfed in the conflict. The protectorates effectively ceased to exist for the next three years, until Jerusalem returned to Christian hands for the first time since the Crusades when the British Army, led by General Allenby, captured the Holy City in December 1917.

69. Norman Bentwich, "The Abrogation of the Turkish Capitulations," *Journal of Comparative Legislation and International Law* 5 (1923): 183.

3

VATICAN WARTIME
FOREIGN POLICY

In wartime, diplomatic relations between governments are experienced at two levels: a level of immediacy, where rapidly evolving political and military developments request constant diplomatic adjustments to strategic objectives, and a level of anticipation of long-term geopolitical and geostrategic changes as the consequence of the war experience. Although not a belligerent in the war, the Holy See was not exempt from this dual level of interaction with both the Ottoman government and the Great Powers involved in the conflict.

From the onset of the war in Arab Ottoman lands on November 5, 1914, to the capture of Jerusalem by General Allenby on December 9, 1917, Pope Benedict crafted and kept adjusting an Eastern policy that aimed to create an immediate and long-term diplomatic environment that ensured the wartime protection of Eastern and Latin Catholic communities in the empire as well as a conducive environment for a future rapprochement with the separated brethren. The Holy See strove to distinguish in this diplomatic process the essential from the ephemeral.[1]

The originality of Pope Benedict's Eastern foreign policy was

---

1. G. R. Berridge, Maurice Keens-Soper, and Thomas G. Otte, *Diplomatic Theory from Machiavelli to Kissinger* (New York: Palgrave, 2001), 133.

manifest in his effort to integrate classic diplomatic functions of negotiation with an ecclesiastical policy that reflected his Eastern ecclesiology. The pontiff engaged in a dynamic diplomacy, assessing the suitability of new paradigms to guide its wartime foreign policy in the Ottoman Empire. This strategy at the geopolitical level was articulated in a comprehensive and cohesive ecclesiological frame. Benedict XV completed and institutionalized the traditional ecclesiological approach in favor of unionism and rapprochement with the separated brethren, previously implemented by Leo XIII, providing a solid theoretical and practical underpinning to his Eastern foreign policy.

ROME AND CONSTANTINOPLE
IN DIPLOMATIC NEGOTIATIONS: THE FUTURE
OF THE FRENCH PROTECTORATE

On November 2, 1914, the tsar opened the hostilities against Constantinople. A few days later, on November 5, France and Britain amended their proclamations of war against the Central Powers to include the Ottoman Empire. In a speech delivered in London on November 9, 1914, British Prime Minister Herbert Asquith foresaw that, now that the conflict had engulfed the Ottoman Empire, "the war had 'rung the death-knell of Ottoman dominion, not only in Europe, but in Asia.'"[2] The road to a new emerging Middle East was being paved.

With the abrogation of the capitulations on September 9, followed by the entry of Constantinople into the war, the French protectorate became de facto ineffectual. Upon his expulsion from Constantinople the French ambassador to the Porte, Maurice Bompard, informed Msgr. Pompilj, vicar general of Rome,

---

2. Herbert Henry Asquith, *Letters to Venetia Stanley*, ed. Michael Brock and Eleanor Brock (Oxford: Oxford University Press, 1982), 402, quoted in David Fromkin, *A Peace to End All Peace* (New York: Henry Holt, 1989), 75. Asquith was prime minister from 1908 to 1916. He was succeeded by David Lloyd George, who served from 1916 to 1922.

that the protection of French interests was transferred to the American ambassador and that of Catholic interests in the Holy Places to Spain, adding that he could not leave Catholic interests in Protestant hands but also knew that the Spanish consul, Count de Ballobar, was lacking the required political influence to protect and take good care of all Catholic interests in the empire.[3] Pompilj relayed the information to Cardinal Gasparri and addressed in the same breath the topical issue of the representation of the Holy See at Constantinople. He acknowledged that it was a delicate subject, sensitive to the reputation of France among the Catholics residing in the empire.[4]

Pope Benedict was facing a difficult situation. The war, which was not expected to last long, had just started. It was too early to predict accurately the final results of the conflict in which two major Catholic countries, France and Austria, were fighting in opposite camps. Meanwhile, the Holy See was weakened on the diplomatic scene because of Benedict's impartial stand in the war and had consequently little political leverage. Was it therefore reasonable for the Holy See to break abruptly with four centuries of tradition and definitively abandon the already weakened French Catholic protectorate?

Any break was complicated by the difficulties presented by each alternative option. The pope and his secretary of state pondered three different diplomatic moves: transferring the French protectorate to Austria-Hungary, the only Catholic country allied to the Ottoman Empire; opening a nunciature in Constantinople, an option strongly supported by the Ottoman government; and finally, maintaining the status quo in the hope of an

3. Pompilj to Gasparri, Nov. 3, 1914, ASV, Segr. Stato, Guerra (1914–18), rubr. 244, fasc. 110; see also "Relazione intorno all'espulsione dei Religiosi dalla Palestina e sullo stato del Patriarcato di Gerusalemme e delle sue missioni, February 22, 1915," AP, N.S., vol. 629 (1919), rub. 126.

4. Pompilj to Gasparri, Nov. 3, 1914, ASV, Segr. Stato, Guerra (1914–18), rubr. 244, fasc. 110.

Entente victory, restoring thereafter the French protectorate. The feasibility of opening a nunciature was the guiding thread in diplomatic discussions between the Holy See, the Porte, and the Great Powers.

The Transfer of the French Protectorate

From the onset of the war until the year 1917, the Western Front was the scene of a war of attrition, a devastating trench war during which neither side was able to deliver the final blow. As Pope Benedict originally believed in a final victory of the Central Powers,[5] the transfer of the French protectorate to Catholic Austria-Hungary was an option worthy of consideration in the early months of the conflict.

In a letter dated December 18, 1914, the nuncio to Austria-Hungary, Msgr. Raffaele Scapinelli, communicated to Cardinal Gasparri the content of an interview he had with Count Berchtold during which the imperial foreign minister asked if the Holy See was planning to transfer the French protectorate to Austria. The nuncio replied that the Holy See was not entertaining the idea and explained that, although the political benefit of becoming responsible for the Catholic protectorate was not to be dismissed, the Austrian Empire was limited in its diplomatic action by its friendly relationship with Constantinople.[6] The Austrian government was prudent and did not want to exercise a right that the Ottoman government no longer recognized. Furthermore, following the annexation of Serbia, the Austrian government was committed to Turkey, as it had promised to support the abolition of capitulations when the time came.[7] The British

---

5. "Le pape n'est pas un *Boche déguisé*; il croit à la victoire finale de l'Allemagne"; Alfred Baudrillart, *Les carnets du Cardinal Baudrillart, 1er août 1914–31 décembre 1918* (Paris: Editions du Cerf, 1994), 258.

6. Scapinelli to Gasparri, Dec. 18, 1914, ASV, Segr. Stato, Guerra (1914–18), rubr. 244, fasc. 110.

7. Ibid.

attaché, Count de Salis, echoed the nuncio's argument, stressing that, in a spirit of Josephinism going back to the Catholic Enlightenment of the late eighteenth century (a spirit greatly resisted by the Holy See throughout the years), Austria was tempted to "treat the Church as a mere department of State," therefore creating friction with the papacy. In addition, the Hungarian element, known for its chauvinism and strong Calvinism, had to be appreciated as an impediment.[8]

The abolition of the capitulations meant the end of all protectorates and the beginning of full independence. Consequently, the Austro-Hungarian government and the Holy See never entered into serious negotiations regarding the possibility of transferring the Catholic protectorate from France to Austria. A dangerous diplomatic vacuum was therefore evident in Constantinople.

The Opening of a Nunciature in Constantinople

The political weakness of the Spanish consul officially in charge of Catholic interests in the Holy Land hindered the diplomatic pressure he could exercise at the Porte on behalf of the Holy See. The new apostolic delegate, Angelo Dolci, a smart and astute diplomat, took advantage of the unstable situation and undertook to demonstrate to Pope Benedict the benefits of entering into official diplomatic relationship with the Ottomans. His insight on the political situation in Constantinople diverged from the view held by the pontiff and his secretary of state. With a broader perspective, the pope advocated more prudence and a wait-and-see attitude.

The plan to establish direct diplomatic ties with the Porte went back to 1896, under Leo XIII's pontificate. The German gov-

8. Thomas E. Hachey, ed., *Great Britain Legation: Anglo-Vatican Relations, 1914–1939, Confidential Annual Reports of the British Ministers to the Holy See, London, England* (Boston: G. K. Hall, 1972), 3.

ernment had taken the issue to heart with the goal of supporting the Latin patriarchate of Jerusalem in its fight against Orthodox expansion in the Ottoman Empire. Arguably, the Franco-Russian alliance impeded French involvement as Paris took a restrained approach to the issue.[9] The German plan was met with French opposition and was thwarted after Pope Leo reaffirmed the authority of the French protectorate in his apostolic letter *Maximo cum Animi* of July 20, 1898.[10] Although the diplomatic situation was different under Benedict's pontificate, the Holy See followed in Leo's steps and considered entering into direct diplomatic relations with Constantinople with hesitation and prudence, eager to avoid confrontation with France.

The pressure to consider direct ties came from the Ottoman government. The Porte entered the negotiations using the fear factor. With the abolition of the capitulations and Constantinople in the war against France, the Holy See was facing a perilous situation. In a dispatch of November 20 addressed to Gasparri, Dolci informed the Holy See that all Catholic institutions (schools, orphanages, and religious houses) in the Holy Land had been confiscated on the ground that they were French property.[11] With the French expelled from the empire and in the absence of official representation, Catholic interests, although under Spanish protection, were at the mercy of Constantinople's temperamental will. Confirming the dire situation in which Catholic interests stood, Giannini wrote that he had heard from the German consul in Damascus that

Most of the hardships facing religious establishments...were an attempt to urge the Holy See to consider direct and official relations with

9. Joseph Hajjar, *Le Vatican, la France et le catholicisme oriental (1878–1914)* (Paris: Beauchesne, 1979), 129.

10. Leo XIII, "Apostolic Letter *Maximo cum Animi* [Aug. 20, 1898]," *ASS* 31 (1898–99): 193–95.

11. Dolci to Gasparri, Nov. 20, 1914, ASV, Segr. Stato, Guerra (1914–18), rubr. 244, fasc. 111.

the Sublime Porte, in order to bring the era of the religious protectorates in the Ottoman Empire to a close.[12]

The Porte used various diplomatic weapons to influence the Holy See. When, in early December 1914, Dolci solemnly introduced himself to the sultan as the new apostolic delegate, he delivered a handwritten letter by Pope Benedict.[13] The Porte immediately raised the question of the diplomatic value of the missive, arguing that it was an official letter of credence, while the Holy See interpreted it as a simple letter of recommendation.[14] Dolci explained to Gasparri that if the missive had been acknowledged by the sultan as a letter of credence, Dolci would have immediately been conferred the official title of representative of the Holy See to the Porte.[15] Dolci's visit to the sultan did not go unnoticed. The European press commented that a historic event had just taken place, with the apostolic delegate in Constantinople meeting with the sultan in the absence of the French ambassador, the century-long representative of the Holy See to the Porte.[16]

A few months later, in September 1915, the Porte used another diplomatic ruse to keep pressure on the Holy See. From September 15 to September 23, the Ottoman office of military censorship blocked the flow of ciphered communications between the apostolic delegation and the Vatican, on the ground that Italy was now a belligerent. Because the Vatican was an enclave in Italian territory, the Italian government was regularly monitoring the communications between the apostolic delegation and the Vati-

12. "Gran parte dei malanni fatti subire adesso agli stabilimenti religiosi...proverebbe dal proposito fermo di volere incurre la Santa Sede a mettersi in directa ed ufficiale relazione con la Sublime Porta, per chiudere in tal guise l'era dei protettorati religiosi nell'Impero ottoman"; Giannini to Gotti, Jan. 16, 1915, AP, N.S., vol. 592 (1917), rub. 126, fol. 44rv (my translation).

13. Dolci to Gasparri, Dec. 12, 1914, ASV, Segr. Stato, 1914, rubr. 257, fasc. 1, ff 19–22.

14. Copy of Benedict XV's letter to the sultan, filed with letter of Dec. 23, 1914, from Dolci to the sultan, ASV, Arch. Deleg. Turchia, Dolci, I.

15. Dolci to Gasparri, Dec. 28, 1914, ASV, Segr. Stato, 1915, rubr. 257, fasc 1.

16. Press article filed with letter of Dec. 23, 1914, from Dolci to the Ottoman sultan, ASV, Arch. Deleg. Turchia. Dolci, I.

can. Dolci interpreted this move as another measure to compel the Holy See to establish official contact with the Porte and enter into formal diplomatic relations. The censorship lasted only a few days after Dolci warned Constantinople that the pontiff was interpreting the measure as a grave offense and a lack of trust. He was then able to convince the Ottoman government to keep corresponding with the Holy See "in view of the great initiative of the Holy Father in favor of universal peace."[17]

While Constantinople was resolute to enter into official diplomatic relations with the Holy See, the pontiff and his secretary of state resisted the offer, acting against the advice of their apostolic delegates in Constantinople and Beirut. Rome made a global geopolitical assessment of the diplomatic scene that conflicted with Dolci and Giannini's regional analysis. Rome pondered the appropriateness of entering into diplomatic relations with the government of a Muslim empire, one whose collapse was anticipated. But even more critical was the risk of angering France, with which the Holy See was hoping to eventually resume diplomatic relations. The political and social situation in France had evolved since the severing of diplomatic ties in 1904. Most Frenchmen were willing to restore good relations with the Holy See, as the break had been damaging to France, especially after the outbreak of the war.[18]

Meanwhile, Dolci preferred to emphasize the good relations existing between the Eastern Catholics and the Muslim population and the urgency to ensure the immediate protection of Catholic interests in the empire. Like his predecessor, Sardi, he questioned maintaining a French religious protectorate that was abused by France to promote its politico-economic interests.

Following closely the developments on the military front,

17. Dolci to Gasparri, Oct. 8, 1915, ASV, AES Austria, 1915, pos. 1061 (my translation).
18. Confidential note about the religious and political situation of France by Mr. Hanoteaux, Jan. 1915, ASV, Segr. Stato, 1918, rubr. 244, fasc. 93.

Pope Benedict tried to buy time. Dolci, aware of Rome's resistance, looked for a diplomatic solution that would satisfy Rome, Paris, and Constantinople. The apostolic delegate tried to convince the Holy See to enter into a lesser form of diplomatic relations, arguing that a rebuttal would create a serious incident with damaging consequences. The sultan would take it as an insult, a grave offense in the world of Ottoman diplomacy. Furthermore, it would anger Djemal Pasha, the head of the Fourth Army in Syria, and trigger persecutions against the significant Catholic population of the region. Dolci proposed the immediate establishment of direct ties with the Ottoman Empire, based on a mini-concordat that would address only a few general points (official recognition of the Catholic Church, election of bishops, matrimonies) in lieu of a full-fledged relationship.[19]

Cardinal Gasparri's response to Dolci came plain and without room for negotiation, making clear that the Holy See was not interested in establishing diplomatic relations or negotiating a concordat with the Ottoman Empire.[20] The secretary of state justified the position of the Holy See in a few points. First and foremost, Pope Benedict wanted to avoid offending France. He thought a simple diplomatic relation (without any form of concordat or convention) would suffice, as it would enhance Dolci's prestige in its relation with the hierarchy of dissident churches. Dolci recognized that although a concordat would be a powerful weapon to ensure the protection of the rights of the church, its future was jeopardized: as soon as the conflict ended, the provisions of the concordat would have to be renegotiated.[21]

On February 7, 1915, in a long letter addressed to Gasparri, an enthusiastic Dolci insisted that the Catholic Church would

19. Dolci to Gasparri, Jan. 15, 1915, ASV, Segr. Stato, 1915, rubr. 257, fasc. 1; see also Dolci to Gasparri, Jan. 31, 1915, ASV, AES Austria, 1915, pos. 1055, fasc. 448.
20. Dolci to Gasparri, Jan. 31, 1915, ASV, Arch. Deleg. Turchia, Dolci 90, II.
21. Dolci to Gasparri, Jan. 17, 1915, ASV, Segr. Stato, 1915, rubr. 257, fasc. 1.

gain prestige in the eyes of the Orthodox churches if the Holy See decided to consider diplomatic ties with Constantinople. He contended that it would be a huge incentive to Latin and Eastern Catholics to strengthen their bonds, therefore generating a strong stimulus in favor of a rapprochement with the schismatic churches. He warned Gasparri that such a unique occasion would not present itself again in their lifetime and challenged the idea that the French Freemason government had any interest in resuming diplomatic ties with the Holy See.[22] Neither Pope Benedict nor Cardinal Gasparri was convinced that establishing direct ties with Constantinople would be a source of satisfaction for the Orthodox churches in the Ottoman Empire. Dolci's optimism was not shared in Rome.

By the beginning of February 1915, Dolci had convinced the Ottoman government to settle for a simple diplomatic relation without any concordat. The Porte had expressed its frustration, and Dolci had to explain that many nations, including Brazil and Belgium, that entertained diplomatic relations with the Holy See were doing so without a concordat.[23] In his dispatch of February to the secretary of state, Dolci presented the Ottoman Empire's official request to engage immediately in the transformation of the apostolic delegation into a nunciature, without the negotiation of a concordat.[24] The Holy See was not interested and asked Dolci to buy time until further notice.

The Holy See knew that its equivocations were misunderstood by Constantinople and had raised concern in Paris. A clear-cut decision had to be made. On March 12, 1915, cardinals Gasparri, Vannutelli, Gotti, Merry del Val, Lorenzelli, and Vico met to discuss the issue.[25] Vico put some order into the different

22. Dolci to Gasparri, Feb. 7, 1915, ASV, Segr. Stato, 1915, rubr. 257, fasc. 1; Dolci to Gasparri, Jan. 31, 1915, ASV, AES Austria, 1915, pos. 1055, fasc. 448.
23. Dolci to Gasparri, Jan. 17, 1915, ASV, Segr. Stato, 1915, rubr. 257, fasc. 1.
24. Dolci to Gasparri, Feb. 7, 1915, ibid.
25. ASV, AES Austria, 1915, pos. 1055, fasc. 448, rapporti sessioni 1915, Sacre Con-

positions taken by the Holy See since the end of 1914, admitting that the pontiff was in a quandary and that a compromise, like the mini-concordat suggested by Dolci, was not workable.

On one hand, the Holy See was eager to prepare a conducive environment for eventually resuming diplomatic relations with France. Any infringement on France's centuries-old religious prerogatives was received with resentment by Paris. On the other hand, as Dolci had repeatedly stressed, the responsibility of the Holy See was to ensure the best protection possible of Catholic interests and populations in Greater Syria, especially against the risk of Muslim persecution. Therefore, the idea of establishing direct ties with Constantinople, with or without a concordat, should theoretically be considered with interest. To end the deadlock, Vico suggested satisfying the Porte by entering into simple diplomatic relations with Constantinople in order to safeguard Catholic interests in the empire. He indirectly dismissed the ability of all countries, Catholic or not, to efficiently protect Catholic interests and, in effect, proposed that the Holy See become responsible for the political and religious national interests of all Catholic countries involved in the war.[26]

A letter was drafted that explained to the French cardinals that, in the midst of rivalries that were endangering the safety of Catholic interests in the empire, the Holy See had decided to take the protection of those interests into its own hands. Gasparri stressed that this move should not be interpreted by the French government as an attempt to get rid of the French protectorate but rather as an act of necessity and duty toward the Catholic populations of the empire.[27] The letter was never sent.

gregazioni Marzo 1915, "Turchia: sulla proposta di stabilire relazioni diplomatiche con la S. Sede"; quoted in Daniela Fabrizio, "Il protettorato religioso sui Cattolici in Oriente: La questione delle relazioni diplomatiche dirette tra Santa Sede e Impero ottomano, 1901–1918"; *Nuovo Rivista Storica* III (1998): 602.

26. Fabrizio, "Protettorato religioso," 603.

27. Ibid.

Pope Benedict had another change of heart and eventually decided to reject the Porte's offer to enter into any kind of official diplomatic relations.[28]

The reaction of the Ottoman government was immediate. On March 13, 1915, Dolci informed Gasparri that the Porte had decided to officially abolish all protectorates and transform the current Latin Chancellery into an autonomous entity.[29] An imperial edict ordered ten Catholic Ottoman subjects to assemble a new Latin Catholic community that the Porte would officially recognize as representing the Latin Catholic Church in the empire. This new community would elect its own patriarch and bishops, all Ottoman subjects. The patriarch would have jurisdiction over all the Latin churches, religious houses, and schools.

In a private note to the Porte, Dolci explained why the Holy See could not even consider a Latin community. In a few points, he listed the main obstacles. Among them, he mentioned the principle of a national church that was in contradiction with the catholic, universal principle of the church, one and united with the Roman pontiff.[30] Dolci further clarified his thought:

This imperial edict sets off an open struggle with the Vatican because the Holy See will never be able to grant the community power to elect the Patriarch and bishops....As for me, as soon as the government will release the edict, I will fill my duty, excommunicating the community organized by the government...by denouncing in all the churches of Constantinople and the Empire this community, which, as it is constituted, is not a catholic community but rather a schismatic body.[31]

28. Ibid., 605.

29. Dolci to Gasparri, Mar. 13, 1915, ASV, AES Austria, 1915, pos. 1057, fasc. 458.

30. Appunti di risposto al Governo Imp. sul progetto della erigenda Comunita Latina. Saggio, Brutta copia, studio (non presentato), ASV, Arch. Deleg. Turchia, Dolci II, Apr. 1915.

31. "Ce tradé impérial engage une lutte ouverte avec le Vatican parce que le Saint Siège ne pourra jamais reconnaître dans la communauté le pouvoir d'élire le Patriarche et les évêques....Quant à moi, aussitôt que le gouvernement publiera ce Tradé, je dois remplir mon devoir en frappant d'excommunication la communauté organisée par le gouvernement...en dénonçant dans toutes les églises de Constantinople et de l'Empire que

On April 5, 1915, barely a month after the plan was launched, Dolci announced to Gasparri that it was to the credit of the German and Austrian ambassadors that the project had failed and the ten members had resigned.[32]

Dolci never abandoned the idea of convincing the Holy See to enter into direct diplomatic relations with Constantinople, even though, with the end of the hostilities, the Porte had become the government of a truncated empire, with Syria-Lebanon and Palestine amputated. In August 1918, three years after the question had been put to rest, the apostolic delegate wrote to Cardinal Gasparri that the rumors, although vehemently denied by the secretary of state, of the establishment of diplomatic ties with China, a non-Christian power, and with the United States were received with dismay by the Imperial government, which from very early on had asked with insistence to tighten its relations with the Holy See.[33] However, Dolci recognized the delicate situation the Holy See was facing and the impossibility of making any decision at this point in the peace process.[34]

A couple of years later, in April 1920, the Turkish government, under the new leadership of Mustafa Kemal, rejected any attempt to establish diplomatic relationships. The political situation had changed dramatically. France had lost its protectorate in the Holy Land but was still adamant about maintaining it in the rest of the crumbling empire and was not ready to tolerate any damaging move coming from the Holy See. As a defeated power, the Porte could not resist France's wishes. Dolci resumed the situation in a letter of April 17, 1920, informing Gasparri that

la communauté constituée de telle façon n'est pas une communauté catholique mais une communauté schismatique"; Progetto Patriarcato Latino, Apr. 1915, ASV, Arch. Deleg. Turchia, Dolci 90, II (my translation).

32. Dolci to Gasparri, Apr. 5, 1915, ASV, AES Austria, 1915, pos. 1057, fasc. 458.

33. Dolci to Gasparri, Rapporti del Delegato Apostolico in Costantinopoli circa l'attivemento di relazioni diplomatiche tra il Governo ottomano e la S. Sede, Aug. 1, 1918, ASV, AES Austria, 1918, pos. 1337, fasc. 529.

34. Ibid.

the minister had forgone all plans to enter into official diplomatic relations with the Holy See, as it was responding positively to France's energic demands to reinstate the protectorate over Christians. The minister justified his decision, arguing that with the Ottomans' loss of the Holy Places, Mesopotamia, and Syria-Lebanon, the remaining Eastern Catholic population was too small to bear heavily on the diplomacy of the Holy See, active in resuming its relationships with France.[35]

Conclusion: Maintaining the Status Quo

In a confidential report of January 1915 to the Holy See, Gabriel Hanoteaux, a French official at the ministry of foreign affairs, addressed the pontiff over maintaining the French protectorate and "asked the Holy See to abstain from any innovation: *quieta non movere.*"[36] Hanoteaux complained to the pontiff about rumors circulating that the Holy See had endorsed a plan to end the French protectorate. Aware that it was accused of being a weapon to support the political and financial interests of France in the Orient, Hanoteaux claimed that

The French Catholic protectorate does not rest only on political interests and historical tradition. The papacy always thought...that the Catholic protectorate was defending in the Orient...the very principle of Catholicism, that is the principle of Unity. If the Catholic establishments and charities were entrusted to all the nations to which the...directors of these charities belong, it would be a dreadful cacophony. The strength and the success of Catholic charities are due to the unity of supervision under the age-long protection of France.[37]

35. Dolci to Gasparri, Apr. 17, 1920, ASV, AES Austria, 1920, pos. 1337, fasc. 529.

36. Confidential note about the religious and political situation of France by Mr. Hanoteaux, Jan. 1915, ASV, Segr. Stato, 1918, rubr. 244, fasc. 93.

37. "Le protectorat catholique de la France ne se fonde pas seulement sur les intérêts politiques et sur les traditions de l'histoire. La papauté a toujours pensé...que le protectorat catholique défendait en Orient...le principe même du Catholicisme, c'est-à-dire le principe de l'Unité. Si les établissements et les oeuvres catholiques étaient confiés à toutes les nations auxquelles les...directeurs de ces œuvres appartiennent, ce serait une cacophonie épouvantable....La force et le succès des oeuvres catholiques tiennent à

The French official went so far as to claim that without France there would be no Catholicism in the Orient.[38]

Pope Benedict, who regarded France as an essential piece on the religious and political European chessboard, chose to maintain the status quo while gaining time with Constantinople. Once the military situation stabilized and the chance of an Entente victory started to materialize, Gasparri informed the French that the Holy See had no intention to abolish or even harm the religious protectorate. Still, its future was directly dependent upon the future of the Ottoman Empire. The collapse of the empire would signify the natural termination of the protectorate.[39]

The decision of the Holy See not to enter into official relations with the Porte was a sign of its own political weakness in European diplomacy but also a sign of Benedict's insight about the future role of the Catholic Church in a devastated Europe and a new, emerging Middle East. The Christian future of Europe was Benedict's first and foremost priority. Early in the war, the pontiff had lamented the "suicide of civilized Europe."[40] He was concerned about the substantial risk of further de-Christianization of a land rooted in Christian tradition. With the Bolshevik Revolution of October 1917 and its impact on Western Europe's social, religious, and political fabric, Benedict XV's worries increased. While engaging in an active diplomacy to bring the war to an end, he looked for diplomatic interactions with European countries, to establish, reestablish, or improve bilateral diplomatic relations. France was an essential piece of this strategy to assist

---

l'unité de direction sous la protection séculaire de la France"; ASV, Segr. Stato, 1918, rubr. 244, fasc. 93, confidential note (my translation).

38. Ibid.

39. Gaparri to Denys Cochin, June 26, 1917, ASV, AES Francia, 1917, pos. 1295–96, fasc. 686.

40. Benedict XV, "Lenten Letter to Cardinal-Vicar Pompili," Mar. 4, 1916, in editorial, "Pope Calls War Suicide of Europe," *New York Times*, Mar. 6, 1916, 1.

the Holy See in the moral reconstruction of Europe after the war. Therefore, keeping France satisfied in the Ottoman Empire became crucial to Benedict's long-term plans. France was not only in charge of the protectorate in the Ottoman Empire but also had a protectorate in China and, as a colonial power, had a strong presence in Africa and in Southeast Asia. Benedict's immediate mission was, in the regional context of the Middle East, to protect the Catholic communities in the empire. But his global mission was the immediate and long-term protection of Catholics all over the world, in countries where France and England were active colonial powers. Thus, reestablishing diplomatic ties with France was far more important to the Holy See than satisfying the Porte.

In a time of turmoil and with little political visibility, Pope Benedict crafted a diplomacy that managed to keep open his political options in Europe for the long term and ensure the immediate protection of the Catholic communities in the Ottoman Empire by keeping the communication channel open with Constantinople. There is little doubt that Pope Benedict never intended to enter into direct diplomatic ties with the Porte.[41] Establishing diplomatic relations with a Muslim country for the first time in the history of the Holy See was a decision that would have had numerous political repercussions and would not have assured the protection of Christians against Muslim persecution. Benedict, although ahead of his time, was not interested in engaging in a Muslim-Christian dialogue. A rapprochement with the Byzantine Orthodox was his main goal, a goal that would have been endangered by the establishment of strong ties between the Catholic Church and the Porte. On a practical

---

41. The Holy See eventually entered into direct diplomatic relations with Turkey in 1960, under the pontificate of John XXIII, who had served as apostolic delegate in Istanbul from 1935 to 1944. The first Muslim country the Holy See established diplomatic relations with was Egypt in 1947, followed by Syria and Iran in 1953.

level, it was anticipated by all governments that the "sick man of Europe" was not going to survive the war as an empire. No sensible government would have taken the risk of establishing diplomatic relations in such an uncertain context.

Benedict's diplomatic talent resided in his using the sensitive issue of direct diplomatic ties to satisfy two powers with opposite interests: France and the Ottoman government. By maintaining an "active status quo" the pontiff gave each government proof of his goodwill while anticipating the future of the geostrategic international scene. Although he had limited options in wartime, Pope Benedict demonstrated the qualities of a talented statesman in the pursuit of his mission. As a political realist, he acted without precipitation and with much prudence. What his contemporaries interpreted as a timid papal diplomacy was actually the mark of his discerning sense of politics.

CONSTANTINOPLE AND THE
RUSSIAN EQUATION

The year 1917 was a military and diplomatic turning point in the unfolding of the war. The Russian Revolution that had broken out in February 1917 dramatically transformed the geopolitical map and put to rest the worst fears of the Holy See. In October 1917, Vladimir Ilyich Lenin, leader of the Bolshevik movement and new head of the Russian government, entered into negotiations with Germany and Austria to secure a peace deal. On March 3, 1918, Russia and the Central Powers signed the Treaty of Brest-Litovsk, which signified the exit of Russia from the war. With this withdrawal the Holy See's worst nightmare faded away. Russia had always been crucial in papal diplomacy and, because of the potential for the expansion of Russian Orthodoxy in Europe and the Ottoman Empire, a source of anxiety.

Constantinople and Russia

Constantinople had always been central to Russian religious culture and geopolitics. Bridging Europe and Asia, its strategic significance lies in its location on the Bosphorus Strait and its proximity to the Dardanelles. The "problem of Constantinople and the Straits," as it became known, was the result of Russian interest in the Black Sea area. With time, it became critical for the Russian Empire to secure a free passage to the warm seas of the south for men and merchandise. This expansionist policy ran up against French and British strategic interests in the region. The hostility of Great Britain endured until the late nineteenth century, given its absolute necessity to protect this vital communication route with India.

As a "commanding point to the Straits,"[42] Constantinople was of strategic significance to both Russia and the European Great Powers, but as "the source of the religion and culture of the Russian people,"[43] as the center of Orthodox Christianity, it was a cause of huge and constant concern to the Holy See. The philosopher Prince Evgeni Trubetskoy illustrated the religious Russian mindset when he declared in 1915 that the question of Constantinople was of vital importance to Russia, declaring that

we are brought to it by all the aspects of our life...the spiritual essence of Russia is involved in this problem. The Cathedral of Sophia is precisely that pearl of the Gospel for which Russia must be prepared to give everything she possesses.[44]

With strong messianic accents, Trubetskoy glorified the spiritual destiny of Russia as sole and true guardian of Eastern Orthodoxy. The Council of Florence of 1439, a last attempt at reconcili-

42. Samuel Kucherov, "The Problem of Constantinople and the Straits," *Russian Review* 8, no. 3 (July 1949): 205.

43. Ibid.

44. Prince E. N. Trubetskoy, *Nationalnyi Vopros* (Petrograd: 1915), 97, quoted in Kucherov, "Problem of Constantinople," 208.

ation with Orthodox Christianity, preceded the fall of Byzantium into Ottoman hands in 1453. It ultimately ended in failure and gave Russia a motive for claiming a unique role as defender of Orthodoxy. Arguing that treason had been committed by the Orthodox Church and the Greek ecumenical patriarch, the tsar contended that Constantinople had lost its position as the Second Rome, the center of Orthodox Christianity. Russian Orthodox doctrine therefore proclaimed Moscow the Third Rome, the guardian of the purity of Orthodox faith.[45]

The tsars had, for the longest time, contemplated the religious and political conquest of Constantinople. To seize the Ottoman capital, Russia waged no less than eleven wars against the empire, but its aspirations were still unfulfilled on the eve of the First World War. The opening of hostilities and the entrance of the Ottomans into the war on the German side offered Russia a clear war aim. Russia and its Entente allies had tried first to prevent the Porte from joining the Central Powers in the conflict. Russia rightly feared that Turkey would become a German satellite, with Constantinople falling under the enemy's military and economic control. It was a situation of immense concern to the Entente. The Allies' failure to keep the Ottoman Empire out of the conflict prompted a new Russian diplomatic approach, focusing on obtaining a direct control of Constantinople and the Straits with the Allies' consent. To this effect, Russia approached France and Great Britain to discuss the future of the Ottoman capital in case of an Entente victory.

In a memorandum of March 4, 1915, delivered to the ambassadors of Great Britain and France in Saint Petersburg, the tsar demanded that Constantinople and the west shore of the Bosphorus, as well as the Sea of Marmara and the Dardanelles, become

45. Marshall Poe, "Moscow, the Third Rome: The Origins and Transformations of a 'Pivotal Moment,'" *Jahrbücher für Geschichte Osteuropas* 49, no. 3 (2001): 412–29; see also chapter 2, footnote 42, of this volume.

part of the Russian Empire. The British government's assent was a complete reversal of its traditional diplomacy in the question of Constantinople. It was a diplomatic act that had to be understood in the larger context of a war waged against a powerful enemy. Keeping Russia satisfied as an ally and avoiding a separate peace between Germany and Russia was paramount to British and French wartime goals. London and Paris imposed a single but essential condition to their consenting to Russia's control of Constantinople. Anticipating the dismemberment of the Ottoman Empire, they wanted to have free rein in its Asiatic part— namely, Greater Syria.[46] The memorandum of March 4 became the basis of the Secret Agreement of 1915. The terms of this agreement reached the Holy See before the Russians made it public in December 1916, only to denounce it in April 1917 after the break of the Bolshevik Revolution. The president of the Council of Ministers, Prince G. E. Lvov, head of the new provisional revolutionary government, proclaimed that Russia's only interest was to promote a stable peace based on the self-determination of peoples. He insisted that his government had no imperialist appetites.[47] With the Treaty of Brest-Litovsk, signed in March 1918 between the Central Powers and Russia, Constantinople came out of Russian hands, and consequently, the Russian Orthodox Church, as the guardian of Eastern Orthodoxy, ceased to be a factor of political and religious importance in the Ottoman Empire.

Russia's determination to seize Constantinople had always been a source of apprehension to the pontiffs. What was new under Pope Benedict's reign was the real possibility of seeing

---

46. "La Francia in Asia avrebbe in compenso la Siria, la Celesiria ed il Libano ed all'Inghilterra si consentirebbe che la ferrovia Bagdad-Golfo Persico avesse il suo sbocco a Gallipoli, anziche a Costantinopoli"; Antonio Scotta, *La conciliazione ufficiosa: Diario del barone Carlo Monti "incarito d'affari" del governo italiano presso la Santa Sede (1914–1922)* (Città del Vaticano: Libreria Editrice Vaticana, 1997), 1:249.

47. E. H. Adamov, *Konstantinopol i prolivy* (Constantinople and the Straits), Document CCCIX, 2 vols. (Moscow: 1925–26), 2:476–77, quoted in Kucherov, "Problem of Constantinople," 212.

Russia achieving its centuries-old goal. The disquiet displayed by the Holy See during the war must be interpreted in the larger context of a long-lasting antagonism between Russian Orthodoxy and Catholicism. A thorough reading of Baron Carlo Monti and French Cardinal Baudrillart's diaries reveals a high level of tension in Benedict XV's diplomatic conduct that sought to avoid, in Cardinal Gasparri's own words, "a threat and desolation equal to that of the Protestant Reformation of the sixteenth century."[48]

Rumors regarding the terms of the Secret Agreement quickly reached the Holy See. A concerned Benedict XV sent an alarmist message to the Entente Powers. Russian possession of Constantinople would widen the schism between Eastern Orthodoxy and Catholicism. He also stressed the negative long-term consequences that such a takeover would have on French and Italian Catholic interests in the Ottoman Empire. But the Holy See was in a diplomatic quandary. Among the Catholic countries involved, Italy had no significant diplomatic influence on the issue. According to Benedict XV, the president of France, Raymond Poincaré, had a personal commitment to Russia and would not budge.[49] In a letter dated March 7, 1915, to Cardinal Amette, Gasparri asked the archbishop of Paris to put pressure on the French government, but to no avail.[50] The French rejected the Holy See's offer to recognize a French Catholic protectorate over Hagia Sophia[51] if the church were returned to Catholic hands in case of an Entente occupation of Constantinople.[52] Great Britain was the nation most implicated in the issue but as a Protestant country had no pressing interests to see Hagia Sophia return to Catholic hands.

48. "Un péril et un malheur égal à celui de la Réforme protestante du XVIème siècle"; Baudrillart, *Carnets*, 230 (my translation).

49. Scotta, *Conciliazione ufficiosa*, 1:250.

50. Ibid., 1:275.

51. The Basilica of Hagia Sophia, a museum since 1935, was originally a church. It was converted into a mosque by Sultan Mehmed II after the fall of Constantinople into Ottoman hands in 1453.

52. Scotta, *Conciliazione ufficiosa*, 1:270.

The End of the Russian Threat

To his great relief, the nightmare that Benedict XV envisioned never unfolded. In April 1917, the new revolutionary provisional government denounced the Secret Agreement that had been drafted in 1915. Rumors surfaced that Constantinople would be given an international status. Cardinal Gasparri immediately informed Carlo Monti that the Holy See would be satisfied if Hagia Sophia were "bestowed to the Eastern Catholic churches, as it was when it was founded."[53]

In April 1919, Benedict XV expressed his concern again, this time related to a lingering fear of seeing Hagia Sophia falling into Greek Orthodox hands. The pontiff lamented that "it would be an offense to the Catholic Church, to tradition, to history."[54] The Holy See made no secret that it would prefer "the Crescent over the Greek Cross on the dome of Hagia Sophia, and that in Asiatic Turkey Muslim indifference was better than Orthodox fanaticism."[55]

The Holy See's diplomatic response to the problem of Constantinople had a direct religious significance. The Russian situation was lucidly described by Prince Kudashev in a letter of February 1915 to Sazonov, the Russian foreign minister.[56] This letter is worth reproducing for its clear insight.

The fundamental problem of the Straits...will not be affected by the sending of one army corps, nor will it change my conviction that neither morally nor physically are we ready for the annexation of the Straits. When I say "morally" or "spiritually" this is what I mean: to settle down in Constantinople, as crusaders proclaiming the triumph of the Ortho-

53. Ibid., 1:81.

54. Ibid., 1:459.

55. Maurice Pernot, *Le Saint-Siège, l'Église catholique et la politique mondiale* (Paris: Armand Colin, 1924), 180 (my translation).

56. Prince Kudashev was the Russian representative of the ministry of foreign affairs at the army headquarters from August 1914 to March 1916.

dox Church, is out of the question because of our Pan-Slavic sympa-thies and affiliations, and our dislike of the Greeks; to add to that, the moral authority of our clergy is hardly very high in the opinion of the Greek clergy. To play the part so brilliantly performed by England in Egypt, we are utterly incapable.[57]

Benedict XV and Gasparri quickly grasped Russia's physical and moral inability to secure its position in Constantinople, as de-scribed by Kudashev.[58] Count de Salis confirmed in a memoran-dum to the Foreign Office that Gasparri was of the opinion that the Russians alone could not take Constantinople. According to him, the pope and his secretary of state would support a British presence in the Ottoman capital or, more reluctantly, a French presence in spite of the anticlerical tendencies of their govern-ment.[59]

The Holy See was not naive and knew that, in wartime, mili-tary necessities were paramount. Keeping Russia satisfied with its main war goal was crucial to the Entente.[60] France and Great Britain could not afford to have Russia sign its own peace treaty with Germany, and they were also resolute to avoid the disaster that a German occupation of Constantinople would have im-plied for their economic interests. That London had reversed its centuries-old policy regarding Russia and the future of Constan-tinople was an unmistakable sign of the shift in its geostrategic policy. In the late nineteenth century, Great Britain had moved the sensitive zone of defense of its empire in Egypt and Pales-tine. Constantinople and the Straits had therefore lost much of their political and military function in the protection of British interests. Still, Great Britain was anxious to contain German ex-

57. Michael T. Florinsky, "A Page of Diplomatic History: Russian Military Leaders and the Problem of Constantinople during the War," *Political Science Quarterly* 44 (Mar. 1929): 113.

58. Hachey, ed., *Great Britain Legation*, 3.

59. Ibid.

60. Scotta, *Conciliazione ufficiosa*, 1:250.

pansionism in the region and was politically ready to transfer the protection of the Straits region to Russia. To this effect, London and Saint Petersburg had signed a convention in 1907, which remained active until November 1917. In this political context, the Holy See had no leverage over France or Great Britain to prevent Russian annexation of the Ottoman capital.

The problem of Constantinople and the Straits found its closure in 1923.[61] Until then, the progresses and setbacks suffered by Russia and the Allies in the resolution of the problem affected the stability of all Christian communities in the rest of the Ottoman Empire. Benedict XV regarded with undisguised apprehension the prospect of a reinvigorated Greek Orthodox Church under Russian control. The sudden and massive disruption brought about by the Bolshevik Revolution in 1917 destroyed the Russian Empire and weakened its church. The new situation did not lessen the Holy See's concern regarding the future ownership of Hagia Sophia. The critical comments of Pope Benedict that "it would be an offense to the Catholic Church, to tradition, to history" if Hagia Sophia would fall into Greek Orthodox hands showed the extent of the ecclesiological gap standing between the Catholic Church and the separated Christians of the East.[62] This attitude illustrates the limit of Benedict XV's praiseworthy efforts in favor of a rapprochement with them.

ECCLESIASTICAL DIPLOMACY AND
UNIONIST ECCLESIOLOGY

Although historiography has reserved the title to his successor, Pius XI, Benedict XV was the "Pope of the East," with high regard for the Eastern Catholic churches and a keen interest in the rapprochement with the separated brethren. In his allocution of

---

61. Mustafa Kemal was the founder and first president of the new Republic of Turkey created after the defeat of the Ottoman Empire and its carving up among the Allies. He renamed Constantinople "Istanbul" and moved the capital to Ankara.

62. Scotta, *Conciliazione ufficiosa*, 1:459.

June 9, 2007, to the Congregation for the Oriental Churches, Pope Benedict XVI reminded his audience that he "began this pilgrimage by taking the name of a Pope who so loved the East."[63] Benedict XV loved and admired the Eastern churches and their traditions. Like Benedict XVI, he believed that "without a constant relationship with the tradition of her origins, in fact, there is no future for Christ's Church. It is the Eastern churches in particular which preserve the echo of the first Gospel proclamation."[64]

In an article published in the *New Republic* in February 1922, the author noted that "in a strictly ecclesiastical field his [Pope Benedict's] handling of the schismatic tendencies in the emancipated nationalisms of...the Near East may prove to be the outstanding feature of his pontificate."[65] The pontiff's Middle Eastern diplomacy was designed to support his ecclesiastical policy, the foundation of his ecclesiological understanding of the church. It was meant to protect the Latin and Eastern Catholic minorities and prepare a conducive environment for a rapprochement with the dissident Orthodox churches.

After the interlude of the reign of Pius X, who showed limited interest in the fate of the Eastern churches, Benedict XV followed in the steps of Leo XIII, completing and institutionalizing Leo's unionist approach. Under Benedict's pontificate, the Sacred Congregation of the Propagation of the Faith for Matters of Oriental Rite, established by Pope Pius IX on January 6, 1862, to oversee the Eastern rite Catholic churches, was detached from the Congregation for the Propagation of the Faith and renamed "Congregation for the Oriental Church."[66] In the same year, 1917,

63. Benedict XVI, "Visit of His Holiness Benedict XVI to the Congregation for the Oriental Churches, 9 June 2007," http://www.vatican.va/holy_father/benedict_xvi/speeches/2007/june/documents/hf_ben-xvi_spe_20070609_congr-orientchurch_en.html.

64. Ibid.

65. Arthur Livingston, "Benedict XV and the New Age," *New Republic*, Feb. 8, 1922, 305.

66. The apostolic constitution *Regimini Ecclesiae Universae* of August 15, 1967, renamed the Congregatio pro Ecclesia Orientali (Congregation for the Oriental Church) to ac-

a Pontifical Oriental Institute dedicated to higher studies in Eastern Christianity completed the structure.

Scholars have raised the question of how to properly qualify the ecclesiastical policy of Benedict XV in the Ottoman Empire. Was it a classic model of unionism, or did he plant the first seeds of a Catholic ecumenism?

The Unionist Tradition and Vatican Foreign Policy

Benedict XV followed in Leo XIII's steps, benefiting from a heritage genuinely concerned with the destiny of the Eastern churches. Leo XIII's project with the Christian East was part of his Great Design, a global policy meant to increase the standing of the Holy See in the world in order to better re-Christianize it. The Eastern Catholic churches, long known as the Uniate churches—a term they rejected as derogatory—were to be the favored instrument for the conversion of the Orthodox Christians to Catholicism. "A form of missionary apostolate," the uniate policy was a springboard for the assimilation of the Orthodox churches into Catholic structures.[67] This policy of assimilation was the stumbling block to any real rapprochement between Catholicism and Orthodoxy. Unionism, as a return to the Catholic fold, was the only model considered for the unity of churches.

Leo XIII's unionist policy was rooted in the conviction that to be successful, a regeneration of the East should come from the East. It concretely meant that he would reject any attempt at Latinization of the Eastern Catholic patriarchates, respecting

---

knowledge the richness and diversity of the different Catholic rites. It is today known as Congregatio pro Ecclesiis Orientalibus (Congregation for the Oriental Churches).

67. The declaration "Uniatism, Method of Union of the Past, and the Present Search for Full Communion" by the Joint International Commission for the Theological Dialogue between the Roman Catholic Church and the Orthodox Church, in its seventh plenary session, which took place at the Balamand School of Theology (Lebanon), June 17–24, 1993, stated that as "a form of missionary apostolate," "'uniatism' can no longer be accepted either as a method to be followed or as a model of the unity our Churches are seeking"; Centro Pro Unione, *Information Service* 83 (1993/II): 96–99.

and conserving their liturgical rites and traditions. If Leo XIII's guiding principles diverged from his predecessor Pius IX's Oriental policy, they were in harmony with Benedict XIV's vision of preservation of the rites of the Eastern Catholics. In his apostolic letter *Allatae Sunt* of July 26, 1755, on the observance of Oriental rites, addressed to the missionaries assigned to the Orient, Pope Benedict declared:

We also wanted to make clear to all the good will, which the Apostolic See feels for Oriental Catholics in commanding them to observe fully their ancient rites which are not at variance with the Catholic religion or with propriety. The Church does not require schismatics to abandon their rites when they return to Catholic unity, but only that they forswear and detest heresy. Its great desire is for the preservation, not the destruction, of different peoples—in short, that all may be Catholic rather than all become Latin.[68]

The interests of these Eastern Catholics were defended by the Congregation for the Propagation of the Faith, established in 1622 to organize the missionary territories in foreign lands. Pope Pius IX recognized the distinctiveness of the Eastern churches and the importance of paying special attention to them, yet favored a return to the Latin rite. Therefore, he created in 1862 a special division in the Congregation, the Sacred Congregation of the Propagation of the Faith for Matters of Oriental Rite.[69] It was a means to separate Oriental affairs from the activities of missionaries among heretics and to exercise a closer control over the Eastern churches, keeping them under the mission territory epithet.

It is against Pius IX's policy of Latinization of the Eastern rite Catholics, a policy strongly resented by these communities and supported by Propaganda Fide, that Leo XIII reacted. Leo

68. Benedict XIV, "Apostolic Letter *Allatae Sunt* on the Observance of Oriental Rites" [July 26, 1755], http://www.ewtn.com/library/encyc/b14allat.htm.

69. Congregatio de Propaganda Fide pro negotiis ritus orientalis established by Pope Pius IX on January 6, 1862, with the apostolic constitution *Romani Pontifices*.

encountered much internal and external resistance against his policy of revival of the Orient by the Orient. The pope received little help from the Curia and predictably from Propaganda Fide, inciting him to work more closely with his secretary of state.[70] Propaganda Fide, which was rarely consulted under Leo's reign, resented the interference of the pope and his disapproval of the pastoral methods used by the missionaries in their ministry to Eastern Christians.

The French diplomatic milieu was also alarmed by Leo XIII's Eastern policy. Any change in the subtle balance established between the Holy See, the Sublime Porte, and France's diplomacy was to bear danger for French cultural, political, and economic interests. For the sake of reconciliation of the dissident Eastern Christians with Rome, Leo XIII was in a somewhat unrealistic way inclined to destroy this balance by entering into direct intercourse with the Porte, supporting at the same time the French protectorate over the Eastern Christians. The French were worried and looked with trepidation at the pontiff's achievements in favor of the Eastern Christians.

Leo XIII outlined his ecclesiological principles in the apostolic letter *Praeclara Gratulationis* of June 20, 1894, in which he invited the Orthodox churches to communion with Rome and reassured them that

there [is not] (any) reason for you to fear on that account that We or any of Our Successors will ever diminish your rights, the privileges of your Patriarchs, or the established Ritual of any one of your Churches.... On the contrary, if you re-establish Union with Us, you will see how, by God's bounty, the glory and dignity of your Churches will be remarkably increased.[71]

In the same breath, the pontiff acted on his promises and organized a series of conferences leading to the publication on No-

70. Hajjar, *Vatican*, 31.

71. Leo XIII, "Apostolic Letter *Praeclara Gratulationis Publicae*" [On the Reunion of Christendom] [June 20, 1894], in *Leonis XIII Acta* 14 (1894): 195–214.

vember 30, 1894, of the famed encyclical *Orientalium Dignitas*, the charter to the Eastern churches.[72] For the healthy development of the Eastern rite Catholic churches as an instrument for the conversion of the separated brethren, the pontiff reacted against the policy of Latinization of the Eastern rite patriarchates. Instead, he safeguarded "the significance of the Eastern traditions for the whole Church."[73]

> The reasons for rivalry and suspicion must be removed, [wrote the pope], then the fullest energies can be marshaled for reconciliation. We consider this of paramount importance to preserving the integrity proper to the discipline of the Eastern Churches.... Their antiquity is august, it is what gives nobility to the different rites, it is a brilliant jewel for the whole Church, it confirms the God-given unity of the Catholic Faith.[74]

The Latin rite priests and missionaries' duty was to assist the patriarchs and bishops, not to encourage conversion to the Latin rite. Any Latinization attempt was punished by deposition and being barred from the priesthood.[75]

The reaction in French and Italian diplomatic circles was fierce, concerned as they were about losing their cultural and political influence over the Eastern Christians of the empire. Propaganda Fide, which had been kept on the side, stayed silent. In the field, the reception of the encyclical by the missionaries was cold. To a sense of superiority, the Latin rite priests and missionaries added a penchant for nationalistic outburst, protecting their country's interests before satisfying their duty toward the universal church.

Leo XIII was instrumental in moving toward a better communication with those he did not call "heretics" or "schismatics"

72. Leo XIII, *Orientalium Dignitas* [On the Churches of the East] [Nov. 30, 1894], *Leonis XIII Acta* 14 (1894), 201–02.

73. John Paul II, "Apostolic Letter *Orientale Lumen*, to mark the Centenary of Orientalium Dignitas of Pope Leo XIII [May 2, 1995]," *AAS* 87 (1995): 745.

74. Leo XIII, *Orientalium Dignitas*, 201–2.

75. Ibid.

anymore but the more courteous term of "dissidents." This, by no means, was a signal to a change of doctrine.[76] Leo's Eastern policy in the Ottoman Empire was idealistic and did not translate well on the ground. Twenty years later, the same stumbling blocks were on Benedict XV's Oriental path when he resumed his predecessor's attempts to bring reconciliation between Rome and the Eastern churches.

Benedict's Ecclesiastical Policy: First Seeds of Catholic Ecumenism?

Benedict XV gave a new depth and breadth to the unionist ecclesiology by taking advantage of the war, which brought the Eastern churches out of the straitjacket in which they were evolving under Ottoman rule and the pressure of Russian Orthodoxy. His first step was to recommend prayers for the return of the Eastern Christians to the Chair of Peter. In the briefs *Romanorum Pontificum* of February 25, 1916,[77] and *Cum Catholicae Ecclesiae* of April 15, 1916, the pontiff made a plea for Christian unity:

Since the truth of the Catholic Church shines mainly through its unity, nothing is more desirable for men unhappily torn from the arms of this Mother to eventually return to you with the correct thoughts and intentions.[78]

The brief was accompanied by a prayer written by the pope himself. "The Holy Father's beautiful prayer[79] composed with such

76. George Tavard, *Ecumenism: Two Centuries of Ecumenism* (Notre Dame, Ind.: Fides Press, 1978), 69.

77. Benedict XV, *"Brief Romanorum Pontificum* [Feb. 25, 1916]," *AAS* 9 I (1917): 61.

78. "Poiché la verità della Chiesa cattolica risplende principalmente per la sua unità, nulla è più auspicabile che gli uomini strappati infelicemente dalle braccia di questa Madre ritornino finalmente a Lei, con pensieri e propositi corretti"; Benedict XV, "Brief *Cum Catholicae Ecclesiae* [Apr. 15, 1916]," *AAS* 8 (1916): 137 (my translation).

79. "O Signore, che avete unito le diverse nazioni nella confessione del Vostro Nome, Vi preghiamo per i popoli Cristiani dell'Oriente. Memori del posto eminente che hanno tenuto nella Vostra Chiesa, Vi supplichiamo d'ispirar loro il desiderio di riprenderlo, per formare con noi un solo ovile sotto la guida di un medesimo Pastore. Fate che essi insieme con noi si compenetrino degl'insegnamenti dei loro santi Dottori, che sono anche

grace for the reunion of the Eastern churches...made the most excellent impression on the schismatics, and many of them [were] really enthusiastic," reported Angelo Dolci after reception and divulgation of the prayer, which he took care to translate into all languages, especially Greek, Armenian, and Turkish.[80] Benedict XV's interest in the issue was too genuine to settle for good intentions and prayers. His ultimate concern was the successful reunion with the dissident churches for which the prayers were offered. To bring fruit, this pastoral step needed to be supported by further concrete actions, which included the creation of an institutional framework.

The idea was not new. In 1894, French Cardinal Langénieux outlined the necessity of creating a special congregation to serve the Eastern Catholic churches. In a note to Leo XIII, he stressed the importance of instituting a congregation independent from Propaganda Fide for three main reasons. First, the Eastern churches were already "alive and constituted" bodies and therefore should not "be submitted to the missionary regimen."[81] Second, their organization supposed consistency and unity of action, impossible to implement if the envisioned congregation were to be maintained as a secondary component of Propaganda Fide. As a third most important point, Langénieux stressed the intertwining of politics and religion in the Orient.[82] Only an autonomous and empowered congregation could efficiently address the sensitive issue of reunion with the separated Christians.

---

nostri Padri nella Fede. Preservateci da ogni fallo che potrebbe allontanarli da noi. Che lo spirito di concordia e di carità, che è indizio della Vostra presenza tra i fedeli, affretti il giorno in cui le nostre si uniscano alle loro preghiere, affinché ogni popolo ed ogni lingua riconosca e glorifichi il nostro Signore Gesù Cristo, Vostro Figlio. Così sia"; brief *Cum Catholicae Ecclesiae*, Preghiera per l'unione dei Cristiani d'Oriente alla Chiesa Romana.

80. Dolci to Gasparri, May 7, 1917, ASV, Segr. Stato, 1917, rubr. 257, fasc. 1.

81. Note du Cardinal Langénieux remise à Sa Sainteté le Pape Léon XIII à l'occasion des Conférences Patriarcales de 1894 et exposant la nécessité d'ériger une Congrégation spéciale pour le gouvernement des Églises Orientales, ASV, AES Stati Ecclesiastici, pos. 1429, fasc. 572.

82. Ibid.

Benedict XV founded this independent congregation, the Congregatio pro Ecclesia Orientali (Congregation for the Oriental Church), with the motu proprio *Dei Providentis* of May 1, 1917, "to forestall the fear that the Orientals might not be held in proper consideration by the Roman Pontiffs."[83] The Eastern churches were no longer considered as "mission fields" under the jurisdiction of Propaganda Fide. The new congregation's first function was to strengthen the position of the Eastern rite Catholic churches and attend their concerns. They were meant to become "centres of contact" with the Eastern Orthodox churches in order to facilitate their ultimate conversion.[84] The pope reserved to himself, a sign of his genuine care, the title of prefect, the head of the congregation serving as secretary. "When our Churches of the East shall see the supreme Pontiff watching in person over their interests," he wrote, "they will without fail understand that it is impossible for the Holy See to give any greater sign of affection for them."[85]

The decision to launch the Congregation for the Oriental Church was the result of a diplomacy that integrated geopolitics with ecclesiastical policy. By the spring of 1917, it became evident that the collapse of both the Ottoman Empire and Austria-Hungary, two empires that regrouped a majority of the Eastern Catholics, was a question of months. It was then time to strengthen these communities and give them the means to become outposts for the conquest of the Greek and Russian Orthodox churches.[86]

The genesis of the Congregation has been well researched and documented. The works of Vincenzo Poggi and Msgr. Giuseppe

83. Benedict XV, "Motu Proprio *Dei Providentis*, de Sacra Congregatione pro Ecclesia Orientali [May 1, 1917],"*AAS* 9 I (1917): 529–31.

84. Tavard, *Ecumenism*,117.

85. Benedict XV, *Dei Providentis*, 529–31.

86. Hervé Legrand, "La fondation de l'Institut Pontifical Oriental en 1917, premier pas vers l'oecuménisme," paper presented at the Pontifical Oriental Institute, Rome, Nov. 9, 2007.

M. Croce have exhausted the subject.[87] If the first seeds are found in Cardinal Langénieux's report, the project's authorship goes to Fr. Delpuche, a White Father.[88] In a series of notes addressed to the pope, he unfolded his vision of the future congregation. He encouraged Benedict XV to take advantage of the state of decomposition of the Russian Empire that until then had acted as a magnet for educated Byzantine Orthodox communities. He correctly anticipated the lack of direction that the Orthodox churches were to suffer after the war, the expected collapse of the Ottoman Empire, and the damage that the Protestant proselytizing would cause.[89]

Politics worked hand in hand with ecclesiastical policy, especially during the war. Delpuche was aware that the power of Great Britain and the rise of the United States were manifest support to Protestant activism in a region politically and militarily dominated by the British. Only by "avoiding unfortunate latinisation, by giving confidence to the dignitaries of these churches, by organizing and by giving to the Catholic Greco-Melchite patriarchate the position it deserves" would any form of success be achieved.[90]

Sensitive to Delpuche's argumentation, Benedict XV founded the new Congregation for the Oriental Church, stating that

the Church of Jesus Christ, since she is neither Latin nor Greek nor Slav but Catholic, makes no distinction between her children, and those,

87. See Vincenzo Poggi, SJ, *Per la storia del Pontificio Istituto Orientale: Saggi sull'istituzione, i suoi uomini e l'Oriente Cristiano* (Rome: Orientalia Christiana Analecta, 2000); Poggi, "Il settantennio del Pontificio Istituto Orientale," in *The Pontifical Oriental Institute: The First Seventy-Five Years; 1917–1992*, ed. Edward G. Farrugia (Rome: Orientalia Christiana, 1993); and Giuseppe M. Croce, "Alle origini della Congregazione Orientale e del Pontificio Istituto Orientale: Il contributo di Mons. Louis Petit," in Farrugia, *Pontifical Oriental Institute*.

88. The White Fathers, founded in 1868 by the first archbishop of Algiers, Cardinal Lavigerie, are also known as the Missionaries of Africa.

89. ACCO, fasc. 541/28, Bizantini-Melchiti; copie d'un rapport remis à sa Sainteté le pape Benoît XV sur la Sacrée Congrégation "Pro Ecclesia Orientali" par le Père Delpuche.

90. Ibid.

whether they are Greeks, Latins, Slavs or members of other national groups, all occupy the same rank in the eyes of the apostolic see.[91]

The Holy See allowed itself a six-month period after the official creation of the congregation to choose its secretary and staff and to devise the scope of the future territory that would be put under its jurisdiction. In a memorandum of September 10, 1917, Delpuche outlined the reasons that worked toward the allocation of a detached territory to the new congregation. Stressing the necessity to restore peace and union, he went on at length to explain how important it was to agree on a specific territory of action for the new institution, apart from the fields covered by Propaganda Fide. He warned the pope of the necessity to give the new congregation jurisdiction over both Latin and Eastern rite Catholics. In a spirit of concord and unity, he pointed out "if each group can appeal to a different authority, each [congregation] listening exclusively to its flock...it will foster among the diverse Catholic groups a discomfort and an uneasiness which will not elude the dissidents."[92]

Other reasons worked toward the establishment of a unique and separate territory regrouping both Latin and Eastern rite Catholics. Another report sent to Pope Benedict highlighted the situation as it was experienced by religious communities, orphanages, hospitals, and schools in the field. These various communities were described as having a "very exclusive Latin character" and resorting to subordination to Latinization as a mean to integrate the Eastern populations.[93] Therefore, the risk that the Latin rite communities would turn to Propaganda Fide instead of the new congregation to solve their problems was not

91. Benedict XV, *Dei Providentis*, 529–31.

92. ACCO, fasc. 541/28, Bizantini-Melchiti, Père Delpuche.

93. ACCO, fasc. 541/28, Bizantini-Melchiti, Institut Pontifical-Sacrée Congrégation Orientale; Travaux Préparatoires, Folder IIC; deux rapports à Sa Sainteté le Pape Benoît XV faits à la suite d'une audience accordée par Sa Sainteté sur l'organisation de la congrégation et sur le choix des personnes. Rapports non datés.

to be lightly dismissed. It was emphasized that, as a most unfortunate consequence, the Congregatio pro Ecclesia Orientali was in danger of starting its mission without the care of any apostolate. Thus there was a need to present a unique and reinforced authority to guarantee unity and avoid a sense of humiliation that the Eastern rite Catholics would not fail to feel.[94]

Regarding the protest that it would be bizarre to put the Latin rite members under the jurisdiction of a congregation dedicated to the Eastern churches, the same report noted that there was no ground for such objection, as "the coexistence of diverse rites in the same place did not mean a plurality of ordinary jurisdiction."[95] The very small numbers considered, "less than 70,000 Latins for 750,000 Eastern Catholics and six million schismatics," were also to be taken into account.[96]

All these reasons combined comforted Fr. Delpuche in his idea of drawing a special map of jurisdiction for the Congregatio pro Ecclesia Orientali, which would rule over both Latin and Eastern rites Catholics. He envisioned a territory that would cover the four Oriental patriarchates. A setback to Delpuche's vision, Pope Benedict opted against his rational argument. Delpuche feared the consequences of a two-headed authority in the same geographical zone but respected the pontiff's decision and understood his motivations as a sensible effort to avoid offending Propaganda Fide by demeaning its competence.[97]

The Pontifical Oriental Institute was established a few months later to offer support to the Congregation for the Oriental Church and to provide the Latin Church with a better understanding of the traditions of the Oriental churches and build a genuine interest in them. The motu proprio *Orientis Catholici* of October 15,

---

94. ACCO, fasc. 541/28, Père Delpuche.   95. ACCO, fasc. 541/28 (my translation).
96. ACCO, fasc. 541/28, Père Delpuche.
97. ACCO, fasc. 541/28, Bizantini-Melchiti, Institut Pontifical-Sacrée Congrégation Orientale, Travaux Préparatoires, Folder IIC, note à Monseigneur Galli, secrétaire des brefs aux princes, sur les deux Motu Propii, Oct. 20, 1917.

1917,[98] gave birth to the pontifical institute conceived to serve a double purpose, educational and ecumenical.[99] As an educational center, it was dedicated to the studies of the dogmatic, liturgical, spiritual, and canonical traditions of the churches of the East. As an ecumenical center, the institute was intended to make the Roman church conversant with all matters concerning the Orient, advocating understanding among the different churches. The Pontifical Oriental Institute started in slow motion. On November 2, 1918, under the administration of Delpuche, it opened its doors to the first students in a palace near St. Peter's Basilica in Rome. It eventually moved to Piazza Santa Maria Maggiore in November 1926. In 1920, forty students enrolled, while in 1921 only twenty-five were sent to the institute. Almost all of them were Franciscans.[100]

In March 1918, Msgr. Batiffol echoed the Holy See's position when he wrote that a potential rapprochement with the dissident churches was in a preparatory stage during which the separated churches would "study each other at a distance with sincere respect for one another."[101]

In a talk delivered in Rome in November 2007 to celebrate the ninetieth anniversary of the Pontifical Oriental Institute, Hervé Legrand, OP, debated whether or not Benedict XV's ecclesiology was akin to a first step toward ecumenism. Legrand stressed the anachronistic use of the term "Catholic ecumenism" in 1914. The ecumenical movement started in 1910 with the World Missionary Conference at Edinburgh, Scotland, and developed outside the Catholic Church. The Roman Church was victim of an al-

---

98. Benedict XV, "Motu proprio *Orientis Catholici* [Oct. 15, 1917]," *AAS* 9 I (1917): 531.

99. Joseph Gill, SJ, "Interessamento della S.C. Orientale per gli studi superiori," in *La Sacra Congregazione per le Chiese Orientali: Nel cinquantesimo della fondazione (1917–1967)* (Rome: Tipografia Italo-Orientale "San Nilo," 1969), 147.

100. Ibid., 151.

101. Pierre Batiffol, "Pope Benedict and the Restoration of Unity," *Constructive Quarterly* 6 (1918): 227. Msgr. Pierre Batiffol (1861–1929) was a prominent French theologian and church historian.

most complete ignorance of the Eastern ecclesiology and of the religious life of the Eastern rite communities. This lack of awareness was partly due to Roman suspicions and to the harsh antimodernist reaction that had distinguished Pius X's pontificate. The antimodernist crusade operated as a damper that froze the development of ecclesiological thought and eventually prevented a fruitful debate about a potential rapprochement with the Eastern Christians.[102]

At that time, Rome considered reunion as the return of erring children to Mother Church, respectful of their traditions and spirituality, a staple of unionism.[103] However, a positive movement toward a better understanding was clearly discernible under Pope Benedict. Propelled by the creation of the Pontifical Oriental Institute, some "principles of ecumenical communication were stated."[104] Although time was not ripe to consider equality in the way both parties were treating one another, the richness of tradition and spirituality of the Orthodox churches was recognized.[105]

Benedict's ecclesiology was not ecumenical. His ecclesiological decisions were the mark of an "intelligent unionism" that sought a better understanding of the separated brethren and promoted a respectful relationship in order to convince them to embrace the Roman Church in an unknown future.[106] Although advocating a rapprochement with the separated brethren, the pontiff missed a unique opportunity to manifest a genuine interest in learning from them. At the close of the war, the Oriental churches, severely weakened by the conflict, recognized

---

102. Legrand, "Fondation de l'Institut Pontifical."

103. Tavard, "Editorial," *Journal of Ecumenical Studies* 1 (1964): 99; see also G. R. Evans, *Method in Ecumenical Theology: The Lessons So Far* (Cambridge: Cambridge University Press, 1996), 21.

104. P. Esterka, "Toward Union: the Congresses at Velehrad," *Journal of Ecumenical Studies* 8 (1971): 13, quoted in Evans, *Ecumenical Theology*, 72.

105. Ibid., 13.

106. Patrice Mahieu, OSB, *Paul VI et les orthodoxes* (Paris: Editions du Cerf, 2012), 267.

the need to act together to ensure their future. To that effect, in January 1919 Archbishop Dorotheos, the metropolitan of Broussa and locum tenens of the ecumenical patriarchate, obtained the authorization from the Holy Synod of the Church of Constantinople to constitute a commission that would discuss the reunion of the Christian churches. In January 1920, an encyclical was promulgated that encouraged the establishment of a *koinônia* regrouping different confessions[107] on a model similar to the newly founded League of Nations. The encyclical listed different points, among them the suggestion to establish an "impartial and deeper historical study of doctrinal differences both by the seminaries and in books."[108] The document, which should have attracted much interest from other denominations, especially from Rome, actually generated little response, as it had been preceded in March 1919 by a similar offer from the Lutheran archbishop Söderblom of Upsal, Sweden, the driving force behind the Life and Work Movement.[109] This ecumenical movement was an attempt to bring Protestants and Orthodox together to envision their practical role and activities in society. On July 4, 1919, the Roman Holy Office issued a decree forbidding Catholics to participate in the London Society for the Union of Christendom,[110] therefore practically rejecting any participation in any new ecumenical movement like the ones evolving within the framework of the Life and Work Movement and the Faith and Order Movement that had grown out of the 1910 World Missionary Conference at Edinburgh.[111] One crucial reason un-

---

107. Greek word for joint participation, Christian fellowship.

108. Ecumenical Patriarchate of Constantinople, "Encyclical Letter *Unto the Churches of Christ Everywhere* [Jan. 1920]," *Ecumenical Review* 12, no. 1 (Oct. 1959): 79–82.

109. Salvador Eyezo'o and Jean-Francois Zorn, eds., *Concurrences en mission: Propagandes, conflits, coexistences (XVIe–XXIe siècle)* (Paris: Karthala, 2011), 269.

110. In September 1864, the Holy Office forbade Catholic participation in the London society. The ban was renewed in July 1919.

111. Suprema Sacra Congregatio S. Officii, "*De Participatione Catholicorum* [July 4, 1919]," *AAS* 11 (1919): 312–16.

derlying this interdict was that the new 1917 Code of Canon Law forbade non-Catholics from joining Catholic associations, therefore severely limiting the spiritual contact between Catholics and those considered as dissidents. Pope Benedict and his successor, Pius XI, adopted a position of "courteous recognition" but never sent delegates to ecumenical conferences.[112]

The most remarkable papal mark of esteem toward Eastern Christianity came on October 5, 1920, when Benedict XV, in his encyclical *Principi Apostolorum*, conferred the title of Doctor of the Church on St. Ephrem, a Syrian monk, deacon of Edessa. The pontiff sought to reach out to all Eastern Christians, pleading that

[He] humbly entreated God to return the Eastern Church at long last to the bosom and embrace of Rome. Their long separation, contrary to the teachings of their ancient Fathers, keeps them miserably from this See of Peter... meanwhile We received letters from the Venerable Brothers Ignatius Ephrem II Rahmani, Patriarch of Syria at Antioch; Elias Petrus Huayek, Maronite Patriarch at Antioch; and Joseph Emmanuel Thomas, Chaldean Patriarch at Babylon. They presented weighty arguments beseeching Us earnestly to bestow upon Ephrem, the Syrian Deacon of Edessa, the title and honors of Doctor of the Universal Church.[113]

Ephrem of Syria was "perhaps, the only theologian-poet to rank beside Dante."[114] Pope Benedict chose him as "a splendid example of learning, of holiness, and of patriotism"[115] and rescued him from oblivion in the West, while he was celebrated as one of the greatest fathers of the church in Orthodox tradition. His writings in the Syriac language were part of the liturgies of

112. James M. Oliver, *Ecumenical Associations: Their Canonical Status with Particular Reference to the United States of America* (Rome: Editrice Pontificia Università Gregoriana, 1999), 19.

113. Benedict XV, "Encyclical Letter *Principi Apostolorum Petro*, on St. Ephrem the Syrian [Oct. 5, 1920]," *AAS* 12 (1920): 457.

114. Robert Murray, "Ephrem Syrus, St.," in *Catholic Dictionary of Theology* (London: Nelson, 1967), 2:222.

115. Benedict XV, *Principi Apostolorum Petro*.

"the Syrian, the Nestorian, the Maronite, the Coptic, the Greek, and the Slavic Rites."[116] His elevation to the rank of Doctor of the Church should be interpreted as evidence of the pontiff's will to improve communication and develop a better understanding between the East and the West. St. Ephrem's writings, a source of ecclesiastical history, were a testimony to the perfect harmony of antiquity with the Catholic voice of the time.[117]

The ultimate goal of the foreign policy crafted by Benedict XV in the Middle East was to serve his unionist ecclesiology and ensure the protection of Catholic interests. In war and postwar turbulent times, the difficulty for the pontiff was to integrate its Eastern ecclesiology and supportive diplomacy in the larger realm of its European policies. As important as the Oriental policy was on the pope's agenda, it was always secondary to its diplomatic relationship with the European powers, which became colonial rulers of the collapsed Ottoman Empire in the early 1920s. Keeping in mind his double responsibility and long-term goal to restore the Eastern rite churches to their ancient glory and to embrace the Orthodox churches,[118] the Holy See's immediate attention was directed to the preservation and protection of the Catholic brethren and properties.

116. Joseph Gorayeb, SJ, "St. Ephrem, the New Doctor of the Universal Church," *Catholic Historical Review* 7 (Oct. 1921): 304.

117. Ibid., 303.

118. Dom Maternus Spitz, OSB, "Pope Benedict XV and the Apostolate," *Catholic Missions, Society for the Propagation of the Faith*, Apr. 1922, 77.

4

PROTECTION OF
CATHOLIC CLERGY AND
PROPERTY

While the Holy See pondered the state of its diplomatic relations with the Ottoman government, the Porte was imposing war measures on the Catholic clergy of belligerent countries present on Ottoman soil, expelling French, British, and Italian missionaries and confiscating their properties. The state of war accelerated a movement that the Porte had been engaged in since the 1908 Young Turk Revolution. In order to enjoy complete independence as a sovereign country, the Ottoman government had launched a diplomatic offensive to eliminate the French protectorate and enter into a direct relationship with the Holy See.

As the Holy See opted for a prudent wait-and-see attitude without officially denouncing the French protectorate, the Porte subjected the pope to diplomatic pressure, deeming all religious establishments under French protection French property. They were therefore confiscated as a war measure, throwing the Holy See into a diplomatic spat with Constantinople. Under German pressure, the Porte expelled most members of the French, British, and Italian clergy, with the plan to substitute German and Austrian missionaries and clergymen. The entry of Italy into the war in May 1915 exacerbated tensions between the Holy See and the Sublime Porte, as many members of the Catholic hierarchy on Ottoman soil were Italian. The arrest and deportation of Msgr. Chibli, Maronite archbishop of Beirut, Msgr. Huyaek, patriarch for the Maronites, and Msgr. Camassei, Latin patriarch of Jerusalem, gave the apostolic delegate Dolci grounds to accuse the Ottoman government of religious persecution against Catholics, a charge rebuffed by Ottoman authorities.

By the end of 1917, after General Allenby's capture of Palestine, the Catholic religious and cultural fabric was badly damaged. Most missionaries had left, and many confiscated Catholic buildings had been sold or secularized. A massive effort to restructure Catholic life and institutions and to adjust to new postwar developments took place under new mandates' rule.

From November 1914 to the end of the war, Dolci and Giannini inundated the secretariat of state and Propaganda Fide with detailed relations, describing the situation at hand. Dolci was given much diplomatic leeway by Cardinal Gasparri, as long as he followed three main guidelines. First, the secretary of state emphasized the need to use prudence in all matters, especially risk taking, as the Holy See was in diplomatic discussion at the highest level with Constantinople. Second, he asked Dolci to divert the question of the French protectorate by arguing that all Catholic institutions were legally property of the Holy See. Finally, Gasparri encouraged the apostolic delegate to stress the moral authority of the papacy. Dolci had often pointed out that Constantinople's war measures could be interpreted as religious persecution, thereby affecting the Porte's reputation among Christians. It was also casting a shadow over the diplomatic discussions regarding the establishment of direct ties between the Holy See and the Ottoman government.

CONFISCATION OF CATHOLIC PROPERTY

War Measures against Catholic Institutions

A few days after Constantinople entered the war, the Ottoman government gave instructions to the provincial governments to confiscate Catholic institutions and expel French, British, and Belgian Catholic clergy. The Holy See immediately reacted and launched diplomatic maneuvers to persuade the Porte to cancel the damaging measures. To that effect, Dolci sought the help of Henry Morgenthau. Although not a Catholic himself, as long as his country remained neutral in the conflict, the American ambassador proved efficient. The German and Austrian ambassadors also intervened often, but as representatives of belligerent countries, their direct interests sometimes collided with those of the Holy See.[1] The apostolic delegates in Constantinople and Syria, supported by the ambassadors, negotiated with a disorganized cabinet in Constantinople, constantly bringing to its attention the harsh measures taken by provincial governments— measures that were not always in phase with Constantinople's decrees.[2] The situation was especially thorny in Syria, a land deemed by Djemal Pasha to be his personal fiefdom. Djemal Pasha, one of the leading Young Turks, was the military governor of Syria, wielding ruthless control over a larger geographic area that included Palestine.

In a series of missives sent to the secretary of state, Cardinal Gasparri, and to the prefect of Propaganda Fide, Cardinal Gotti, Dolci and Giannini informed the Holy See of the evolution of the situation regarding the protection of Catholic interests. The situation varied depending on the area and the type of establish-

---

1. Giuseppe Pompilj to Gasparri, Nov. 15, 1914, ASV, Segr. Stato, 1915, rubr. 257, fasc. 1.
2. Dolci to Gasparri, Sept. 21, 1915, ASV, Segr. Stato, 1915, rubr. 257, fasc. 1. Dolci mentions "la disorganizzazione del Gabinetto, ogni dicastero nella sua sfera d'azione essendo assolutamente indipendente dal Gran Vizirato e dal Ministero degli Esteri"; see also Dolci to Gasparri, Oct. 10, 1915, ASV, Segr. Stato, Guerra (1914–18), rubr. 244, fasc. 110.

ments concerned. Churches and chapels, as places of worship, were treated differently than schools or hospitals.

A few weeks into the conflict, most French missionaries toiling on Ottoman soil had been expelled and their properties confiscated. One of the most sensitive issues was the closure of Catholic schools run by French missionaries. Giannini mentioned the Jesuits in Adana, whose schools had been converted into military hospitals. Other schools like the schools of the Brothers of the Christian Schools were converted into Muslim schools.[3] In a letter of November 17, 1914, Giannini noted that only "the establishments under the flag of belligerent countries [essentially France] are concerned."[4] The Ottoman government was convinced, long before the start of the war, that Catholic schools protected by the French protectorate were a vehicle used by France to promote its political, economic, and cultural interests and impose its *mission civilisatrice*, rather than places to educate Catholic students in the faith.

After meeting with the grand vizier on December 12, 1914, Dolci sent a dispatch to Cardinal Gasparri in which he explained that, in the Ottoman view, the schools were a means for political propaganda.[5] The American ambassador Morgenthau confirmed that, among the many establishments confiscated by the Ottoman government, "the Jesuit University at Beirut was closed and confiscated by the government...a large part of the furniture was taken by the government. The French medical buildings at Beirut were also confiscated by the Turkish government....In fact all the establishments belonging to the Jesuits in Beirut were confiscated."[6]

3. Relazione intorno all'espulsione dei Religiosi dalla Palestina e sullo stato del Patriarcato di Gerusalemme e delle sue mission, from the Patriarchate of Jerusalem, Feb. 22, 1915, AP, N.S., vol. 629 (1919), rub. 126.

4. Giannini to Gotti, November 17, 1914, AP, N.S., vol. 592 (1917), rub. 126, fol. 18rv–19rv.

5. Dolci to Gasparri, Dec. 12, 1914, ASV, Segr. Stato, 1914, rubr. 257, fasc. 1.

6. Letter from Ambassador Morgenthau, Jan. 20, 1915, ASV, Segr. Stato, Guerra (1914–18), rubr. 244, fasc. 110.

With a few exceptions, Catholic churches and chapels met a different fate and were protected by the authorities as places of worship. Dolci reaffirmed in a dispatch of February 4, 1916, that, per the decision of the cabinet, the churches should not be closed, as they were considered chapels of worship.[7] Often, churches were closed by local governors and then reopened after the intervention of the apostolic delegate and the German or Austrian ambassador to the Porte. Giannini noted the closure of Latin and Eastern Catholic churches in Aleppo that were confiscated to host the military.[8] He reported that the Jesuit church in Beirut was closed and reopened twice. The motive given to close it was that "it was not convenient to have a Christian church on the same premise as a Muslim school."[9] The building was reopened after the intervention of the Austrian ambassador.

Giannini shared his insight about the future of the Catholic churches in Syria, suggesting that the measures taken by the Ottoman government were meant to prevent any future attempt at restoring Catholic life after the war.[10] Although the Porte insisted that all measures were politically motivated war measures, numerous examples in Syria and Palestine painted a different picture. The Holy See was wary that behind the excuse of war measures, Catholics were facing actual religious persecution, intended to put pressure on the Holy See and bring it to seriously considering entering into direct diplomatic relations with the Porte.[11]

The situation of Catholic establishments deteriorated further after the entrance of Italy into the war in May 1915. The apostolic delegates, Dolci and Giannini, were both Italian. The welfare of the Custody of the Holy Land, entrusted to Italian Franciscans,

---

7. Dolci to Gasparri, Feb. 4, 1916, ASV, Segr. Stato, Guerra (1914–18), rubr. 244, fasc. 110.
8. Giannini to Dolci, Oct. 11, 1916, ASV, Arch. Deleg. Turchia, Dolci II, fasc. 2.
9. Giannini to Dolci, Oct. 25, 1916, ibid. (my translation).
10. Ibid.
11. Giannini to Gotti, Jan. 16, 1915, AP, N.S., vol. 592 (1917), rub. 126, fol. 44rv.

also experienced significant deterioration. In the early days of 1915, the Ottoman government ordered the closing of twelve convents belonging to the Custody of the Holy Land on the theory that they were under French protection. Dolci explained in a letter to Gotti, the prefect for Propaganda Fide, that the Italian and Spanish consuls in Jerusalem had negotiated with the Porte, the Spanish official explaining that the institutions were overwhelmingly staffed with Italians and were therefore the property of the King of Italy. Dolci lamented that this nationalist attitude of the Spanish minister not only offended the government but also aroused the susceptibility of other powers, with disastrous consequences.[12] The Italian and Spanish consuls' attempts to replace the French protectorate with a new Italian or Spanish protectorate was forcefully rejected by a government eager to assert its absolute sovereignty.

To obtain the reopening of the convents, Dolci accused the Ottoman government of instigating religious persecution. He insisted that the Porte had the duty to protect the Catholic religion because the church was transnational and impartial. The apostolic delegate used political arguments to solve a religious problem. In a meeting with the grand vizier, Dolci explained why the Porte should refrain from engaging in measures that damaged Catholic religious interests, a move that was to the exclusive advantage of the Orthodox churches, the Ottoman government's "arch-enemy." He suggested that the reopening of the convents would have no political meaning because it had no bearing on the question of the protectorate.[13] The arguments convinced the vizier, and the convents were reopened shortly after the meeting.

With the expulsion of French and Italian missionaries, most religious establishments were in jeopardy. The Ottoman gov-

12. Dolci to Gotti, Mar. 28, 1915, AP, N.S., vol. 592 (1917), rub. 126, fol. 59–63.
13. Ibid.

ernment closed and confiscated the buildings on the grounds that they were French property because they had been under French protection for centuries. To counter the measures of confiscation, the Holy See raised the legal issue of ownership, arguing that all establishments, although protected by the French, were the property of the Holy See. There was, therefore, no legal ground to confiscate them. The legal status of convents, schools, and other religious buildings became the crux of most diplomatic exchanges between the Holy See and Constantinople.

The Legal Status of Catholic Institutions

Early in the war, on November 17, 1914, Giannini wrote to the general governor of Beirut, Bekir Sami Bey, to raise the issue of the legal status of Catholic institutions in Syria and Palestine. He contended that the buildings belonged to the Holy See, since all Catholic missions come under the Holy See regardless of the nationality of their occupants.[14]

The legal status of Catholic establishments was an issue going back to the Treaty of Mytilene of 1901 by which the Ottoman government acknowledged the legal existence of all Catholic institutions under French protectorate, allowing most of them to be exempted from municipal taxes and custom duties.[15] A list of all establishments concerned was compiled with a clause allowing the addition of new establishments in the future. Nevertheless, the legal situation was never fully clarified, as the official acknowledgment of these institutions was based on the presentation of deeds, which were often nonexistent. Most of the establishments ruled by French missionaries had de facto and not de jure existence, as many of them had been built illegally.[16] A new

14. Giannini to Gotti, Nov. 17, 1914, AP, N.S., vol. 592 (1917), rub. 126.

15. Alexander Mombelli, "Palestine: Catholics Affirm Principle of Their Rights," *Catholic News*, Jerusalem, N.C.W.C., Dec. 7, 1935, http://www.catholicnews.sg/index.php?option=com_content&view=article&id=4266&Itemid=78.

16. Jean-Paul Durand, OP, "Les accords de Mytilène de 1901 entre le gouvernement

agreement was signed in 1913, alluding to the specific privileges of the Catholics in the Holy Land.

In a relation written on February 22, 1915, the patriarch of Jerusalem developed the legal interpretation given by the Holy See regarding the establishments of the Latin patriarchate of Jerusalem under French protectorate. He explained that

since the Ottoman government has abolished the French protectorate, it could be said that the establishments that are not French, but only under the protection of France, would certainly have to come back under Ottoman administration, unless France presents these establishments as purely French, which would be an inaccuracy in respect to missions and schools under the patriarchate.[17]

The Ottoman government accepted the argument and kept the schools and missions belonging to the Latin patriarchate open.

While the Porte was justifying its confiscating Catholic establishments, considering the Catholic buildings to be French property, the Holy See argued that there was a difference, with huge legal implications, between French property and property protected by France. On these grounds, Dolci was instructed by Cardinal Gasparri to defend Catholic establishments as being the sole property of the Holy See.[18]

In many cases, the situation was complicated by the sale of Catholic property by Ottoman authorities to local buyers. In February 1916, Dolci wrote to Gasparri regarding the confiscation of

français et la Sublime Porte," in *Le pontificat de Léon XIII, renaissances du Saint–Siège?* ed. Philippe Levillain and Jean–Marc Ticchi (Rome: Ecole française de Rome, 2006), 185–202.

17. "(A ciò si risponde che) avendo il governo ottomano abolito il protettorato francese, si direbbe che ne verrebbe di conseguenza che gli stabilimenti non francesi, ma protetti soltanto, avessero da tornare sotto il regime ottomano senz'altro, ameno che la Francia non avesse presentati tali stabilimenti come puramente francesi, ciò che sarebbe stato un'inesattezza per riguardo alle mission e scuole del Patriarcato"; *Relazione intorno all'espulsione dei Religiosi dalla Palestina e sullo stato del Patriarcato di Gerusalemme e delle sue mission*, patriarchate of Jerusalem, Feb. 22, 1915, AP, N.S., vol. 629 (1919), rub. 126 (my translation).

18. Gasparri to Giannini, July 28, 1915, ASV, Segr. Stato, Guerra (1914–18), rubr. 244, fasc. 111.

the mission belonging to the Sisters of St. Joseph in Beirut. Dolci was able to prove the ownership of the mission by the Holy See, presenting documents showing that the mission had been built with money sent by Pope Pius IX. Nevertheless, the rumor was that the mission had already been sold, which, as Dolci noted, "would complicate the transactions."[19] Diplomatic discussions were especially tense regarding those establishments under the care of the Custody of the Holy Land and buildings in Syria shared by Catholic and Orthodox communities.

The Custody of the Holy Land presented a unique situation. Although entrusted to Italian Franciscans, the Porte considered the establishments under the guardianship of the Custody as French property and closed the majority of them. An exception was granted to the rare members of the Custody who were citizens of a neutral country. In a decree of April 1915, transmitted by Giannini to Dolci, the Ottoman government stated that

although it is not possible to recognize otherwise than French the convents of the Holy Land, of Jerusalem, and *its surroundings*... religious members from neutral countries are allowed, out of gracious kindness, to stay from now on in the convents under the protection of the Ottoman government.[20]

Giannini questioned the content of the decree. He observed that the Porte considered as belonging to the Custody convents and other religious institutions situated in the surroundings (*e dintorni*) of the Custody, which, according to Giannini, raised a serious issue, as it would also justify the closure of convents situated far away from Jerusalem.[21]

19. Dolci to Gasparri, Feb. 4, 1916, ASV, Segr. Stato, Guerra (1914–18), rubr. 244, fasc. 110.

20. "Benche non sia possible riconoscere altrimenti che come stabilimenti francesi i conventi di Terra Santa di Gerusalemme *e dintorni* (emphasis mine)... e stato concesso..., per graziosa gentilezza, ai religiosi sudditi delle nazioni neutre di dimorar per adesso nei loro conventi rilevanti unicamente dal Governo Ottomano"; Giannini to Dolci, May 25, 1915, ASV, Segr. Stato, Guerra (1914–18), rubr. 244, fasc. 111 (my translation).

21. Ibid.

As for the French ownership of all establishments under the Custody of the Holy Land, Giannini dismissed the Ottoman statement on two main grounds. First, he argued that there was an important legal distinction between French establishments and establishments under French protection. Second, he noted that the Custody of the Holy Land was established by imperial decree long before the signature of the first capitulations between Sultan Suleiman the Magnificent and King Francis of France, capitulations that were the foundational basis for the establishment of the French protectorate. In the *firman* establishing the Custody, Giannini stressed that no mention was made of French property. That the imperial decree was promulgated upon French request did not imply that the establishments referred to in the decree became French property automatically. If that were the case, the Republic of Venice or Spain, both of which were also accorded *firmans* by the Porte, could also claim ownership of institutions under the guardianship of the Custody of the Holy Land.[22]

Then Giannini gave a legal explanation to justify the ownership of the Custody of the Holy Land by the Holy See. The Franciscan Custody has always been deemed an autonomous entity.

Its properties…enjoyed the privileged status given to pious legacies by the legislation of the Ottoman Empire. And as under canon law, the Franciscans possess nothing, the true and lawful owner of the convents of the Custody and their belongings has always been and is still today the Holy See as a result of papal bulls, and has never been France or any other nation.[23]

Giannini's legal demonstration was ratified by Djemal Pasha, who admitted in one specific instance that a hospice in the Holy Land was not French property. Building on this unexpected

22. Ibid.
23. "Le sue proprieta…godevano dello stato giuridico privilegiato assegnato ai legati pii dalla Legislazione dell'Impero Ottomano. E poiche per legge canonica I Francescani nulla possiedono in proprio, la vera e legittima proprietaria dei conventi della Custodia e delle loro appartenenze fu sempre ed e anche oggi la Santa Sede, come risulta dale relative Bolle Pontificie, e nom mai la Francia o altra nazione"; ibid. (my translation).

acknowledgment, Giannini dismissed any further discussion about French ownership and centered his reasoning on the legal repercussions that the French protectorate entailed for the Custody of the Holy Land. The responsibilities attached to the protectorate belonged to the nation ensuring the protection—namely, France—and not to those benefiting from the protection. Therefore, any retribution or war measure had to be addressed to France, the nation that had signed the capitulations, the foundation of the protectorate, and not to those under its protection, like the Italians, guardians of the Custody of the Holy Land.[24]

Msgr. Dolci had thereafter to convince the Ottoman government of the validity of Giannini's legal demonstration. According to Fr. Tonizza, writing from the Custody, Dolci was confident that he would be able to prove the full ownership of the Holy See over the establishments of the Custody of the Holy Land and would also try to obtain a new *firman* to recognize and confirm this right officially.[25]

Pope Benedict followed the situation in the Holy Land closely. He waited until July 23, 1915, a couple of months after Italy had entered the war, to give his official consent to Dolci to "declare that the Holy See is the sole owner" of the establishments under the guardianship of the Custody.[26] With France and Italy fighting against Constantinople, the Holy See, which until then had chosen a prudent policy, had to become more proactive in defending its ownership over Catholic institutions in the Ottoman Empire, especially in the Holy Land. Therefore, the pontiff engaged in a balanced diplomacy with the Porte, working to find a way to obtain satisfaction without budging on its wait-and-see prudent policy regarding the establishment of direct ties with the Ottoman government.

24. Ibid.
25. Giacinto Tonizza to Serafino Cimino, minister general of the Franciscan Order, June 27, 1915, ASV, Segr. Stato, 1915, rubr. 257, fasc. 3.
26. Dolci to Gasparri, July 27, 1915, ASV, Segr. Stato, Guerra (1914–18), rubr. 244, fasc. 111.

Despite Dolci's reassuring dispatches, the diplomatic spat between the Holy See and Constantinople did not find an easy solution. In November 1915 the menace from the Ottoman government to close and confiscate more Catholic establishments still lingered. In a letter dated November 25, Dolci acknowledged that the Porte had adopted a new stance. He informed Gasparri that he had met with the new minister, who promised to protect the convents of the Custody of the Holy Land situated in Palestine but, with regard to the other convents, asked that a study regarding their ownership be done.[27] The Ottoman government was not satisfied with oral or written general declarations of ownership by the Holy See and now required legal documents to prove its rights over Catholic establishments. The minister was convinced that they legally belonged to the Holy See, but unfortunately that was not enough to serve as legal proof of ownership.[28] The minister suggested to Dolci that the Holy See was placing too much hope in the return of the old regime and that they would be better protected if they could present the necessary documents. This statement was a veiled threat, understood as such by Dolci, who could not find any better immediate response than to gain time. He begged the minister to reopen the churches belonging to convents that had been closed, arguing that the collection of legal deeds proving the Holy See's ownership over Catholic establishments would take time. In the meantime, Catholic worship and life had to be maintained to avoid further disintegration of the Catholic fabric in the area. The minister accepted the request to keep churches open and to wait for proof of ownership before reopening the convents themselves.[29]

Dolci noted two important points in the new direction taken by the Ottoman government. First, he recognized the subtlety

---

27. Dolci to Gasparri, Nov. 20, 1915, ASV, Segr. Stato, 1918, rubr. 244, fasc. 111.
28. Ibid.
29. Ibid.

of Turkish diplomacy in its distinguishing, among the convents of the Custody, between those located in Palestine and those in areas like Beirut, Damascus, and Aleppo, respecting the former and closing the latter. Dolci explained to Gasparri that the government had chosen a double-edged diplomacy. On one hand, it was maintaining the pressure on the Holy See to present legal deeds and enter into direct diplomatic relations if Rome wanted to halt the confiscation of more Catholic institutions. But on the other hand, since the Holy Places were famous all over the world, the Porte was eager to avoid direct confrontation with Christians worldwide, therefore keeping the convents of the Holy Land open.

Second, Dolci interpreted the order to present legal deeds of ownership as a way to give a legal and final answer to an old problem and avoid future claims of ownership or protectorate by other nations. In the same letter, Dolci lamented the passing away of Baron von Wangenheim, the German ambassador who had been supportive of Dolci. The new ambassador, Count Metternich, did not have the intuition and energy of his predecessor and could not help in this difficult matter. Therefore, Dolci gave his advice to Gasparri: considering the foolishness of the new political orientation of the government, the uncertainty of the future, and the omnipotence of Djemal Pasha in Syria—who did not comply with any disposition taken by the central government—Dolci suggested that it would be wiser to keep a low profile and wait until the end of the hostilities.[30]

Gasparri's response came in early January 1916. He thanked Dolci for his advice and thorough account but asked him to be more proactive and keep the discussion open with the Ottoman government. As a canon lawyer Gasparri was comfortable arguing on legal grounds. He circumvented the delicate topic of ownership acquired through distinctive deeds for each property and

30. Ibid.

appealed to canon law to resolve the matter. He emphasized the legal nuance between ownership (*proprieta*) and the use of this property (*uso*), arguing that the Mendicant orders, in this case the Franciscans, had the use of the convents that were legally owned by the Holy See.[31] According to Gasparri, this argument should suffice to convince the Ottoman government to abandon the idea of presenting deeds for each property. If Constantinople persisted, Gasparri then recommended, to gain time, begging the government to reopen all the convents, a step necessary to provide spiritual assistance to Catholics in the area, arguing of the difficulty in collecting the information.[32]

The Holy See was never convinced of the Porte's good will and feared that behind legalistic subtleties loomed religious persecution against Catholics. The fate of the monastery of Mar-Elias, in Syria, was one situation that reinforced the Holy See's accusation that the Porte had engaged in an anti-Catholic campaign.

On January 24, 1915, the patriarch of the Syriac Catholic Church of Antioch, Ignatius Ephrem Rahmani, wrote to Cardinal Gasparri to lament the treatment reserved to Eastern Catholics, especially to the Syriac Catholic Church.[33] He complained that two of its religious establishments, the monastery of Mar-Elias and a local church, had not only been confiscated but had been transferred to the Syriac Orthodox Church. The patriarch explained in a memo the historical background of the issue. There was a time, he wrote, when the Ottoman government, denying Christians the right to build new churches, had ordered the two branches of the Syriac Church (Catholics and Jacobites) to share the same buildings.[34] When the community became overwhelm-

---

31. Gasparri to Dolci, Jan. 8, 1916, ASV, Segr. Stato, 1918, rubr. 244, fasc. 111.

32. Ibid.

33. Rahmani, patriarch of the Syriac Church, to Gasparri, Jan. 24, 1915, ASV, Segr. Stato, Guerra (1914–18), rubr. 244, fasc. 110.

34. The Jacobites are the members of the Syriac Orthodox Church.

ingly Catholic, the religious establishments became its exclusive property. The patriarch stressed that the Syriac Catholic Church had never recognized the French protectorate and had always paid taxes to the Ottoman government.[35] On March 14, 1915, Gasparri wrote to Msgr. Scapinelli, pronuncio in Vienna, asking him to solicit the support of the Austrian government via its ambassador in Constantinople.[36] The Austrian and German ambassadors promised to mediate in favor of the Syriac Catholic community of Mar-Elias.[37] Rejecting the accusations of deliberate religious persecution of Catholic communities, the Ottoman government presented the decision to evict the Syriac Catholic community and favor the Jacobites as a war measure against religious establishments under the French protectorate. The Porte dismissed the fact that the religious were actually Ottoman subjects living in a territory, under a special *firman* from the Ottoman government, exempted from French protection. The contested measures exacerbated the tensions between Catholic and Orthodox communities at a time when Pope Benedict was promoting a rapprochement with the separated brethren.

THE EXPULSION AND PERSECUTION
OF CATHOLIC CLERGY
War Measures or Religious Persecution?

While Catholic churches, convents, schools, and other buildings were closed, confiscated, and reallocated for Ottoman purposes, Catholic clergy were expelled and sent back to their country of origin or deported to different areas of the Otto-

35. Rahmani to Gasparri, Jan. 24, 1915, ASV, Segr. Stato, Guerra (1914–18), rubr. 244, fasc. 110.

36. Gasparri to Pro–Nunzio in Vienna, Scapinelli, Mar. 14, 1915, ASV, Segr. Stato, Guerra (1914–18), rubr. 244, fasc. 110.

37. Dolci to Gasparri, Apr. 8, 1915, ASV, Segr. Stato, Guerra (1914–18), rubr. 244, fasc. 110.

man Empire. The Holy See immediately expressed its fear that war measures against members of belligerent countries would soon transform into a religious persecution against Catholics. The apostolic delegate, Angelo Dolci, sought the help of Baron von Wangenheim to avoid violent deportation of French clergymen, but also recognized that Germany had provided the impulse needed against the French missions in order to destroy their national influence.[38] Von Wangenheim reinforced the Holy See's apprehension when he dismissed any religious persecution against Christians in Syria, although he admitted that the Ottoman government had taken some tough measures against French missionaries.[39]

A flurry of missives from clergymen in Palestine and Syria, as well as press articles, denounced the expulsions and bad treatment suffered by the Catholic clergy. The *New York Times* of January 11, 1915, worried that

hundreds of missionaries and other religious workers in the Holy Land are facing starvation, according to reports received…by the Rev. Godfrey Schilling of the Franciscan order, Commissary General for the Holy Land in the United States. The reports show that the Turks have turned the Franciscans out of nearly all of their convents in Armenia, Upper Syria, and Galilee.…In Jerusalem flourishing communities of the Assumptionists, Dominicans…the Poor Clares and other orders are said to have been put out into the streets.[40]

A few days later, the patriarchate in Jerusalem informed Propaganda Fide that the expulsion of religious members of belligerent countries had been sudden and brutal and had been accompanied by many unnecessary vexations. Nevertheless, he praised the kind attitude of government agents and the Muslim

38. Dolci to Gasparri, Dec. 12, 1914, ASV, Segr. Stato, Guerra (1914–18), rubr. 244, fasc. 110.

39. Baron von Wangenheim to Dolci, Dec. 9, 1914, ASV, Segr. Stato, Guerra (1914–18), rubr. 244, fasc. 110.

40. "Oust Religious Workers," *New York Times*, Jan. 11, 1915.

population, insisting on the reverential treatment received by the patriarch.[41]

With the entrance of Italy into the war, the situation of the Catholic clergy further deteriorated. Dolci noticed that the treatment of Italian clergy was much harsher than what the French, Belgian, and British were enduring due to a subtle distinction established by the Porte, not on religious but political grounds. In a meeting with Dolci, the director for political affairs explained that if the hostile attitude of France and England against Turkey was warranted, he could not justify the conduct of the Italian government. Recalling the Libyan War of 1911 and the Italian occupation of the Dodecanese Islands, he complained that, not satisfied to have reduced the territorial integrity of the Ottoman Empire, Italy was now taking advantage of the international military situation, unfazed at the idea of shedding new blood in Turkey.[42]

The decrees against Italian clergymen had a powerful effect, as most members of the Catholic hierarchy in the Ottoman Empire were Italian. Dolci obtained assurance from the Porte that Giannini, the Italian apostolic delegate in Beirut, would be protected and would maintain his position.[43] Yet, Giannini's security was never fully assured, as Djemal Pasha, the commander of the Syrian army, who accused most Italian and French clergymen of spying for their country, threatened to imprison him.

With the expulsion of French and Italian clerics and missionaries, the Catholic network was threatened and weakened. Dolci pointed out that the eventual expulsion of religious members of belligerent countries was a disaster for religious worship, parish

41. Relazione intorno all'espulsione dei Religiosi dalla Palestina e sullo stato del Patriarcato di Gerusalemme e delle sue mission, Feb. 22, 1915, AP, N.S., vol. 629 (1919), rub. 126.

42. Dolci to Gasparri, Sept. 16, 1915, ASV, Segr. Stato, Guerra (1914–18), rubr. 244, fasc. 111.

43. Dolci to Gasparri, Sept. 19, 1915, ASV, Segr. Stato, Guerra (1914–18), rubr. 244, fasc. 110.

life, and the safe running of hospitals. Yet, he was able to avoid the worst and, with the support of the German ambassador, obtained the cancellation of the order of expulsion for a selected few clergymen.[44]

Dolci was adamant that the war measures presented by the Ottoman government against clergymen belonging to the Entente countries were, in their focus on the clergy as well as in their scope and brutality, repressive measures characteristic of religious persecution. By the end of 1915, little doubt was left. In a dispatch of December 12, Giannini described to Msgr. Scapinelli, the nuncio in Vienna, what amounted to clear religious persecution. Giannini recounted that the *vali* of Beirut, the Turkish governor of the region, had ordered the Sisters of St. Vincent and other congregations, the great majority being Ottoman subjects, to change their religious habit on the grounds that "it was a sign of foreign fashion."[45] He addressed this letter to the nuncio in Vienna with the hope that Scapinelli would intervene directly, as Giannini was forbidden to write to the *vali* or any other authority or to ask for police intervention. Informed by the nuncio of the dangerous situation arising in Syria, Gasparri asked Dolci to step in while using great diplomatic skill and showing respect to the Ottoman government.[46]

A few days later, it was the Jesuits' turn to face persecution. The governor of Mount Lebanon commanded them to abandon their religious habit and opt for an Oriental religious outfit. They were summoned to leave their house in Zahle, and those without an Ottoman citizenship were to return to their respective countries, as the governor was not willing to recognize the Latin Catholic worship.[47]

44. Dolci to Gasparri, Oct.6, 1915, ibid.

45. Giannini to Scapinelli, Dec. 12, 1915, and Scapinelli to Gasparri, Jan. 4, 1916, ASV, Arch. Deleg. Turchia, Dolci II, fasc. 2.

46. Gasparri to Dolci, Jan. 18, 1916, ASV, Arch. Deleg. Turchia, Dolci II, fasc. 2.

47. Dolci to Gasparri, Jan. 15, 1916, ASV, Segr. Stato, Guerra (1914–18), fasc. 305–1.

In March 1916, the governor of Lebanon promulgated a decree enjoining all Latin Catholic priests, monks, and nuns of Ottoman nationality, members of a congregation whose headquarters were abroad, to break all ties with their order and leave their habit and any mark distinctive of their religious order. He allowed Lebanese religious men and women to keep their religious status as long as they would rejoin their former community, Maronite or Melchite.[48]

That the headquarters of these congregations were in France and not in Rome complicated the situation. In a follow-up letter to Gasparri, Scapinelli noted that it would be easy to successfully demonstrate to the Ottoman government that although most religious congregations had their headquarters abroad, the center of these congregations was the Catholic Church itself and therefore pointed toward Rome and the Holy See. Unfortunately, several general superiors of these congregations resided in France, a location that obviously did not coincide with the central power of the church concentrated in Rome.[49]

Pope Benedict received the news of the enforcement of these repressive measures with dismay. Well aware of the key influence that public opinion was slowly gaining in public policy making, the pontiff asked Dolci to become more proactive and put pressure on the Sublime Porte to stop this persecution, arguing that they were sparking outrage from the world against the Ottoman Empire.[50] But, as happened often in the empire, hostility toward Catholics was the result of the provincial governors' harsh interpretation of Constantinople's orders. While the Porte was using the threat of religious persecution as a diplomatic

48. Instructions given by the Lebanese government, Mar. 7 [1916], (1) 332, ASV, Arch. Deleg. Turchia, Dolci II, fasc. 2.

49. Scapinelli to Gasparri, Sept. 25, 1916, ASV, Segr. Stato, Guerra (1914–18), rubr. 244, fasc. 112.

50. Dolci to Gasparri, June 2, 1916, copying Gasparri's dispatch of May 28, 1916, ASV, Segr. Stato, Guerra (1914–18), rubr. 244, fasc. 110.

weapon to force the Holy See to establish diplomatic ties with them, local officials were promulgating decrees that fit their own immediate interests and beliefs. The *valis* were regularly receiving orders from Constantinople to cancel measures they had taken against Catholic members of the clergy—orders that were not always followed. Giannini and Dolci frequently complained about the internal tensions and state of disorganization of the Ottoman government in this matter.[51]

Dolci pointed out that by letting local governors in Syria and Lebanon enforce measures of persecution without efficient control Constantinople was acting against its own interest. An organized and adequate protection of the Catholic communities by the Porte itself would be a testimony to the world that Christian worship did not need the protection of foreign powers, its natural protector being the Ottoman government.[52]

Throughout the war Dolci appealed to the German ambassador to act with energy in order to obtain the liberation of the religious men and women, victims of Ottoman persecution. The apostolic delegate grasped the ambiguity of the role played by the ambassador. On one hand, Germany, as a European Christian power, was supporting the Holy See in its attempt to protect all clergy victims of expulsion or deportation. On the other hand, as an ally to the Porte, Germany was offered a chance to impose its political and religious presence in the Ottoman Empire by substituting a German and Austrian clergy to the French and Italian one.

In the wake of the expulsion of the French, British, and Italians from the empire, Berlin, Vienna, and Budapest created committees to discuss the most appropriate way to support the Catholic missions and other establishments that had been sur-

---

51. Dolci to Gasparri and Serafini, Apr. 15, 1916, ASV, Arch. Deleg. Turchia, Dolci II, fasc. 2.

52. Dolci to Gasparri, June 2, 1916, ASV, Segr. Stato, Guerra (1914–18), rubr. 244, fasc. 110.

rendered to the Ottoman government.[53] That Berlin and Vienna had as their main and ultimate goal the protection of Catholic interests in Greater Syria was not in doubt. By taking over establishments that had been in Italian and French hands for centuries, Berlin, and to a lesser measure Vienna, were also aiming at political and cultural gain. Scapinelli warned Gasparri that sending German and Austrian clergy members to the Ottoman Empire would support the "grand design of Germany," which was to replace the old political influence of France in Greater Syria, but also to expand its own power in the immense region from Constantinople to Baghdad through the German railway project.[54] Scapinelli feared that allowing German clergy to substitute for French and Italian clergy would anger France, which, in return, would accuse the Holy See of taking sides in the conflict through this means.

A few weeks later, the papal nuncio at Munich, Cardinal Frühwirth, wrote to Gasparri along the same lines. Cardinal von Hartmann, the archbishop of Cologne, had written to Frühwirth regarding the spiritual care of Catholics in the empire. Von Hartmann reported that the German ambassador had confided that Dolci, as an Italian citizen, would not obtain any favorable response to his requests without the support of Germany. Therefore, a German bishop or at least a bishop from a neutral country should be sent to Constantinople to facilitate the resolution of conflicts between the Holy See and the Porte.[55] While exchanging missives with the Holy See, Cardinal von Hartmann launched a German Catholic propaganda campaign in the Otto-

53. Scapinelli to Gasparri, Dec. 17, 1915, ASV, AES, Austria, 1915–16, pos. 1071, fasc. 465.

54. Ibid. The Berlin-Baghdad railway project began in 1888 and gained momentum in the early 1900s, stimulated by the newly revived German slogan *Drang nach Osten* [yearning for the East]. The railway was central to German's national hope, as it was a manifestation of the government's ambition to achieve economic and political hegemony in the crumbling Ottoman Empire.

55. Frühwirth to Gasparri, Jan. 25, 1916, ASV, AES Austria, 1915–16, pos. 1071, fasc. 465.

man Empire. He dispatched a clergyman, Dr. Straubinger, whose official mission was to deliver a letter of recommendation to the military chaplaincy. He had actually been sent to investigate the current state of affairs in order to initiate German Catholic propaganda in the Orient. Dolci dismissed a report, *Relazione sulle missioni e scuole cattoliche in Turchia e i cattolichi tedeschi*, written by the German agent, criticizing its lack of accuracy and saying that it was flawed due to a lack of genuine information. The conclusions of the report had been drafted so as to justify sending German clerics. Consequently, Cardinal von Hartmann sent a doctor in theology, Enrico Zimmermann, to Constantinople.[56] A few other German clerics followed.

With Gasparri's approval, Dolci allowed the German clergymen to work in Catholic institutions while avoiding upsetting France.[57] He tempered the activism of Dr. Straubinger, whose energy was concentrated in converting French schools belonging to the Brothers of the Christian Schools into German missions, and convinced him to consider the schools as Ottoman institutions.[58] He also suggested, with Gasparri's approval, that he open schools with German Catholic features that would serve the German colony.[59]

Dolci was successful in curbing German propaganda in the Ottoman Empire but was not able to assuage Italian and French fears. Carlo Monti expressed his concern to Gasparri about the German religious offensive in Palestine, which aimed at overruling the Italians in the Custody of the Holy Land and establishing a German guardianship. As a proof of the collusion between the German government and the German bishops, Monti pointed out that the Protestant German government was paying all the Catholic missionaries' travel expenses.[60]

56. Dolci to Gasparri, Feb. 10, 1916, ibid.   57. Gasparri to Dolci, Mar. 3, 1916, ibid.
58. Dolci to Gasparri, Feb. 10, 1916, ibid.
59. Gasparri to Dolci, Mar. 3, 1916, ibid.; Dolci to Gasparri, Feb. 10, 1916, ibid.
60. Carlo Monti to Gasparri, May 14, 1916, ibid.

This assault on Catholic missions and schools backed by the German government did not bear much fruit. The Holy See was attentive to maintaining the status quo with the French and the Italians, sending German and Austrian clergy toward a case-by-case agreement. From Constantinople, Dolci was enrolling the help of the German ambassador in settling diplomatic quarrels and welcomed the support of the few German clergymen that were sent to Greater Syria to sustain Catholic life and worship in a time of religious persecution against clerics from belligerent countries.

Ottoman Persecution of High-Ranking Catholic Ecclesiastics

Whether the vexations that accompanied the arrest and deportation of French and Italian clerics were proof of religious persecution and not the mere result of war measures against citizens of belligerent countries is open for discussion. In contrast, the treatment reserved for members of the Catholic hierarchy left little room for doubt. The Maronite archbishop of Beirut, Msgr. Chibli, the Latin patriarch of Jerusalem, Msgr. Camassei, and the Maronite patriarch, Msgr. Huayek, were victims of persecution because of their religious status and not because they were citizens of a belligerent country. With the exception of the Latin patriarch of Jerusalem, Msgr. Filippo Camassei, who was Italian, none of them was of European extraction, neither French nor Italian.

Msgr. Chibli was the Maronite archbishop of Beirut. Although not a Catholic of Latin rite, the rumor spread in the first days of July 1916 that he had been condemned to death by the Martial Court of the City of Beirut. When Dolci protested to the minister of foreign affairs against the measure, the minister questioned the veracity of the information and promised the apostolic delegate that he would intervene and stop the execution. Dolci pointed out the lack of communication between Constantinople and the governor of Syria, saying that the measure was "another stupid act from the Governor of Syria," to which the minister of foreign affairs replied that it was true indeed.[61] Chibli was actually not condemned to death but to deportation, along with other Maronite notables. He eventually died on March 20, 1917.

More sensitive was the situation faced by Msgr. Huayek, the Maronite patriarch who was forced with other high-ranking members of the Catholic Church in Syria and Palestine to cosign a statement praising the commander in chief of Syria, Djemal Pasha.[62] The language used was typical of propaganda communiqués. The text, written in French, was a rhetorical exercise that hid a veiled threat against the Catholic Church. The signatories of the statement praised General Djemal Pasha,

well-known for his wisdom, and whose arrival in the area is considered as a true blessing and a kindliness from the Most High who, in the critical circumstances of human things knows how to create men instrumental for the consolation of peoples.[63]

The panegyric of Djemal Pasha was accompanied by personal letters written by different prelates, among them Msgr. Huyaek.[64] The Maronite patriarch stopped short of praising the great heart and magnanimity of Djemal Pasha, concentrating instead on tarnishing the image of France among Maronites, dismissing any beneficial role the nation had ever played in Syria-Lebanon.[65] This denigration of France was a step to ensure the

61. Dolci to Gasparri, July 8, 1916, ASV, AES Austria, 1916, pos. 1104, fasc. 470.

62. Opuscule "Réponse à la presse française––Démentis opposés par le Clergé supérieur de la Syrie et de la Palestine aux mensonges des journaux français," Jérusalem, Nov. 14, 1916, ASV, Segr. Stato, Guerra (1914–18), rubr. 244, fasc. 111.

63. "Bien connu pour sa sagacité, et dont l'arrivée dans ces parages est considérée tout à fait comme un bienfait et une bienveillance du Très-Haut qui dans les circonstances critiques des choses humaines sait créer des hommes utiles pour la consolation des peuples"; Réponse à la presse française, Nov. 14, 1916 (my translation).

64. Letters from Gregory IV, patriarch of Antioch, and Dimitrios Cady, Kaimakam patriarchal for the Greek Catholics, were also attached.

65. Réponse à la presse française, Nov. 14, 1916.

safety of the Maronite population, which was accused, often without any evidence, of collaboration and friendship with the French. Praising the Ottoman government and blaming France for all ills did not help Msgr. Huyaek, who was sentenced to deportation in July 1917. Dolci complained to the war minister that Patriarch Huyaek, a high-ranking ecclesiatic who had just celebrated his seventy-fifth birthday, had received orders to leave his summer residence of Diman nestled in the north of Lebanon and move to Zahleh in the Beka, where there were no Maronites to minister to and no adequate place to live.[66] He stressed the negative repercussions that the measure would have on the image the Ottoman government was eager to maintain with Catholics worldwide,[67] as well as with the Maronites who could enter into rebellion and reopen the longstanding question of Lebanese independence.[68]

The deportation of Huyaek was managed with much care and subtlety. Djemal Pasha did not order a violent arrest. He invited the patriarch to different meetings in distant locations, each time pushing him farther away from his seat in Lebanon. When Huyaek received the invitation to join Djemal Pasha in Zahle in August 1917, he presented excuses on account of his health and offered to be at the disposal of the governor at the residence of the Maronite archbishop of Cyprus in Shewan.[69] He was eventually released after the intervention of the Holy See and the emperor of Austria.

With British troops approaching Jerusalem, tension in the Ottoman government rose. After subjecting Msgr. Chibli and Msgr. Huyaek to persecution, Djemal Pasha turned his attention to the Latin patriarch in Jerusalem, Msgr. Camassei. While Huyaek was moved into exile but never arrested, Camassei met a more brutal fate. Dolci informed Cardinal Serafini at Propaganda Fide

66. The Beka or Beqaa is a farming valley in East Lebanon.
67. Dolci to Ottoman minister of war, July 26, 1917, ASV, Arch. Deleg. Turchia, Dolci III.
68. Dolci to Gasparri, Oct. 24, 1917, ASV, Segr. Stato, Guerra (1914–18), fasc. 130–1.
69. Zahle is today the capital and largest city of the Beka.

that Msgr. Camassei and his vicar, Msgr. Piccardo, had been arrested by order of Djemal Pasha and sent to an unknown location.[70] Conflicting reports reached Dolci. On December 2, 1917, General Bronsart, head of the German military mission in the Ottoman Empire, reported to Dolci that Camassei had been sent to Angora for military reasons,[71] but also because the climate was better for his health.[72] Bronsart insisted that the patriarch had traveled in an automobile in the most comfortable manner. In the meantime, British general Sir Reginald Wingate alerted Count de Salis, the British representative to the Holy See, that Msgr. Camassei had been deported with much violence to Nablus, Palestine, on November 19, 1917.[73] While in exile, Camassei was ordered by Djemal Pasha to write a letter to Pope Benedict with the request to publish it in the *Osservatore Romano*.[74] In this letter, preserved in the Secret Vatican Archives, Camassei engaged in a forced propaganda exercise similar to his previous panegyric of the Ottoman government and the military commander of Syria, Djemal Pasha.[75] After lamenting the many calamities that had affected Lebanon, he expressed gratitude to Pope Benedict's actions to alleviate the Lebanese suffering and praised "the famous Djemal Pacha…[who] actually took care of our situation and tried to alleviate our misery," stressing that he had always been "surrounded with the most kind gestures and the most benevolent consideration."[76]

According to Giannini's letter to Cardinal Serafini of December 6, 1917, Msgr. Camassei was exiled neither to Nablus nor

70. Dolci to Serafini, Nov. 25, 1917, AP, N.S., vol. 629 (1919), rub. 126.

71. Angora, today known as Ankara, is situated in the heart of Anatolia.

72. Dolci to Serafini, Dec. 2, 1917, AP, N.S., vol. 629 (1919), rub. 126.

73. Telegram from Sir Reginald Wingate to Count of Salis, Dec. 5, 1917, ibid.

74. Dolci to Gasparri (with letter from Msgr. Camassei of Nov. 2, 1917), Dec. 5, 1917, ASV, AES Austria, 1917, pos. 1211, fasc. 496.

75. Réponse à la presse française, Nov. 14, 1916.

76. Dolci to Gasparri, Dec. 5, 1917, ASV, AES Austria, 1917, pos. 1211, fasc. 496 (my translation).

Angora but was staying with a wealthy Melchite family from Damascus.[77] He announced in the same note the death of Msgr. Piccardo. To complicate the situation further, the pro-vicar for the Latin patriarch, François Fellinger, informed Gasparri that Msgr. Camassei had been deported on November 19, 1917, to Nazareth. On November 24, Msgr. Piccardo had been sent to Damascus, where he died on December 2, after a long trip. He was seventy-four years old.[78]

After the British troops entered Jerusalem on December 9, 1917, Cardinal Gasparri officially requested the return of Patriarch Camassei to his seat. The situation was complicated by his probable sojourn in Nazareth, the headquarters for the German expeditionary force, still in Ottoman hands. General Bronsart advised Dolci not to insist on Camassei's return to Jerusalem because military reasons forbade it.[79] More to the point, the minister of foreign affairs criticized Pope Benedict's congratulatory message sent after the fall of Jerusalem to the British that explained his lack of eagerness to meet the pope's request to free Msgr. Camassei. "The pope has become our enemy," the minister complained to Dolci.[80]

In view of the deadlock reached with Ottoman and German officials, the Holy See turned to Italy for help, which provoked the astonishment of the German ambassador to Constantinople.[81] Msgr. Camassei was eventually freed in November 1918.[82] Writing to the Society for the Propagation of the Faith, the patriarch declared that his forced exile was the means chosen by Providence to bestow great honor on Catholicism.[83]

77. Giannini to Serafini, Dec. 6, 1917, AP, N.S., vol. 629 (1919), rub. 126.

78. Telegram from Sir Reginald Wingate to Count of Salis, Dec. 24, 1917, ASV, Segr. Stato, Guerra (1914–18), fasc. 111.

79. Dolci to Serafini, Dec. 30, 1917, AP, N.S., vol. 629 (1919), rub. 126.

80. Dolci to Serafini, Jan. 28, 1918, ibid. (my translation).

81. Dolci to Gasparri, Feb. 24, 1918, ASV, Segr. Stato, Guerra (1914–18), fasc. 130–1.

82. François Fellinger to van Rossum, Sept. 29, 1918, AP, N.S., vol. 629 (1919), rub. 126.

83. "Missionary Notes and News," *Catholic Missions*, May 1919, 119.

The ill treatment of high-ranking ecclesiastics in Syria and Palestine was directly ordered by Djemal Pasha. He was aware of the diplomatic tension he had created with the deportation of Msgr. Camassei, whom he accused of being an Italian spy. In all his actions, he proved independent from Constantinople while ruling Syria as his fiefdom. With time, he became more belligerent, especially after the British troops started their successful approach to Jerusalem.

AN ASSESSMENT: THE

DISINTEGRATION OF THE CATHOLIC RELIGIOUS

AND CULTURAL NETWORK

Both Dolci and Giannini regularly expressed their fear that after years of war and religious persecution, and although the central government was willing to protect Catholic churches, only traces of Catholicism would remain following the war.[84] The closing of schools, convents, and other Catholic establishments, accompanied by the expulsion of most missionaries and clerics, weakened and shrank the Catholic religious, social, and cultural life.

With the capture of Jerusalem came the time to assess the state of Catholic interests in Palestine and Syria. On March 2, 1918, Dolci informed Gasparri that he had heard rumors from the Greek Orthodox clergy that the Ottoman government was preparing a law regarding church property. The government did not intend to return the properties that had been confiscated during the war, many having already been sold or used for other purposes. Rather, it planned to confiscate the remaining establishments while undertaking to maintain Christian worship.[85] Some details of the future law were leaked. Dolci informed Gasparri that in addition to the confiscation of ecclesiastical property, the

84. Dolci to Gotti, Sept. 21, 1915, ASV, Segr. Stato, 1915, rubr. 257, fasc. 1.
85. Dolci to Gasparri, Mar. 23, 1918, ASV, AES Austria, 1918–19, pos. 1314, fasc. 517.

Porte was elaborating a policy addressing non-Muslim religious bodies that suppressed the attributes and prerogatives of all patriarchs. The various administrative bodies were to be replaced by one small committee whose task was to run all schools, charitable institutions, and churches.[86]

Rome's reaction was swift. Gasparri instructed Dolci to protest with energy but prudence against the new bill. The apostolic delegate met with the minister of cults, who did not share much about the content of the bill. It had been prepared by a German adviser whose task was to study the German and Austrian legislation on church property and draw his inspiration from it. Dolci described the German adviser as a "fanatic protestant" and questioned the authority of the German or Austrian law in this matter, arguing that neither in Germany nor in Austria had religious property been subjected to a regime similar to the sacred Muslim law.[87]

Entering into the legal aspects of the bill, Dolci complained that he had been left in the dark regarding the particulars of the text, but he was able to articulate two hypotheses. If the law referred to properties that in the future would be bequeathed by Christians to the Catholic Church, it was then essential to recognize the legal identity (*personalité juridique*) of the church so that it would acquire properties legally and manage them independently. On the other hand, if the law addressed already existing church properties, Dolci argued that it would create a delicate situation with hazardous diplomatic repercussions.[88]

The Holy See claimed that the Catholic Eastern churches could not be compared or identified with the other dissident Eastern churches. Their constitution was different. While the Orthodox Eastern churches were autonomous, the Catholic Eastern churches were under the authority of the pope, which

86. Dolci to Gasparri, May 11, 1918, ibid.   87. Dolci to Gasparri, Sept. 27, 1918, ibid.
88. Ibid.

prevented any interference from a third party.[89] With the surrender of the Ottoman army and the signing of the Mudros armistice on October 30, 1918, that spelled the end of the conflict on Ottoman soil, the law never came into effect.

The time came for the Holy See to supervise the reopening of religious establishments— both Latin and Eastern Catholic properties that had been closed or confiscated by the Ottoman government during the war. The religious network had been badly damaged and needed a thorough investigation before relaunching Catholic life to its fullest. Propaganda Fide and the newly established Congregation for the Oriental Church took over the task.

Acting in line with his predecessors, Pope Benedict's diplomacy in the Ottoman Empire had two main objectives: the protection of lay and religious Catholic communities and the protection of Catholic properties in a Muslim environment. The safeguarding and strengthening of Catholic minorities' presence in the Ottoman Empire had been supported throughout the centuries by France and later by France and Great Britain, who fought for their welfare and status as protected religious minorities. The ultimate goal of the Holy See had always been to ensure the continuity of a Catholic presence in the cradle of Christianity despite the modest numbers that represented the Catholic communities. The protection of Catholic communities was tied to the Holy See's strategy to guarantee the integrity of Catholic properties, especially the Holy Places to which all Christians turn with deep reverence and devotion.

Pope Benedict was the first pontiff to experience a war conflict of this scope and violence and to witness the forces of fragmentation at work in the Ottoman Empire. Therefore, he had no example of past experience to rely on. The impact of his person-

89. Ibid.

ality and of his personal understanding of the relationship between the Catholic Church and the world and the church and other religions was therefore more accentuated. He was a pioneer in this domain.

Although remaining impartial throughout the war, the pontiff chose to lead a vocal and active diplomacy that carried the risk of further endangering the welfare of both Catholic communities and institutions in a time of political instability. Refusing to remain silent to avoid the persecution of Catholic communities on Ottoman soil, Pope Benedict chose to intervene as a spiritual leader in the affairs of the world. Instead of silence, which is often held by the Holy See to be more effective than direct condemnation, he encouraged the apostolic delegate to move the diplomatic discussion from the purely political plane to the religious one by arguing on the basis of his moral authority and his love for all.

Pope Benedict went beyond the simple acknowledgment of wartime measures against the Christian populations and elevated the debate to encompass the future of the relationship between Muslims and Catholics, arguing that the persecution of Christians would have the worst effect on worldwide public opinion. At a time when diplomacy of reciprocity was not possible, this strategy was the one that carried a greater chance of success. It was a move that entailed risks, especially after the Ottoman minister declared that the pope was now their enemy; but it was also courageous, a sign of how Pope Benedict understood the role of the Catholic Church in a world in the process of being completely reshaped.

5

BENEDICT XV'S HUMANITARIAN ASSISTANCE

Humanitarian relief efforts relayed by governments on a foreign theatre of war are often interpreted as diplomatic efforts meant to support and sometimes validate specific foreign policy objectives.[1] Seldom are they recognized as charitable efforts per se. Pope Benedict's humanitarian policy during the First World War was a genuine charitable endeavor, answering the foundational moral precepts of true Catholic charity. But although the Holy See had as its main objectives the relief of war victims and a will to radiate ethical convictions, it also hoped to enhance its influence and prestige in Greater Syria, a schismatic land to be won back.

It was only through well-oiled diplomatic channels that humanitarian assistance could be safely provided. Situated in essence above the political realm, papal humanitarian relief efforts were directly dependent upon the evolution of the political situation on the war theatre and the diplomatic ability of the Holy See's representatives on the scene. Pope Benedict's humanitarian policy was innovative. The pontiff designed an original relief policy, a third path between purely charitable acts and a humanitarian

1. See Gary J. Bass, *Freedom's Battle: The Origins of Humanitarian Intervention* (New York: Knopf, 2008); Bruno Cabanes, *The Great War and the Origins of Humanitarianism, 1918–1924* (Cambridge: Cambridge University Press, 2014).

diplomacy that furthered foreign policy objectives. His diplomacy was at the crossroad of idealist and realist policies. His humanitarian assistance diplomacy was not a substitute for political action. While providing relief to all in need, in Europe and in the Ottoman Empire, Pope Benedict was diplomatically very active on the European scene trying to secure peace. Political action and humanitarian assistance strategy were developed hand in hand.

The main actors in humanitarian relief efforts in the Ottoman Empire were the Holy See and the American government through the American Red Cross and Near East Relief. The collaboration between the two was difficult and eventually resulted in accusations of discrimination against the Catholic population by Near East Relief workers.

CATHOLIC HUMANITARIAN ASSISTANCE: A PHANTOM?

Foundations and Motivations of the Holy See's Humanitarian Assistance

From Europe to the end of the Ottoman Empire, conditions were chaotic. Civil victims and prisoners of war suffered, dying of illnesses, starvation, or exhaustion after deportation. Through its closely knitted network of parishes and missions—although most had been confiscated and French and Italian missionaries had been expelled—the Catholic Church reached every corner of the war theatre, offering the pope and his secretary of state a unique listening post in spite of difficulties of communication and the large amount of disinformation and numbers of false rumors circulating. The missionaries became the "cornerstones of humanitarianism,"[2] and their influence at the policy-making level increased during the war.[3]

---

2. David Rieff, *A Bed for the Night: Humanitarianism in Crisis* (New York: Simon and Schuster, 2002), 67.

3. Thomas A. Bryson, *American Diplomatic Relations with the Middle East, 1784–1975: A Survey* (Metuchen, N.J.: Scarecrow Press, 1977), 61.

The Holy See spent more than eighty million gold lire, including the majority of Benedict's personal wealth, to fund humanitarian assistance.[4] The French essayist Romain Rolland dubbed it the "Second Red Cross."[5] It tracked and secured the exchanges of thousands of prisoners of war. In the Ottoman Empire, it rescued civil populations from complete destitution and starvation and tried to prevent massacres in Armenia.

In Greater Syria, it alleviated daily sufferings, tending the sick and negotiating the shipment of food and medicine to sick and starving populations. Designed by Pope Benedict and his secretary of state in Rome, the humanitarian assistance was implemented by Catholic missionaries under the guidance of the apostolic delegates Dolci and Giannini. The commitment of the church to bringing relief to suffering populations also originated from the lower level. It was the combination of a strong sense of purpose at the Vatican and the devotion of missionaries relayed by apostolic delegates on the ground that transformed the Catholic Church into an original and dedicated humanitarian world agency.

Until the 1870s, the cornerstones of humanitarian relief were the Catholic and Protestant missionaries who understood their actions as charity. Answering the moral imperative of service to humanity, they acted upon the belief that every human being was a gift of God without regard to his race or religion. With the introduction of the Swiss-inspired International Red Cross movement in 1863, civil officers with no religious affiliation increased the ranks of humanitarian workers. The Red Cross rapidly became the "legally recognized guardian" of the international humanitarian law of war.[6]

4. Anne Cipriano Venzon, ed., *The United States in the First World War: An Encyclopedia* (New York: Garland, 1999), 78.

5. Romain Rolland, a pacifist, left France at the outbreak of the war and joined the Red Cross in Switzerland. He worked for the International Agency for Prisoners of War and shared Pope Benedict's concern for the future of Europe.

6. Rieff, *Bed for the Night*, 70.

The openings of hostilities in 1914, a conflict of unknown violence and scope, called for an unprecedented level of involvement. Relief workers from the International Red Cross joined missionaries, both Catholic and Protestant, who were enrolled by the Holy See and the American government respectively, to alleviate the suffering of starving populations. The missionaries became, willingly or not, intelligence agents. Their firsthand reports and the personalities of some of them influenced the policy-making of their native countries. This was particularly true of the American Protestant missionaries toiling on Ottoman soil. To their government, humanitarian relief efforts were at once a charitable endeavor and a diplomatic tool to use against the Ottoman government.

When the American ambassador Henry Morgenthau initiated "a kind of national crusade" in his home country that intended to raise funds to alleviate the sufferings of Ottoman subjects in the empire,[7] the impressive success of his charitable endeavor was regarded as a piece of a larger diplomatic effort. The ultimate goal was to put pressure on the Ottoman government to stop the massacre of Christian and Jewish Armenian populations. As the representative of the only great power still neutral in the conflict, he had firsthand knowledge of the atrocities committed in the Ottoman Empire. Information officially meant for the State Department was leaked to the American public, which rapidly demanded American involvement. Morgenthau, pressing the moral and political power of his country upon the Ottoman government, tried to convince the Porte that they would greatly suffer in reputation for not taking American public opinion into account.

7. John A. deNovo, *American Interests and Policies in the Middle East, 1900–1939* (Minneapolis: University of Minnesota Press, 1963), 103.

Benedict XV's Humanitarian Assistance:
Divergent Assessments

The Holy See also used the leverage of international Catholic opinion to dissuade the Ottoman government from carrying out massacres and to convince it to open its frontiers to food shipments. Although a respected source of morality and wisdom, the papacy found itself in a complicated position facing another esteemed source of morality in the persons of the American president, Woodrow Wilson, and Ambassador Morgenthau. Their humanitarian relief efforts sustained by large donations made by American citizens were publicly acknowledged and regularly praised in contemporary newspapers. English-language literature on the subject commended American humanitarian relief as well as the International Red Cross's dedication to saving lives. The Holy See was rarely mentioned. Ambassador Morgenthau's seminal book, a narrated *Personal Account of the Armenian Genocide* published in 1918, mentioned the apostolic delegate at Constantinople, Msgr. Dolci, once in passing.[8] Ten years later, James L. Barton, in his *Story of Near East Relief*, gave no acknowledgment of Catholic involvement. Cardinal Gibbons, the archbishop of Baltimore, is cited in the American context.[9] Neither Dolci nor Giannini is acknowledged as a personality worthy of mention. The commitment of the church at the highest hierarchical level, as well as at the lower level represented by priests and missionaries, is ignored.

During the world conflict, the public picture of humanitarian relief portrayed the American Protestant assistance in its center working hand in hand with the American Red Cross while keeping the Holy See's diplomatic and practical involvement at the

8. Henry Morgenthau, *Ambassador Morgenthau's Story: A Personal Account of the Armenian Genocide* (Garden City, N.Y.: Doubleday, 1918).

9. James L. Barton, *Story of Near East Relief (1915–1930): An Interpretation* (New York: Macmillan, 1930).

periphery. Was this a distortion of reality or did it represent the truth of the times? How should we then assess the content of numerous envelopes and boxes kept in the Secret Vatican Archives as well as those at the Congregation for the Oriental Churches and Propaganda Fide that methodically depict the struggle of the apostolic delegate at Constantinople to obtain assistance, the various conversations he had with officials at the Porte, the responses from Cardinal Gasparri, and the voluminous amount of letters written by missionaries crying for help? How should we appreciate the significance of the erection in Constantinople of a statue of Pope Benedict a few weeks before his death in 1922, bearing the inscription "To the great pope of the world's tragic hour, Benedict XV, benefactor of the people, without discrimination of nationality or religion, a token of gratitude from the Orient, 1914–1919"?[10] How should we value the gratitude bestowed upon the pontiff by the sultan, the vice-king of Egypt, the great rabbi of Turkey, the Armenian, Gregorian, and Georgian patriarchs—all Muslims, Jews, or schismatic patriarchs—while the pope's involvement is only mentioned in passing by European and American governments?

A few answers can be offered. First and foremost, Pope Benedict XV greatly disappointed European governments and public opinion—Catholic and non-Catholic alike—when he declined to take sides in the world conflict. His impartial stance cost him tremendously in terms of moral authority and the ability to significantly influence the course of events. The American president, Woodrow Wilson, benefited from the situation and gained a new status as moral leader. In addition, the pope's choice of impartiality left the Holy See in an uncomfortable position to ask for military support for its relief efforts. The Allies were convinced

---

10. Robert John Araujo and John A. Lucal, *Papal Diplomacy and the Quest for Peace: The Vatican and International Organizations from the Early Years to the League of Nations* (Ann Arbor, Mich.: Sapientia Press of Ave Maria University, 2004), 159.

that behind a public impartial façade, the Holy See had always been hoping for the victory of the Central Powers.

But what was perceived as a liability in Europe and in the United States became an asset from the Ottoman perspective. Papal neutrality allowed greater efficiency, although few missionaries were able to remain on Ottoman soil, after those native to the Entente countries were deported. The pontiff was able to devise a new approach to humanitarian relief in a context of greater freedom. The French protectorate was in shambles, and the majority of French missionaries had left the Ottoman Empire. The so-called *mission civilisatrice* that France had impressed on the Ottoman Empire through the work of its missionaries had no other goal than to establish political, economic, and cultural control under the cover of humanitarianism. This centuries-long policy had hurt the Holy See's universal charitable mission. But since November 1914, France had joined the ranks of the Ottoman Empire's enemies, opening a legitimate and unique door of action to the papacy.

BENEDICT XV: "BENEFACTOR OF THE PEOPLE"

The International Red Cross and the American Red Cross, the American Jewish Committee, Near East Relief, and the Holy See, all neutral parties in the conflict until the break of diplomatic relations between Washington and Constantinople in April 1917, were energetic actors in humanitarian relief efforts. Early in the hostilities, alarming information about the destitute state of Syria and Palestine had reached the American continent. On January 30, 1915, the *New York Times* announced that an American ship loaded with food was to be dispatched by the provisional Zionist Committee to alleviate the sufferings of Jews, Muslims, and Christians of Palestine and Syria.[11] In another article of July 7, 1916, lamenting the lack of cooperation of Ottoman offi-

11. "Americans to Send Aid to Palestine," *New York Times*, Jan. 30, 1915.

cials, the *New York Times* reported that "from 50,000 to 80,000 Syrians already have perished, and that the Turkish military authorities still are draining the country of its food."[12] A year later, the *New York Times* of October 22, 1917, revealed that in the absence of organized relief, the number of famine-stricken in Syria had reached 1,200,000. The situation differed depending on the areas. If the condition of the civil population was bearable inland, the situation was catastrophic in Lebanon and on the coast. Food channeled by ships never arrived. Isolation from the outside world was almost complete.[13]

The Papal Project for Supply to Populations of Syria and Lebanon

The famine in Syria developed in 1915 out of a shortage of food especially felt in Lebanon. Its population, predominantly Catholic, the Maronites of Mount Lebanon, was accused of supporting the Entente countries and was therefore neglected by the Ottoman government, especially by Djemal Pasha, the military commander for Syria and Palestine. In a dispatch of June 19, 1916, the apostolic delegate in the United States, Giovanni Bonzano, conveyed to Cardinal Gasparri the fears of American emigrated Lebanese about the fate of their Maronite families and friends.[14] The American press and the mail that was able to reach that side of the Atlantic reported numerous arrests, deportations, and executions among the Christian population. Distraught men and women begged the apostolic delegate to ask for the Holy See's humanitarian and diplomatic intervention. A few months later, on September 26, 1916, Cardinal Amette, the archbishop of Paris,

---

12. "Turkey Will Permit Relief for Syrians," *New York Times*, July 7, 1916.

13. Stephen Hemsley Longrigg, *Syria and Lebanon under French Mandate* (New York: Octagon, 1972), 48.

14. Apostolic delegate in the United States, Giovanni Bonzano, to Gasparri, June 19, 1916, ASV, AES Austria, 1916, pos. 1099, fasc. 469; see also "Fear of Massacre of Syrians," *New York Times*, May 21, 1916.

transmitted a missive to Gasparri from the Comité d'action française en Syrie pleading for papal involvement.[15] He lamented that the population was not the victim of organized massacre but was simply being allowed to die by forbidding the distribution of cereals.[16]

The response given by Gasparri to both Bonzano and Amette sheds light on the diplomatic visibility of the Holy See on the humanitarian scene in Syria in mid-1916. In a reassuring tone, the secretary of state pointed out that the pope was aware of the situation faced by the Christian population in Syria and especially in Lebanon and, trusting the word of the Ottoman minister, asserted that those Christians who had been arrested were political agitators. The government assured the Holy See that there had been neither persecutions nor massacres against the Christian population.[17] In Beirut, among twenty-nine people who had been arrested and executed, twenty-six were Muslims and only three were Christians.[18]

In his reply to Amette, Gasparri positioned the Holy See in the shadow of the American government, asking Dolci to intercede with the Ottoman government in favor of the American Committee,[19] which had been established to organize the sending of a supply ship from the United States to the Syrian coast. Unlike the American government, the Holy See did not own any ship able to navigate to Syria, nor did it have the ability to raise significant funds. At this stage of the conflict, the most efficient papal diplomacy was one of support for the American govern-

15. The letter is dated May 22, 1916. The Comité d'action française en Syrie was composed of important personalities, including senators and members of the Institut de France.

16. Cardinal Amette to Gasparri, Sept. 21, 1916, ASV, AES Stati Ecclesiastici 1916–22, pos. 1418, fasc. 562.

17. Gasparri to Bonzano, July 21, 1916, ASV, AES Austria, 1916, pos. 1099, fasc. 469.

18. Frühwirth to Gasparri, June 20, 1916, ASV, Segr. Stato, Guerra (1914–18), fasc. 110.

19. Gasparri to Amette, Sept. 30, 1916, ASV, AES Stati Ecclesiastici, pos. 1418, fasc. 562; see also Gasparri to Dolci, June 27, 1916, ibid.

ment, whose moral authority had not yet been undermined by the break of diplomatic relations between Washington and Constantinople.

In Constantinople, the Holy See, represented by Angelo Dolci, was well respected. Its impartiality was not challenged there as it was in Europe. Its moral authority was not weakened by Ottoman fears of military or politico-economic appetites. Unlike the Holy See, the American government was accused by the Porte of harboring political goals under the cloak of humanitarian assistance. The accusation was not without foundations. Wyndham Deedes, a British army officer, had alluded in his conversations about American relief shipments to "how much there is 'political' at the back of all relief."[20] On July 24, 1916, Dolci met with the Turkish minister of foreign affairs to convince him that the joint relief effort was a real act of philanthropy and was not harboring any political motives. His efforts were in vain. The Turkish minister questioned the Entente Powers and the United States' sudden interest in the welfare of Muslim Ottoman populations. According to him, the governments of the Entente were trying to encourage a revolt in Syria as they had already attempted with Sharif Hussein bin Ali, the emir of Mecca.[21]

Dolci's mission of support of American humanitarian endeavors with the Ottoman government had reached a dead end. Per-

---

20. Vivian D. Lipman, "America-Holy Land Material in British Archives, 1820–1930," in *With Eyes toward Zion*, vol. 2, *Themes and Sources in the Archives of the United States, Great Britain, Turkey and Israel*, ed. Moshe Davis, 42 (New York: Praeger, 1986).

21. Dolci to Gasparri, July 29, 1916, ASV, AES Stati Ecclesiatici, pos. 1418, fasc. 562. Dolci reproduces the content of his interview with the minister, quoting him: "Perche l'America, cosi il Ministro all'Incaricato d'Affari Americano, e piu chiaramente l'Inghilterra e la Francia non commuovono per i poveri di Costantinopoli e di Smirne? Perche si sentono impietositi solamente per gli abitante della Siria?...I governi dell'entente con questo progetto tentano favorire delle rivolte come hanno fatto per quella dell'Emir della Mecca." In June 1916, the sharif of Mecca, allied with the British, initiated an Arab revolt against the Ottoman Empire. The account of the Arab revolt is chronicled in T. E. Lawrence's seminal book; T. E. Lawrence, *Seven Pillars of Wisdom: A Triumph* (Garden City, N.Y.: Doubleday, 1935).

sonal papal intervention on behalf of the starving population of Syria was then the last resort. On August 31, 1916, the apostolic delegate reported to Gasparri that he had written to Cardinal Gibbons asking him to use his tremendous influence with the American government. He eventually got the American ambassador in Constantinople to support Dolci's relief endeavors.[22] Cardinal Gibbons confirmed to Gasparri that the new American ambassador, Abram I. Elkus, had received orders from his government to help the apostolic delegate.[23] In the meantime, Washington was still contemplating dispatching its own humanitarian relief with the help of the American Red Cross. In its edition of September 15, 1916, the *New York Times* reversed its previous attitude and announced that the Porte had consented to American shipment of relief supplies to the famine-stricken population of Syria.[24]

By the end of 1916, neither the American government nor the Holy See had succeeded in their attempts to organize an official grand-scale operation to alleviate the sufferings of the Syrian population. The Ottoman Empire was not to blame, as it had given authorization to the American Committee for Armenian and Syrian Relief for the shipment of relief supplies. In a letter to Cardinal Gasparri on January 31, 1917, Giannini accused the British of detaining an American ship in Alexandria with the excuse that they didn't have all the security guarantees for this relief supply effort.[25] The British fleet, the dominant naval force in the war, enforced the naval blockade. But according to the *New York Times*, it was the refusal of Germany and Austria-Hungary to grant safe passage to Beirut for the American relief ship *Caesar* that was responsible.[26]

22. Dolci to Gasparri, Aug. 31, 1916, ASV, AES Austria, 1916, pos. 1123, fasc. 476.

23. Gibbons to Gasparri, Nov. 1, 1916, ibid.

24. "Turkey Will Permit Relief for Syrians," *New York Times*, Sept. 15, 1916.

25. Giannini to Gasparri, Jan. 31, 1917, ASV, AES Stati Ecclesiastici, 1916–22, pos. 1418, fasc. 563.

26. "1,200,000 Starving in Syria," *New York Times*, Oct. 22, 1917.

The situation changed dramatically with the break of diplomatic relations between Washington and Constantinople on
April 2, 1917. Although the American government never declared
war on the Ottoman Empire, the Porte ceased allowing the delivery of relief by American means. Therefore, the Holy See became the privileged interlocutor of the Ottoman government to
discuss humanitarian assistance in Syria and Palestine.

Dolci seized the opportunity. A couple of months earlier, on
February 6, 1917, in a letter addressed to Gasparri, he suggested
that the Ottoman government be asked to allow humanitarian
relief to be dispatched by ships sailing under the pontifical flag.
With this goal in view, he planned the creation of a commission
represented by the consuls of the powers still present in Beirut
under the presidency of Msgr. Giannini. The project specified
that the central committee would be under the presidency of
the apostolic delegate in Syria and the vice presidency of the
procurator of the Custody of the Holy Land. Eight others members would be chosen by both the Ottoman government (two
members) and by the apostolic delegate in Constantinople (six
priests of different nationalities).[27] A series of meetings ensued
between Dolci and Ottoman officials. Enver Pasha, the minister
of war, approved Dolci's suggestion that the relief supply would
be done "directly by the Holy Father and in the name of the Holy
Father."[28] The moral authority of the papacy and the complete
impartiality demonstrated by the Holy See since the beginning
of the hostilities convinced the Ottoman government to accept
that the relief transportation be done with a ship from a neutral
country, under the pontifical flag.[29] After a series of secret meet-

---

27. Dolci to Gasparri, Feb. 6, 1917, ASV, AES Stati Ecclesiastici, 1916–22, pos. 1418, fasc.
563; see also Projet de ravitaillement approuvé par le gouvernement ottoman le 22 juillet
1917, ASV, Arch. Deleg. Turchia, Dolci II, fasc.2.
    28. Dolci to Gasparri, Feb. 11, 1917, ASV, AES Stati Ecclesiastici, 1916–22, pos. 1418,
fasc. 563.
    29. Ibid.

ings between Dolci and its ambassador at Constantinople, the Spanish government offered to charter a ship to deliver the relief supplies. Dolci was pleased with the results of his interviews with Ottoman officials. Although the operation was without any doubt a genuine charitable endeavor, the apostolic delegate didn't lose sight of the politico-religious profit that the Holy See could gain from its humanitarian efforts. "If the Holy See can send one ship to Beirut's harbor," wrote an enthusiastic Dolci to Gasparri, this

deed in favor of the poor wretched Christians [will bring] so much greater glory to the Roman Pontiff in these schismatic regions! The prestige of the Holy See...will shine with so much radiance. All the...admirable initiatives of the Holy Father, which have dried out so many tears and relieved many pains, have always aroused great admiration, not only among the Catholics, but among all without distinction of nationality and religion.[30]

The apostolic delegate was aware that the position of the Holy See was envied. He had always felt a sentiment of jealousy coming from the American embassy.[31] Commenting on the food supplied by the American ship *Caesar*, Dolci complained that he had been kept in the dark. He had already raised this issue in August 1916, when the apostolic delegate had informed Gasparri that the American chargé d'affaires had complained to an Ottoman minister that the liberation of Italian prisoners had been granted to Pope Benedict through his apostolic delegate and not to the American embassy in Constantinople.[32]

Once the Ottoman government had given its authorization in

30. "Carita per quei poveri infelici cristiani...quanta maggior Gloria per il Pontificato romano in queste regioni scismatiche! Il prestigio della S. Sede...ha brillato di tanto fulgore. Tutte...admirabili iniziative del S. Padre, che hanno asciugato tante lagrime ed alleviati tanti dolori, hanno sempre suscitato un'ammirazione indicibile, non tra i cattolici..., ma in tuti senza distinzione di nazionalita e di religione"; Dolci to Gasparri, Feb. 11, 1917, ibid. (my translation).

31. Dolci to Gasparri, Feb. 17, 1917, ibid.

32. Dolci to Gasparri, Aug. 22, 1916, ASV, Segr. Stato, Guerra (1914–18), fasc. 1.

principle to proceed with dispatching relief supplies,[33] the Holy See needed to secure the authorization of the belligerent countries active in the region. Since the British fleet had imposed a naval blockade, it was to the government of His Majesty that the Holy See officially asked for the authorization to dispatch the relief supplies. The British government forwarded the demand to the French, who, in a dispatch of April 16, 1917, gave their approval. The permission note stated that

the supplying of Syrian populations having already been accepted in principle by the Allied governments last October, and the circumstances not having allowed the American government to perform this task under the conditions laid down, the French government makes no objection to the passage through the blockade of ships chartered by the Spanish government to ensure the supplying.[34]

An agreement in principle, although a steppingstone, was not a final deal. The Vatican philanthropic endeavor needed all the security guarantees necessary in wartime, guarantees that, in British eyes, were not met at that point. The British wanted a guarantee that the relief supplies would not be used by the enemy, which was an assurance that the Holy See could not provide.[35]

The British government asked for more details about the committee in charge of dispatching the relief. Dolci was politically savvy and immediately understood the need to include preeminent non-Catholic ecclesiastics in the committee to satisfy

---

33. The official authorization came on July 22, 1917.

34. "Le ravitaillement des populations syriennes ayant déja été admis en principe par les Gouvernements Alliés en Octobre dernier et les circonstances n'ayant pas permis au gouvernement des États-Unis de l'effectuer dans les conditions prévues, le Gouvernement français ne fait aucune objection au passage à travers la ligne de blocus des navires affrêtés par le Gouvernement espagnol pour assurer ce ravitaillement"; French Ministry for Foreign Affairs to His Majesty's Embassy, Paris, Apr. 16, 1917, ASV, AES Stati Ecclesiastici, 1916–22, pos. 1418, fasc. 563 (my translation).

35. French Ministry for Foreign Affairs to His Majesty's Embassy, Paris, May 11, 1917, ibid.

Protestant England, without budging on the necessity to have the relief supplies delivered in the name of the pope. "May I recommend [wrote Dolci to Gasparri] that the relief be done under pontifical banner and be distributed in the name of the Holy Father, these two conditions being absolutely essential for the prestige of the pontificate."[36]

After months of back-and-forth correspondence between British officials and Gasparri, papal efforts reached a dead end. In a final message from Lord Balfour transmitted to Gasparri by Hugh Gaisford, a British official attached to the British legation to the Holy See, the Holy See's request was met with a flat refusal. The British foreign secretary brought the hopes of the pope to an end, explaining that the operation did not meet the essential guarantees necessary to move forward.[37] The Holy Father had gone so far as to ask the American cardinal Gibbons to use his influence to get President Wilson to intercede with the British government on the issue of relief delivery, but to no avail.

The argument behind the dismissal was reasonable but not the fundamental reason justifying the British refusal. The Holy See's philanthropic action ran against British interests in the region at that time. On June 28, 1917, Prime Minister Lloyd George had appointed General Edmund Allenby commander of the Egyptian Expeditionary Force, with one mission: "to take Jerusalem as a Christmas present for the nation."[38] A policy designed to protect the British Empire and maintain its prestige among those faithful to the British flag, the military campaign led by Allenby was a great achievement after a decisive victory at Gaza against the Ottomans in early November 1917 and the capture

36. Dolci to Gasparri, July 24, 1917, ASV, AES Stati Ecclesiastici, 1916–22, pos. 1418, fasc. 563.
37. Hugh Gaisford to Gasparri, Oct. 11, 1917, ibid; see also Benedict XV to Cardinal Gibbons, Oct. 18, 1917, ibid.
38. David F. Burg and L. Edward Purcell, *Almanac of World War I* (Lexington: University Press of Kentucky, 1998), 176.

of Jerusalem on December 9, 1917. A papal relief effort was thus unthinkable in such circumstances. Turkish troops were concentrated in the area and would have without a doubt seized any food supply provided by the Holy See for the destitute populations of Syria. The anticipated capture of Jerusalem did not necessitate papal intervention.

Beyond the tactical military considerations, the Allies' negative response also acknowledged the weakened position of Pope Benedict, who, since the ignored Peace Note of August 1, 1917, was going through a momentary crisis of moral authority in Europe. In such circumstances, the Holy See had no political leverage. Military reasons prevailed over charitable considerations in the decision taken by the Entente governments.

Although the papacy was not able to provide relief support on a grand scale, especially in Syria, it was nevertheless highly active in Constantinople. Under the enlightened guidance of Angelo Dolci, less ambitious projects were created to help the poor. Pope Benedict's charity, Essuyer les larmes cachées, was founded to provide food to the destitute of Constantinople, without distinction of nationality or religion. Funds were sent from Rome to support the charity under the presidency of Marquess Pallavicini and Countess Bernstorff, the Austrian-Hungarian and German ambassadors' wives.[39] The pontiff's devotion to the destitute in the Ottoman Empire earned him a respected and strong positive reputation among the local populations.

Rumors of Persecution of the Jewish
Population in Palestine

In 1914, the estimated population of Palestine was 700,000. Of this population, the Jews numbered around 85,000 souls.[40] American newspapers repeatedly reported rumors of wide-

---

39. Dolci to Serafini, Dec. 11, 1917, AP, N.S., vol. 630 (1919), rub. 126, fol. 137rv–38r.
40. Bryson, *American Diplomatic Relations*, 61.

spread persecution of the Jewish population. Between 1915 and 1917, the *New York Times* devoted its columns to numerous articles describing the mistreatment of the Jews in the Ottoman Empire, especially in Palestine.[41] After the American consul at Jerusalem, Otis Glazebrook, informed Morgenthau of their destitute state, the American ambassador appealed for relief supplies.[42] Millions of Jews in America joined by other concerned American citizens responded with great generosity to the American Jewish Committee's appeal to bring help to the Jewish population of Palestine and other areas, particularly Eastern Europe.[43]

Especially appalled by the treatment reserved by the Poles for their Jewish population, the Jewish Committee published *The Jews in the Eastern War Zone*, written to better inform the American population. In December 1915, a copy of the report was sent to Pope Benedict. Although the pamphlet focused exclusively on the condition of the Jews in the Eastern war zone, it gave a good insight into the expectations of American Jewish leaders regarding the potential involvement of the Holy See in relief efforts in favor of their coreligionists. The *10th Annual Report of the American Jewish Committee* was published with a petition to the Holy Father begging him to exert his powerful influence to alleviate Jewish sufferings. It was signed by Louis Marshall, the president of the American Jewish Committee, and by its executive committee. Stressing "the profound moral, ethical, and religious influence" of the Catholic Church and the long tradition of the Vatican to provide relief to every soul in distress without discrimination of nationality or religion, the committee recalled with "admiration and gratitude" that, on numerous occasions in the past, the papacy had always been benevolent and had ex-

41. See "Turks Killing Jews Who Resist Pillage," *New York Times*, May 20, 1917, and "Cruelties to Jews Deported in Jaffa," *New York Times*, June 3, 1917.

42. Bryson, *American Diplomatic Relations*, 61.

43. Ibid., 62. Bryson stresses that "the initial Jewish problem centered about the fate of some 50,000 Russian Jews in Palestine."

tended its protection to the Jewish population in the name of justice and right.[44]

The Holy See's reply came on February 9, 1916, from Secretary of State Gasparri to the president of the American Jewish Committee, Louis Marshall. In the committee's eyes, the papal response was akin to an "encyclical against anti-Jewish prejudices."[45] Gasparri's response, published in their annual report, reaffirmed that the popes had always considered all men as brethren. The editor of the French newspaper La libre parole, Edouard Drumont, who was a notorious anti-Semite, evaluated the papal statement as a response that "has been what it should have been—cordial, charitable, and consoling. One cannot help feeling a sentiment of pity for those who suffer [he wrote], no matter who they are, and we are not permitted to doubt the sincerity of the declarations expressed by the American Jewish Committee. We are rather inclined to recognize the wisdom of its initiative in rendering such respectful homage to the wisdom and the sense of justice of the head of the Christian Church."[46]

Rumors of persecution and massacre of the Jewish population of Palestine were sometimes just rumors. Ambassador Elkus met with Rabbi Messinger, second chairman of the Swiss Zionist Society, to inform him that the reports of discrimination, maltreatment, and even massacre of the Jews in the Ottoman Empire, specifically in Palestine, were entirely unfounded. Msgr. Camassei, Latin patriarch in Jerusalem, confirmed the information in a dispatch to Dolci, stating that the deportation of the Jewish population was very limited and done for military reasons to avoid casualties in case of bombardment by the Entente troops.[47] Dolci

44. American Jewish Committee, "10th Annual Report of the American Jewish Committee, 12 November, 1916," in American Jewish Year Book 19 (1916): 453–54.

45. Ibid., 453.

46. Édouard Drumont, editorial, in La Libre Parole (1916), quoted in "10th Annual Report," 19: 457–58.

47. Dolci to Serafini, June 1, 1917, AP, N.S., vol. 629 (1919), rub. 126.

also wrote to the prefect of Propaganda Fide, Cardinal Serafini, affirming that, according to the German ambassador, who had been informed by his consuls in Palestine, the Jewish population was not the object of any form of persecution. The deportations that had been alluded to and amplified by the European and American media concerned all the inhabitants of Jaffa and were not reserved to the Jews. In a follow-up dispatch, Dolci added that there were 50,000 inhabitants in Jaffa with fewer than 7,000 of Jewish faith. The consuls in Palestine had witnessed neither persecution nor destruction of villages.[48] This information was confirmed by diplomatic officials of Austria, Spain, and Holland.

On the other hand, the American consul Garrels, sojourning in Alexandria, Egypt, described the Jaffa deportation under a different light. His report published in the *New York Times* noted that

the orders of evacuation were aimed chiefly at the Jewish population. Even German, Austro-Hungarian, and Bulgarian Jews were ordered to leave the town. Mohammedans and Christians were allowed to remain provided they were holders of individual permits. The Jews who sought the permits were refused.[49]

Dolci met with the great rabbi of Turkey, Haim Nahum, to inform him that he had received instructions from the Holy Father to intercede with the Ottoman government in favor of the Jewish population, ensuring their protection.[50]

When a statue of Benedict XV was erected in Constantinople, Haim Nahum was among the notable contributors. The statue bears the inscription "To the great pope of the world's tragic hour, Benedict XV, benefactor of the people, without discrimination of nationality or religion, a token of gratitude from the Orient, 1914–1919." In a few words, Benedict XV's achievements

48. Ibid., June 3, 1917.
49. "Cruelties to Jews Deported in Jaffa," *New York Times*, June 3, 1917.
50. Dolci to Serafini, June 5, 1917, AP, N.S., vol. 629 (1919), rub. 126.

are summed up. There is no similar monument in Western Europe to honor his dedication and charity. But with all the good will of the contributors, the statue stands in the courtyard of the Cathedral of the Holy Spirit "completely hidden from passersby, visible only to those going to the office, which means only the Catholics."[51] Even the Turkish newspaper *L'Atti*, in its edition of November 1, 1918, lamented the location of the future statue, arguing that "It [would] be a pleasure for all, instead of raising the statue of the Pope in the courtyard of the Cathedral, to erect it on one of the largest boulevard of Pera."[52] Benedict's humanitarian assistance to the civil populations of the Ottoman Empire was hailed by those who recognized in the pontiff his moral authority, his sense of solidarity beyond nations, and his respect for human dignity.

AMERICAN NEAR EAST RELIEF AND
THE ACCUSATIONS OF DISCRIMINATION
AGAINST CATHOLICS

The literature that chronicles the many relief efforts for the destitute populations of Syria and Palestine praises the role of the United States through the ambassador Henry Morgenthau and the consuls in the region. The contribution of the Holy See to the vast humanitarian relief endeavors is never mentioned.[53] Not only was the widespread involvement of the Catholic Church under the leadership of the pope ignored, but also by the end of 1917, rumors spread in Syria and Palestine that Catholics were discriminated against by American and British officials in charge of American Near East Relief. As a result, collections from Catholics in the United States fell off sharply. While collec-

---

51. "Notre première statue," *Le Soir*, Oct. 28, 1918, AP, N.S., vol. 658 (1920), rub. 126, fol. 377 (my translation).

52. "Prière à la Préfecture de la ville," *L'Atti*, Nov. 1, 1918, ibid. (my translation).

53. See Lipman, "America-Holy Land Material," or Bryson, *American Diplomatic Relations*.

tions reached a peak in 1919 with $19.4 million, they fell off to $13 million in 1920 and still further in 1921.[54]

American Near East Relief and
Catholic Contribution

The American Committee for Armenian and Syrian Relief was founded in September 1915 in the wake of the Turkish onslaught on the Armenian population.[55] Congress later incorporated the committee in 1919 as Near East Relief. An outstanding story of American philanthropy, the history of Near East Relief is one of tremendous success. According to James Barton, the biographer and first chairman of the organization, Near East Relief, "irrespective of religion and creed, (it) clothed the naked, fed the starving and provided shelter, care and practical schooling for more than a hundred and thirty thousand fatherless waifs left as wreckage from the Great War."[56] It raised more than $90 million during the war years that were dispatched essentially in Europe and in the Ottoman Empire. Until the entry of General Allenby in Jerusalem in December 1917, the relief efforts were under the chairmanship of Bishop McInnis, the Anglican bishop in Jerusalem.[57]

Near East Relief was rooted in the missionary work of Protestants, but after two months in existence, it became clear that the contribution of American Catholics was necessary in order to expand the basis for the fundraising campaigns. Therefore,

---

54. Bryson, "A Note on Near East Relief: Walter George Smith, Cardinal Gibbons, and the Question of Discrimination against Catholics," *Muslim World* 61 (July 1971): 202.

55. Bryson wrote, "On 3 September, Morgenthau cabled the State Department the grim news [of the Armenian massacre], and suggested that Cleveland Dodge, a wealthy American industrialist and philanthropist, organize a relief committee to save the Armenians. In mid-September Dodge convened a group in his New York office and there founded one of the most effective relief organizations in modern history"; Bryson, *American Diplomatic Relations*, 60.

56. Barton, *Story of Near East Relief.*

57. Ibid., 76.

Barton's interest turned to Cardinal Gibbons. James Cardinal Gibbons, archbishop of Baltimore, a respected eighty-year-old clergyman, enjoyed an international reputation.[58] His efforts for relief of the victims of war were already known and widespread, from Belgium to Poland. His becoming a board member of Near East Relief, along with representatives of Judaism, gave the committee a larger scope.

The solicitation of Catholic funds did not prevent Barton from utterly ignoring the physical presence of Catholic missionaries and clergy and the diplomatic activity of the Holy See in the Ottoman Empire. He expressed his fear that the expected entrance of the United States into the war on the side of the Entente Powers and with it the withdrawal of Protestant missionaries, teachers, and heads of institutions would leave the Christian population at the mercy of a hostile government.[59] This statement was a startling denial of the role and influence exerted by the apostolic delegates in Constantinople and Syria on the Ottoman government in their efforts to alleviate the suffering of the population.

In April 1918, the American Red Cross announced that a commission of sixty members was heading to Palestine to study the needs of the population of the Holy Land and assist in their relief. Its mission was to work with General Allenby to prepare the future in the region. To that effect, the commission was to receive the support of the British Syria and Palestine Relief Fund and the American Armenian and Syrian Relief Committee.[60] No mention was made of any Catholic participation through the channel of the apostolic delegates.

One reason for ostracizing the Holy See could be that there was no independent Catholic structured organization analogous

---

58. John Tracy Ellis, *The Life of James Cardinal Gibbons, Archbishop of Baltimore, 1834–1921* (Milwaukee, Wisc.: Bruce, 1952), 2:222.

59. Barton, *Story of Near East Relief*, 5.

60. "Finley Heads Palestine Mission," *New York Times*, Apr. 17, 1918.

to the British and American relief committees. The Holy See was counting on an already existent network through its missions, schools, and hospitals. The Catholic Near East Welfare Association (CNEWA) would not be founded by Pius XI until 1926 in response to Near East Relief. The association, whose purpose was to provide humanitarian assistance to those in need without regard to nationality and creed, followed criteria set out by Benedict XV. Another reason offered at the time to explain the lack of consideration of Catholic humanitarian assistance was the deliberate will of Near East Relief to discriminate against Catholics.

Accusations of Discrimination
against Catholics

The first report of discrimination by Near East Relief workers against Catholics in Syria and Palestine went back to the spring of 1919. The accusation was grave enough that Cardinal Gibbons considered withdrawing American Catholic support from Near East Relief. Although he never officially quit the executive committee, arguing that he had received enough evidence that there had been no discrimination against Catholics, the rumor spread in the United States, and the collections fell sharply. In 1919, $19.4 million were collected. The number fell to $13 million in 1920.

The task to prove that there had been no discrimination against Catholics fell on Walter George Smith, a Roman Catholic attorney in Philadelphia and a member of the Near East Relief committee. Stationed in Constantinople to determine the needs of the destitute population, he started his investigation. Eager to defend Near East Relief, which he considered a "worthy institution,"[61] he appealed to Dolci and requested that he write to Cardinal Gibbons to reassert that relief was given without distinc-

---

61. Bryson, "Note on Near East Relief," 203.

tion of race or religion to anyone in need.[62] In early June 1919, he visited Cardinal Gasparri in Rome to put an end to the rumors. Both Dolci and Gasparri trusted Smith's report that there was no organized or voluntary discrimination against Catholics from Near East Relief. In their eyes, the case was closed.

By the end of 1919, the situation remained tense. Not only were Near East Relief workers accused of discrimination against Catholics, they were also accused of using the relief efforts as a means for proselytizing among the Catholic community. In a letter addressed to Cardinal Marini, the secretary of the Congregation for the Oriental Church, Giannini, in a veiled criticism of Dolci's credulity, refuted the apostolic delegate's assertion that the distribution of goods by the American Red Cross and Near East Relief was done with complete impartiality and without distinction of race or religion. He explained that it was difficult for Dolci, being stationed in Constantinople, to obtain reliable and regular information regarding the situation in Syria and Palestine. Giannini bluntly criticized the "subjectivity and the bias displayed by the American Red Cross in this region" and "the spirit of Protestant proselytizing."[63] A few months later he wrote to Cardinal Gasparri to complain that the Americans had transformed a genuine philanthropic enterprise into a work of Protestant proselytizing and a weapon against Catholicism.[64] In a letter to Smith, he alerted the attorney that

Major Nicol who is...the current director of the "Near East Relief Association" is purely and simply a member of the protestant Regular Mission, established in Turkey for many years, transformed for the occasion into an officer of the American Red Cross.[65]

62. Dolci to Cardinal Gibbons, June 10, 1919, Walter George Smith, unpublished "Journal of a Journey to the Near East," Walter George Smith Manuscript Collection, St. Charles Borromeo Seminary, Philadelphia, Pa., quoted in Bryson, "Note on Near East Relief," 205.
63. Giannini to Marini, Nov. 1, 1919, ACCO, fasc. 115/5, 2803 (my translation).
64. Giannini to Gasparri, Mar. 11, 1920, ASV, AES Stati Ecclesiastici, 1916–22, pos. 1418, fasc. 565 (my translation).
65. "Le major Nicol qui est...l'actuel directeur du 'Near East Relief Association' est

Therefore, a simple change of label was sufficient for the Protestant mission to acquire the supervision and the monopoly over the resources of Near East Relief.

Giannini provided ample evidence of discrimination against the Catholic community. Reports piled up on his desk. The Jesuit fathers of St. Joseph University in Beirut published in their periodical *Al Bechir* (The Messenger) a letter they had received from Zahle relating "that some priests, anxious to instruct Catholic orphans in their faith, had been refused admittance into a shelter controlled by the Committee for Near East Relief."[66] The facts were confirmed by the managing director in Beirut, who apologized for these occurrences, which were not the fact of some personal prejudice but a line of conduct decided by the executive bureau.[67] Count de Ballobar, the Spanish consul in Jerusalem, was also indignant about Protestant conduct. Bitterly complaining about "the hypocrisy of which all the Protestants are masters," he noted in his wartime diary, "They have made a very bad impression on the city, by having transformed the Austrian hospice, a purely Catholic institution, into a Protestant orphanage."[68]

Giannini's complaint shed light on the new challenges and dangers facing the Catholic Church in Syria and Palestine at the end of World War I in the form of an increased Protestant proselytizing facilitated by the capture of Palestine by the British.[69]

---

purement et simplement un membre de la Regular Mission protestante établie en Turquie depuis de nombreuses années, transformé pour le besoin de la cause en officier de la Croix Rouge Américaine"; Giannini to Walter George Smith, Mar. 13, 1920, ibid. (my translation).

66. "Near East Relief Orphan Asylums Barred to Priests," *Catholic Missions*, Jan. 1921, 8; see also "Editorial, Notes, Near East," *Catholic Missions*, Feb. 1921, 46.

67. The director of the asylum said to the visiting priests, "This is our line of conduct; it has been traced by my superiors, and I will follow it to the end"; "Near East Relief Orphan Asylums Barred to Priests," 8.

68. Eduardo Moreno and Roberto Mazza, eds., *Jerusalem in World War I: The Palestine Diary of a European Diplomat, Conde de Ballobar* (London: I. B. Tauris, 2011), 200.

69. See Ussama Makdisi, *Artillery of Heaven: American Missionaries and the Failed Conversion of the Middle East* (Ithaca, N.Y.: Cornell University Press, 2007).

At the end of the war, regardless of its dismissal by contemporary observers, the scope of Pope Benedict's humanitarian assistance in Europe and in the Ottoman Empire appeared as a monumental achievement by the papacy. Pope Benedict chose a vocal diplomacy in favor of the destitute population of Syria and Palestine. Against the expectations of European and American public opinion but faithful to his impartial position, he offered no encyclical or official statement reproving Ottoman actions on their own soil.[70] Instead of a general and almost certainly ineffectual condemnation of persecution and organized massacre, he favored a method of systematic denunciation on a case-by-case basis through the channel of his apostolic delegates in Constantinople and Syria, who often obtained concrete and positive results for their demands. It was difficult for the public in Europe and America to appreciate or even be aware of the multitude of separate and small achievements of the papacy that, once summed up, amounted to a remarkable accomplishment. Benedict was accused of supporting a barbarous government, and his position became less and less defensible to many observers, Catholics and non-Catholics alike, after the Armenian massacre of 1915 became known to the world. Benedict's appeal to the Ottoman government was never a vague appeal without concrete consequences, but each request was a practical commitment with expected positive results. By his actions, the destitute populations of Syria and Palestine, an image of the suffering humanity, were touched by the love of Christ for his neighbor. Pope Benedict chose to exhibit pure charity to all in need. He exemplified the motto of the International Committee of the Red Cross, "Inter arma caritas."[71]

70. ASV, Arch. Deleg. Turchia, Dolci 90, fasc. 2.

71. "In war, charity" (my translation); see Yves de la Brière, "Le règne pontifical de Benoît XV," *Études* (Feb. 5, 1922): 261.

2

POSTWAR
PROTECTION
OF CATHOLIC
INTERESTS,
1917-1922

6

THE HOLY SEE AND
THE POSTWAR WORLD
ORDER

THE HOLY SEE AT THE
CENTER OF THE DIPLOMATIC
WORLD

The postwar collapse of empires and monarchies and the emergence of non-European political players such as the United States, Japan, and Brazil initiated a major cultural, social, and political shift in Europe. The status quo *ante bellum* characterized by Eurocentrism and colonial expansion was defunct. Benedict XV understood that the long nineteenth century had come to an end and that the Holy See would have to develop a new diplomatic approach that took into account the new complexion of the diplomatic chessboard in Europe and beyond.

Two main evolutions had taken place after the close of the war. The creation of the League of Nations expanded the political map to embrace the world, which encouraged the pontiff to think in larger terms than the nineteenth-century Eurocentric model. Pope Benedict also acknowledged the fading away of most Catholic kingdoms and embraced the democratic nation-states that issued forth from the collapse of the Austro-Hungarian, Russian, and Ottoman empires by establishing official diplomatic relations with most of them. The papacy became the center of the emerging world and acquired a renewed spiritual and political prestige.

The New Diplomatic Prestige of the Papacy

In a speech delivered at the National Catholic Congress held at Liverpool, England, in July 1920, Cardinal Gasquet echoed a British minister's remark that "the man who best came out of the war was the pope."[1] The sudden surge of civil governments entering into diplomatic relations with the Holy See startled contemporary religious and political observers alike, as the common agreement was that, with a foreign policy decried during the war, the Holy See's diplomatic standing had reached its nadir. After the resounding failure of the papal diplomatic attempt to bring the world conflict to an end with Benedict XV's Peace Note of August 1917, Vatican diplomacy, still wearing the shackles of the so-called Roman Question, had been fading into oblivion. As stipulated in article 15 of the Treaty of London of 1915, the Holy See was barred from the postwar decision-making process. It did not get a seat at the Paris Peace Conference that convened on January 18, 1919, to establish the peace terms for the defeated powers and devise the rules of the new international order. As a last resort, the secretary of the Congregation for Extraordinary Ecclesiastical Affairs, Msgr. Bonaventura Cerretti, was sent to Paris as a secret representative of the Holy See to the Paris Peace Conference.

In this political climate, the absence of the Holy See at the postwar settlement table would have had grave consequences on Catholic interests worldwide were it not for the surge in bilateral relationships between the Holy See and new and old states that eventually built a solid and enviable diplomatic network. On the threshold of war, a dozen states were represented at the Vatican. After four years of the conflict that the pontiff lamented

1. Georges Goyau, *Papauté et chrétienté sous Benoît XV* (Paris: Perrin, 1922), 17.

as the "suicide of civilized Europe,"[2] the international geopolitical scene had changed dramatically. The demise of the Austro-Hungarian and Ottoman Empires gave birth to new independent states that looked for diplomatic recognition at the Vatican. The Holy See welcomed with open arms the new governments of Poland, Serbia, Czechoslovakia, and other nation-states that issued from the dismemberment of the defeated empires.[3] The natural increase of states only partially explained that in 1921 twenty-five chancelleries had established ties with the Vatican.[4] The rise in the quality of already existing diplomatic relations was also a source of satisfaction to the Holy See. Belgium, Chile, and Brazil, who were states that enjoyed second-rank diplomatic ties, raised their legations to full-rank embassies.[5]

Most noticeable for the international prestige of the Holy See and its influence over the future political developments of the new world order outside the world of multilateral diplomacy was the transformation of the British Special Mission into a permanent legation and, even more critical, the reestablishment of diplomatic relations with anticlerical but Catholic France in May 1921. In Cardinal Merry del Val's own words, "France was too great a lady to come up the backstairs."[6] During the presidential campaign of 1920, the Socialist candidate and future president Alexandre Millerand had expressed his willingness to reestab-

2. Benedict XV, "Lenten Letter to Cardinal-Vicar Pompilj *Al Tremendo Conflitto* [Mar. 4, 1916]," *AAS* 8 (1916): 59.

3. Lithuania and Poland were reconstituted in 1918, while Czechoslovakia, the Kingdom of Serbs, Croats, and Slovenes (future Yugoslavia), Estonia, and Latvia were founded in 1918, and Turkey in 1923. The Holy See reestablished diplomatic relations with Poland in 1919, sending Achille Ratti, the future Pius XI, as its first papal nuncio. It recognized Estonia and Latvia in 1921. A concordat was signed with both countries in 1922. A nunciature was opened in Czechoslovakia and Yugoslavia in 1920.

4. Eight ambassadors and seventeen ministers.

5. L. J. S. Wood, "Vatican Politics and Policies," *Atlantic Monthly*, Sept. 1921, 404.

6. Quoted in Wood, "Vatican Politics and Policies," 398. Rafael Cardinal Merry del Val was the secretary of state of Pius X, under whom diplomatic ties with France were severed.

lish diplomatic ties with the Holy See. Once elected president, he openly and publicly engaged in debates to this aim. On March 21, 1920, Jean Doulcet was sent to Rome as minister plenipotentiary. On May 18, 1921, the chief of government, Aristide Briand, dispatched Charles Jonnart as ambassador extraordinary.[7]

France's decision to resume diplomatic relations with the Holy See was essentially driven by considerations of foreign policy. In a dispatch of May 29, 1921, Jonnart reported on the meeting he had with Pope Benedict, Cardinal Gasparri, and Msgr. Cerretti, the new nuncio to Paris. The pontiff indicated that he would support France's efforts in favor of the "reconciliation of peoples" and facilitate the role of the French missions in the Middle East.[8] To comfort its political, financial, and cultural standing, Paris was eager to maintain its religious protectorate in a newly reshaped Middle East and was hoping to enroll the Holy See in its undertaking.

As for the Holy See, it never concealed its intention to rebuild trust and confidence with France and eventually reenter into healthy diplomatic intercourse. With the demise of the Austro-Hungarian Empire and the blocked political situation with Italy, France, although anticlerical, was the only imposing Catholic nation and could not be ignored. The canonizations of Joan of Arc, the patron of France, on May 16, 1920, and Margaret Marie Alacoque on May 13, 1920, were demonstrations of the pontiff's goodwill toward the "eldest daughter of the Church."[9]

7. Raymond L. Buell, "The Vatican and the New World," *Current History* 16 (Sept. 1922): 981.

8. M. Jonnart, ambassadeur extraordinaire de France près le Saint-Siège à M. Briand, ministre des affaires étrangères, Rome, 29 mai 1921, in *Documents diplomatiques français, 1921*, ed. Commission de publication des documents diplomatiques français, Série 1920–32 (16 Janvier–30 Juin) (Bruxelles: Peterlang: 2004), 4:669.

9. In 496, the Frankish ruler Clovis was baptized by the archbishop of Reims, taking the title of "His Most Christian Majesty." The conversion of Clovis meant the conversion of the Frankish kingdom. Catholicism became the state religion, and future France became known as the "eldest daughter of the Church."

At the end of Benedict XV's pontificate, Italy was one of the few politically noteworthy European nations without an official representative at the Roman court. In *Pacem Dei Munus*, his encyclical on peace and Christian reconciliation, published on May 23, 1920,[10] the pontiff renounced the papal decree prohibiting Catholic heads of states to make official visits to the Quirinal. This decision was understood as a first step toward reconciliation, although Benedict, reiterating the message of his first encyclical, *Ad Beatissimi*, made clear that it "must not be interpreted as a tacit renunciation of its sacrosanct rights by the Apostolic See, as it acquiesced in the unlawful situation in which it is placed."[11] As soon as France resumed diplomatic relations with the Holy See, the Quirinal expressed through its national press its willingness to consider further steps on the road to official reconciliation.[12]

Most European powers had established, reestablished, or upgraded their diplomatic relations with the Holy See. They were driven not only by foreign political motivations but also by significant domestic considerations. The risk of being swept up by the revolutionary turmoil that was spreading throughout the European continent in the wake of the militantly atheist Bolshevik Revolution led many nations to turn to the Holy See for political and social support. Pacifist socialists had long thought that their time had come to export the Petrograd riots over Europe, transcending all nationalistic barriers. Communist uprisings were spreading to Hungary and Bavaria. Recognized as the only powerful transnational institution, the Holy See's assistance was welcomed by European nations to act as a buffer against the Bolshevik wave. As a result, the postwar years saw a

---

10. Benedict XV, "Encyclical Letter *Pacem Dei Munus Pulcherrimum* [May 23, 1920]," *AAS* 12 (1920): 209–18.

11. Ibid.

12. Charles Loiseau, *Politique romaine et sentiment français* (Paris: Grasset, 1923).

resurgence of Catholic politics in Europe, supported by the Holy See. It represented a third path between Marxist socialism validated by the Bolshevik Revolution and the individualism born of Anglo-Saxon liberal capitalism.[13]

Under Pius X, the Vatican had been consigned to relative diplomatic oblivion. Benedict's impartial stance during the war years accentuated the Holy See's isolation and crisis of moral authority. Therefore, the unexpected strengthening of its prestige and influence on the postwar international diplomatic scene became a source of speculation and the favorite topic of discussion in many newspapers and reviews of the time. Looking beyond domestic and international political motivations, observers of Vatican politics conjectured on what other reasons could explain the renewed influence that the Holy See was exerting on the course of European diplomacy.[14]

The Holy See emerged from the war as a spiritual force to be reckoned with. In order to combat the disillusionment of the postwar age, many felt a need to reconnect Europe with its Christian cultural heritage. Pope Benedict was setting an example for other nations on how to approach the world of international relations in order to guarantee long-term peaceful results, conducting a diplomacy grounded in patience, hope, and charity. The Holy See's new postwar prestige was built on a twofold paradox. With the nineteenth-century demise of the Papal States, the Holy See lacked a territorial realm, which from a secular political point of view should have signified its exclusion from the diplomatic sphere of international relations. However, the loss of the Papal States became a gain in papal hands as it reinforced the Vatican's spiritual kingdom worldwide. Moreover, rather than confining the Vatican to a second-class political role, the Holy

13. Michael Burleigh, *Sacred Causes: The Clash of Religion and Politics from the Great War to the War on Terror* (New York: HarperCollins, 2007), 33.

14. Sisley Huddleston, "The Revival of the Vatican," *Fortnightly Review*, July 1920, 67–77; Alexis François, *Semaine littéraire de Genève*, Oct. 29, 1921.

See's exclusion from all postwar peace negotiations reinforced its universal appeal and allowed the pope to act in foreign affairs as the universal pastor of a global church.[15] It is the universality and transnationality of the Catholic Church that allowed the Holy See to address the universal craving for order and moral authority that fostered a rebirth of religious sentiment.[16]

Pope Benedict had been physically and politically isolated from the European diplomatic scene during the war years. After the guns fell silent, the personal moral qualities of the pontiff started to shine through, enhancing his prestige and influence. After years of carnage, which he tried to stop by all means in his power, Benedict was recognized for his humanitarian efforts, if not his peace activism. In this domain, he was unrivaled. His compassion for humankind became a source of reflection and attraction. Acknowledging the inviolability of human dignity as foundational to human relations, he had depleted the Vatican's revenues to assist those in need, without regard to race or religion. He was praised for his large-scale efforts to provide for "spiritual and material assistance to prisoners."[17] He fed the starving and protected widows and young orphans. The humanitarian network he led was akin to a second Red Cross. On the European front, he pursued his humanitarian efforts long after the war had come to an end. In the wake of the Bolshevik Revolution, he made appeals for the relief of famine in Eastern and Central Europe as well as in Russia. On December 1, 1920, in his role as father to all, he dedicated a special encyclical, *Annus Iam Plenus* to the children of Central Europe.[18]

The pope eventually reaped the reward of his impartiality

15. Huddleston, "Vatican's New Place in World Politics," *New York Times Current History*, Oct. 1920–Mar. 1921, 199.

16. "Two Internationals: Red and Black," *New Republic*, Aug. 30–Nov. 22, 1922, 123.

17. John F. Pollard, *The Unknown Pope: Benedict XV (1914–1922) and the Pursuit of Peace* (New York: Geoffrey Chapman, 1999), 113.

18. Benedict XV, "Encyclical Letter *Annus Iam Plenus* [Dec., 1, 1920]," *AAS* 12 (1920): 554.

and consistency during the world conflict. The numerous bilateral diplomatic ties established with Catholic and non-Catholic nations bore testimony to the newly rediscovered charisma of the papacy. Moreover, a few of Pope Benedict's contemporaries eventually acknowledged him as the most notable moral force active in international politics, debating on the influence the pontiff could exert on the newly created League of Nations.[19] Yet, the Holy See did not obtain a seat at the league. The pontiff's newfound spiritual authority on peoples did not translate well in the confined political world of powers devising the covenant for the newly founded institution.

The Exclusion of the Holy See
from the League of Nations

The Paris Peace Conference opened on January 18, 1919. As stipulated, upon Italy's insistence, in article 15 of the secret Treaty of London of 1915 the Holy See was excluded from the peace negotiations. The pope lamented this situation, although he publicly denied any interest in getting a seat at the table of negotiations.[20] The Holy See was also denied membership in the League of Nations, the new center of multilateral diplomacy.

In January 1919, just before the opening of the Peace Conference, Pope Benedict and President Woodrow Wilson met at the Vatican. Although nothing transpired from their meeting, the encounter did not pass unnoticed, as Wilson was the first American president to meet a Roman pontiff. With the mediation of Cardinal Gibbons, Pope Benedict and President Wilson had come to respect and trust each other. Excluded from the Paris Peace Conference and still diplomatically at odds with France, the pontiff put his trust in "this former professor who was the

19. Huddleston, "Revival of the Vatican," 74.
20. Pollard, *Unknown Pope*, 141.

moralistic son of a Presbyterian minister."[21] Later in the year, in July 1919, in an effort to influence the negotiations from which he was barred, Benedict wrote to Wilson asking the president's help to ensure the protection and freedom of the Catholic missions in the former German colonies. Wilson agreed to use his political and moral authority in support of the pope's query.[22]

During the war, the prestige and moral authority of the United States were esteemed, supplanting the Holy See's influence on the unfolding of the conflict. The French novelist Romain Rolland, in an article of October 1, 1914, published in the *Journal de Genève*, implored President Wilson's help.[23] The American president eventually answered the call. The United States entered the war in April 1917, on the side of the Entente powers.

A few months later, Pope Benedict published his Peace Note of August 1, 1917, his greatest effort to end the war. President Wilson followed in his footsteps and delivered, on January 8, 1918, a message to the U.S. Congress laying out his peace aims. He stated fourteen points, which "were to be the United States' blueprint for the securing of a lasting and just world peace."[24] While

21. Michael P. Riccards, *Vicars of Christ: Popes, Power, and Politics in the Modern World* (New York: Crossroad, 1998), 90.

22. See Letter of Benedict XV of July 1, 1919, to Woodrow Wilson and Wilson's response of August 15, 1919, in Joseph P. Tumulty, *Woodrow Wilson as I Know Him* (Garden City, N.Y.: Doubleday, 1921), 482–83.

23. Between 1914 and 1919, Romain Rolland, future Nobel prizewinner in literature, published a series of articles in the *Journal de Genève* that were later gathered in two books: *Au-dessus de la mêlée* and *Les précurseurs*. On October 1, 1914, he wrote an open letter to President Wilson: "Monsieur le Président, dans cette guerre néfaste, dont le résultat, quel qu'il soit, sera la ruine de l'Europe, les yeux de ceux qui ont le triste privilège d'échapper aux passions de la mêlée, se tournent vers votre pays et vers vous. Puissiez-vous bientôt faire entendre votre voix juste et ferme au milieu des frères ennemis! Il n'y a pas seulement de l'intérêt des peuples qui sont aux prises, mais de la civilisation tout entière, menacée par ces luttes sacrilèges. Que les États-Unis d'Amérique rappellent à l'Europe démente qu'aucun peuple n'a le droit, pour satisfaire son orgueil et ses haines, d'ébranler l'édifice du progrès humain, qu'il a fallu tant de siècles de génie et de peines pour élever"; Rolland, *Les précurseurs* (Paris: Editions de l'Humanité, 1920), 216.

24. Joel S. Poetker, *The Fourteen Points* (Colombus, Ohio: Charles E. Merrill, 1969), prologue.

Pope Benedict's Peace Note was decried and ignored, President Wilson's Fourteen Points were widely acclaimed as a "generous and non-punitive postwar settlement"[25] and established the American president as the new moral leader of the world. Two main guidelines shaped Wilson's Fourteen Points. Points six to thirteen advocated self-determination for national minorities in Europe. But it was point fourteen that became paramount, as it endorsed the foundation of "a general association of nations [that] must be formed...for the purpose of affording mutual guarantees of political independence and territorial integrity to great and small states alike."[26] The underlying philosophy behind the covenant for the new League of Nations can be traced back to the Fourteen Points outlined by Wilson. The draft for the covenant was presented by the Paris Peace Conference in April 1919 and officially ratified on June 28, 1919, when the Treaty of Versailles was signed.[27] The league started to operate on January 10, 1920.

Pope Benedict and President Wilson shared a common view of the postwar world, a view that rejected colonialist expansion and favored self-determination of nationalities.[28] Eventually, neither the pontiff nor the American president was able to defend his position at the newly established League of Nations, as neither of them became a member. Although most Americans saw the league as "without doubt the most important feature of the peace treaty" and "'an absolutely necessary piece of machin-

25. Thomas Paterson, J. Garry Clifford, and Shane J. Maddock, *American Foreign Relations: A History to 1920* (Boston, Mass.: Wadsworth, 2010), 1:290.

26. Christine Compston and Rachel F. Seidman eds., *Our Documents: 100 Milestone Documents from the National Archives* (New York: Oxford University Press, 2003), 150.

27. Robert John Araujo and John A. Lucal, *Papal Diplomacy and the Quest for Peace: The Vatican and International Organizations from the Early Years to the League of Nations* (Ann Arbor, Mich.: Sapientia Press of Ave Maria University, 2004), 116. The league covenant was an integral part of the Treaty of Versailles.

28. See Eres Manela, *The Wilsonian Moment: Self-Determination and the International Origins of Anticolonial Nationalism* (Oxford: Oxford University Press, 2007).

ery' for carrying out the terms of peace,"[29] the U.S. Senate twice rejected a resolution of ratification of the Treaty of Versailles. To be ratified, the treaty had to be approved by two-thirds of the Senate. The resolution was first rejected on November 19, 1919, and in a subsequent vote on March 19, 1920. The United States did not become a member of the league, which weakened the international prestige and credibility of the new institution dedicated to promote peace and stability worldwide. The pope had also lost a potential supporter at the league.

Article 1 of the covenant of the league restricted membership to self-governing states, therefore eliminating the Holy See as a potential member. However, acknowledging the newfound prestige of the government of the Catholic Church, contemporary observers of Benedict XV's pontificate wondered if the league would not gain at admitting among its ranks a representative of the Holy See.[30] The new international body could benefit from Benedict's unexpected and new political and spiritual standing. But it was argued, since the league was essentially a moral authority, that the pope would have to be the head of such a body, an option that could not be considered by secular nations, especially by Italy.[31]

The pontiff had also alluded to the creation of a community of nations in his Peace Note of August 1917, stating that "instead of armies, [he was calling for] the institution of arbitration, with its lofty peacemaking function, according to the standards to be agreed upon and with sanctions to be decided against the State which might refuse to submit international questions to arbitration or to accept its decisions."[32] The pontiff's thoughts on the concept of a league of nations evolved and matured. In his en-

---

29. "A Review of the World," *Current Opinion*, June 1919, 344.
30. Huddleston, "Revival of the Vatican," 74.
31. Ibid., 75.
32. Benedict XV, "Apostolic Exhortation *Dès le début* [Aug. 1, 1917]." *AAS* 9 I (1917): 417–20.

cyclical *Pacem Dei Munus*, published on May 23, 1920, Pope Benedict broached the topic of a Christian league, voluntarily omitting mention of the already existing League of Nations. Calling for an "association of nations," the pontiff stated: "all States, putting aside mutual suspicion, should unite in one league, or rather a sort of family of peoples, calculated both to maintain their own independence and safeguard the order of human society."[33]

The pope was calling for a league inspired by Christian principles of morality, integrity, and forgiveness. "The Church will certainly not refuse her zealous aid," he wrote, "to states united under the Christian law in any of their undertakings inspired by justice and charity, inasmuch as she is herself the most perfect type of universal society."[34] Pope Benedict's statement can be read as the first modern papal statement devoted to peace, asking a secular international body to recognize the universal nature of the church and the Christian roots of the European continent as a foundation for worldwide peace and stability.

Although many unsuccessful attempts were made in this direction, the final draft of the covenant of the League of Nations did not include any reference to religion "as a means of determining the physical boundaries of the state" or guarantees of religious freedom.[35] While self-determination, equality of nations, and justice were concepts listed as foundational principles, religious factors such as freedom of conscience and worship that could have substantially influenced the international social peace were dismissed. Wilson had lobbied in favor of religious freedom, but he was absent from the meeting where the provision was deleted upon the request of the French legal adviser.[36] Instead, separate Minorities treaties were instituted to protect

33. Benedict XV, *Pacem Dei Munus*, 209–18.
34. Ibid., 216.
35. Malcolm D. Evans, *Religious Liberty and International Law in Europe* (Cambridge: Cambridge University Press, 1997), 82–83.
36. Ibid., 96.

the minorities' rights, but the opportunity to give those rights an international stature was lost.[37]

The decision to omit mentioning religion or Christian principles in the covenant of the League of Nations disappointed Pope Benedict, as it did not reflect the newly restored prestige and influence enjoyed by the Holy See on the diplomatic scene. However, it is the league's failure to lay down solid foundations to secure world peace and collective security that concerned Pope Benedict. By refusing to include all the major powers, defeated or not, in the organization, the new body was closing the door on the opportunity to become a universal organization that, as another moral authority, could have competed with the universality of the church. The founders' vindictive choice to rebuff Germany was in complete opposition to the moral principles expounded by Pope Benedict since the beginning of the war. It was therefore to the benefit of the Holy See to stay aloof and keep developing a unique moral and political aura. The Holy See lost an opportunity to officially join the international body of sovereign nations through the newly founded League of Nations and be an active participant in international politics. However, remaining outside this international body while maintaining bilateral diplomatic relations with most of its members gave the papacy more freedom in its diplomatic undertakings, as the Holy See could exert its influence at the league through the conduit of members of the league amenable to the Holy See's policies.

37. Manfred Franz Boemeke, Gerald D. Feldman, and Elisabeth Gläser, eds., *The Treaty of Versailles: A Reassessment after 75 Years* (Cambridge: Cambridge University Press, 1998), 258. The first of these Minorities treaties was the Polish Minorities Treaty intended to protect the Jewish population in Poland. It then came to embrace the welfare of all the Jews in Central and Eastern Europe.

THE MANDATE SYSTEM: CONCEALED COLONIZATION?

Mandate System and Imperialism

Pope Benedict had little time left to follow the development of the League of Nations, as he died a couple of years after it began full operation. During these years, he established private and unofficial contacts with its members in order to monitor decisions that would have a direct influence on the future of Catholic interests in the world.[38] The pontiff's primary concern was to ensure the protection of Catholic rights in the emerging Middle East.

The birth of the mandate system, a system meant to govern the colonies or territories that once belonged to the defeated powers, put a lid on France and Britain's claims to share the spoils of wars in the collapsed Ottoman Empire.[39] The British and French demands for annexation of those territories were firmly opposed by Woodrow Wilson as being in contradiction with the philosophy underlying the League of Nations. The mandate system emerged as a compromise between the powers' imperialistic intentions and Woodrow Wilson's opposition to annexationist policies and his promise to national minorities that they would be granted the right to self-determination.[40] Pope Benedict was following with keen interest the deliberations regarding the organization of the mandate system, as he supported Wilson's call in favor of self-determination of national minorities.

As a compromise, the mandate system did not clearly answer the question of its finality. Was it aiming at the future abolition of colonialism, or was it creating a system that would allow the

---

38. Araujo and Lucal, *Papal Diplomacy*, 146.
39. Nele Matz, "Civilization and the Mandate System under the League of Nations as Origin of Trusteeship," in *Max Planck Yearbook of United Nations Law*, ed. A. Von Bogdandy and R. Wolfrum (Leiden: Brill, 2005), 9:48.
40. M. Evans, *Religious Liberty*, 105.

colonial powers to amend and redesign their colonial politics?[41] In point twelve of his Fourteen Points, dealing specifically with Turkey, Wilson had implicitly notified France, Britain, and Italy that the United States would not accept any wartime agreement on the carving up of the Ottoman Empire and the attribution of spheres of influence between the Allied powers.[42] Point twelve stated:

> The Turkish portions of the present Ottoman Empire should be assured a secure sovereignty, but the other nationalities which are now under Turkish rule should be assured an undoubted security of life and an absolutely unmolested opportunity of autonomous development, and the Dardanelles should be permanently opened as a free passage to the ships and commerce of all nations under international guarantees.[43]

Considering the political prestige enjoyed by the American president in Europe and the Middle East, France and Britain had no other choice than to verbally adopt Wilson's call for self-determination in the region while, at the same time, making sure that it would be practically impossible to implement.[44] On November 9, 1918, France and Britain issued an ambiguous joint declaration tackling the issue of self-determination:

> The object aimed at by France and Great Britain in prosecuting in the East the war let loose by the ambition of Germany is the complete and definite emancipation of the peoples so long oppressed by the Turks and the establishment of national governments and administrations deriving their authority from the initiative and free choice of the indigenous populations.[45]

---

41. Matz, "Civilization and the Mandate System," 54.

42. John A. deNovo, *American Interests and Policies in the Middle East, 1900–1939* (Minneapolis: University of Minenesota Press, 1963), 110.

43. Compston and Seidman, *Our Documents*, 151.

44. James Gelvin, "The Ironic Legacy of the King-Crane Commission," in *The Middle East and the United States: A Historical and Political Reassessment*, ed. David W. Lesch (Boulder, Colo.: Westview Press, 2007), 14.

45. Ibid., 15.

But the same statement was pouring cold water on indigenes' dreams of self-determination, making France and Britain's support conditional on their acceptance of guidance from "advanced nations," a statement with colonial connotations, foreshadowing the institution of future mandates.

French and British Mandates in Greater Syria

In his *History of Syria*, the late historian Philip K. Hitti described Greater Syria as "the largest small country on the map, microscopic in size but cosmic in influence."[46] Lacking in natural resources, it is its strategic geographical location and its history that explain its disproportionate role in the region.[47] Syria lies at the meeting point of three continents and has served as a trade and culture route between the Occident and the Orient for over 3,500 years. In an address delivered in 1934, George Antonius, author of the seminal book *The Arab Awakening*,[48] defined geographical Syria—also known as Greater Syria—as a "rectangle of land which forms the eastern boundary of the Mediterranean Sea, and is bounded on the north by the Taurus Mountains, on the east by the Syrian Desert, on the south by the Sinai Desert and Peninsula, and on the west by the Mediterranean Sea."[49]

From the nineteenth century onward, geographical Syria had been the battlefield where French and British empires vied for domination of the Middle East. The capture of Jerusalem by British troops in December 1917 signaled the collapse of the Ottoman Empire and the partitioning of Greater Syria between the rival empires.

Article 22 of the covenant of the League of Nations estab-

46. Philip K. Hitti, *History of Syria including Lebanon and Palestine* (Piscataway, N.J.: First Gorgias, 2002), 1:3.

47. Neil Quilliam, *Syria and the New World Order* (Reading, UK: Gamer, 1999), 28.

48. George Antonius, *The Arab Awakening: The Story of the Arab National Movement* (London: Hamish Hamilton, 1945).

49. Antonius, "Syria and the French Mandate," *International Affairs* (July 1934): 523–24.

lished the mandate system, emphasizing that "the well-being and development" of people living in the former colonies of defeated countries "form a sacred trust of civilization."[50] France and Britain were therefore offered mandates on the basis of a "tutelage [that] should be exercised by them as mandatories on behalf of the league."[51]

Article 22 of the covenant classified the mandates into three groups, depending on the stage of development of the territories. Palestine, Lebanon, and Syria received a Class A mandate as representing non-self-governing societies that would need supervision for a short period of time before being granted independence.[52] The mandatory's mission was essentially to provide advice and support to allow these territories to be granted independence after reaching an advanced stage of political, economic, and social maturity.

The implementation of the new mandate system went through different phases. On April 24 and 25, 1920, at the Conference of San Remo, the Supreme Council of the Allied Powers confirmed the Allied Mandates Commission's resolution to partition Greater Syria and allot a civil mandate for Syria to France, while Great Britain was entrusted with a mandate for Palestine. The details of the mandates remained to be drafted and approved by the League of Nations, and the borders of the new entities were defined by the French and British governments at a conference in London on December 4, 1920.[53] The final terms of the British

50. Covenant of the League of Nations, art. 22, par. 1, quoted in J. A. S. Grenville, ed., *Major International Treaties, 1914–1973: A History and Guide with Texts* (London: Methuen, 1974), 24–27.

51. Ibid., art.22, par. 2.

52. Three types of mandates were created by the League of Nations. Class A mandates consisted of former Ottoman Empire territories, including Palestine, Lebanon, Syria, Iraq, and Transjordan. Class B mandates covered German colonies in Central Africa. As for class C mandates, they consisted of South-West Africa territories and some Pacific Islands.

53. Howard Grief, *The Legal Foundation and Borders of Israel under International Law*

and French mandates were eventually approved by the league on July 24, 1922, a few months after Benedict XV's passing away, and became operational on September 29, 1923.

The principle of decolonization was not explicitly mentioned in article 22, but it could be inferred, after close reading, that the mandate system was intended to be a first step on the way to the abrogation of the colonial system. The Class A mandates of Great Britain and France regarding the former possessions of the Ottoman Empire stipulated that Syria, Palestine, Iraq, and Transjordan were deemed to "have reached a stage of development where their existence as independent nations can be provisionally recognized subject to the rendering of administrative advice and assistance by a Mandatory until such time as they are able to stand alone. The wishes of these communities must be a principal consideration in the selection of the Mandatory."[54]

However, in practice, the Wilsonian ideal of self-determination was met with reticence by both France and Great Britain. The practical implementation of the two mandates was dictated by the state of Anglo-French relations and their respective colonial interests. The importance of the Class A mandates was essentially due to their strategic position for both the French and British empires. The welfare of the Arab populations of the area and their training for future independence was secondary in the global imperialistic schemes of the two Great Powers.

The mandate years were a time of growing tension between the rules imposed by the mandatories and the growing demand for independence of the populations under foreign governance. The resistance against colonial behaviors was fueled by the development of nationalist movements that had gained in matu-

---

(Jerusalem: Mazo, 2008), 55. The final Franco-British boundary agreement was signed in Paris on December 23, 1920.

54. Covenant of the League of Nations, art. 22, par. 4, in Grenville, *Major International Treaties*, 24–27.

rity after the war.[55] The Holy See, with its network of Catholic institutions, churches, and missions, was directly concerned by the model of control adopted by the mandatories and its effect on the local populations. It had a direct bearing on Pope Benedict's ecclesiastical and diplomatic policy, as the pontiff was in the midst of devising a new approach to the relations between the Catholic missionaries in the world and their allegiance to their country of origin, most often one with colonial territories worldwide.

THE HOLY SEE'S POLICY OF EMANCIPATION

Pope Benedict was not alone in judging that the mandate system had answered the imperialistic cravings of powers like France and Great Britain but had also sown the seeds of future decolonization. However, it was to the pontiff's credit to foresee the consequences that this first step in the process of decolonization would have on the universal church and its mission network worldwide. Pope Benedict acted upon this unique opportunity to emancipate the missionary world from the shackles of the Great Powers. He liberated the Catholic Church from its identification with the Eurocentric model, which the postwar scene had rendered geopolitically inadequate and morally untenable.

A Universal Call to Emancipation:
Encyclical *Maximum Illud*

After four years of a war that saw Christian nations fighting against each other, the "credit of European civilization" in the colonies was gone.[56] In September 1920, the Orientalist Gertrude Bell evoked the danger of this moral collapse bluntly: "Over and

---

55. David K. Fieldhouse, *Western Imperialism in the Middle East, 1914–1958* (Oxford: Oxford University Press, 2006), 3.

56. Lady Francis Bell, ed., *The Letters of Gertrude Bell* (New York: Boni and Liveright, 1927), 2:404.

over again, people have said to me [she wrote] that it has been a shock and a surprise to them to see Europe relapse into barbarism. I had no reply—what else can you call the war? How can we, who managed our affairs so badly, claim to teach others to manage theirs better?"[57] In the same vein, the American historian Lothrop Stoddard pointed out in 1922 that "the Western rulers will always remain an alien caste: tolerated, even respected but never loved, and never regarded as anything than foreigners."[58]

In this context, Benedict grasped the need for the church to emancipate itself from the colonial powers, especially France and its Catholic protectorate. For centuries, in the colonies, France had been associated with Catholicism and Catholicism with France, regardless of the state of the diplomatic relations between the Holy See and Paris. Against the Eurocentric and nationalist positivism of the nineteenth century the pontiff affirmed the unity and universality of the church. To the positivist philosophy that assumed the superiority of European civilization and culture, the pope opposed a vision of society based on the equality of men and cultures, nurtured by Catholic missions. With much insight, Benedict foresaw that the expansion of the world, embodied in the new League of Nations, would challenge the secular Eurocentric political and cultural model. He contemplated a world in which the Catholic Church, a universal and transnational institution, would rethink and reorganize the missionary world in order to strengthen harmonious international relations and world peace. The international missionary network, free from the control of the Great Powers, was moving away, slowly and gradually, from a nationalistic spirit, eventually becoming the cornerstone on which Pope Benedict anchored the church in the modern world.[59]

57. Ibid.
58. Lothrop Stoddard, "Islam Aflame with Revolt," *World's Work*, May–Oct. 1922, 138.
59. Matz, "Civilization and the Mandate System," 60.

Most of the measures Benedict XV took to protect the missions in lands under French and British mandates are expressed in his apostolic letter *Maximum Illud*, on the propagation of the faith throughout the world, promulgated on November 30, 1919.[60] The covenant for the League of Nations creating the mandate system had already been approved as of July 28, 1919, but the league was not in full operation. The Conference of San Remo of April 1920 had not yet authorized the mandates for Palestine and Syria to Great Britain and France.

Maximum Illud was not an apostolic letter about missions in the Middle East. It was a document written to respond to the concern of a Belgian missionary in China, Vincent Lebbe, who in 1918 had complained to Propaganda Fide about the rising conflict between Chinese nationalism and the French Catholic protectorate, criticizing the exacerbated nationalism of French missionaries.[61] The apostolic letter was the first papal document to provide an international and comprehensive approach to the missionary world.

Maximum Illud identified three main priorities for the missionary clergy: the formation of a native clergy, the recognition of human dignity of all men and cultures, and the missionaries' renunciation of nationalistic endeavors. Pope Benedict highlighted the need to train an indigenous clergy with "the same kind of education for the priesthood that a European would receive," so "that some day they will be able to enter upon the spiritual leadership of their people." By training indigenous missionaries, Benedict's hope was to get access to "places where a foreign priest would not be tolerated," often because he was associated with a European colonial enterprise.[62] It was a revolutionary document,

---

60. Benedict XV, "Apostolic Letter" *Maximum Illud* [Nov. 30, 1919]," *AAS* 11(1919): 440–55.

61. Jacques Leclercq, *Thunder in the Distance: The Life of Père Lebbe* (New York: Sheed and Ward, 1958); see also Ernest P. Young, *Ecclesiastical Colony: China's Catholic Church and the French Religious Protectorate* (Oxford: Oxford University Press, 2013).

62. Benedict XV, *Maximum Illud*, 445.

as it directly challenged the missionaries and their hierarchy to rethink their relationship with the colonial rulers and engaged them to draw a clear line between their Catholic and nationalist allegiance, cutting ties between the missionary and his country.

In *Maximum Illud*, Pope Benedict sternly denounced missionary nationalism.

It would be tragic indeed [wrote the pope] if any of our missionaries forgot the dignity of their office so completely as to busy themselves with the interests of their terrestrial homeland instead of with those of their homeland in heaven.... Such behaviour would infect his apostolate like a plague. It would destroy in him, the representative of the Gospel, the sinews of his love for souls and it would destroy his reputation with the populace.[63]

The message was especially intended for French missionaries, who provided most of the Catholic missionary force.

Pope Benedict was careful not to use a vocabulary that could be misunderstood by the missionaries, as the nuance was subtle between the ideas of nationalism and patriotism. The term "nationalism" is difficult to define. One definition is given by Professor Maurizio Viroli, who points out that

nationalism is not to be confused with patriotism.... By "patriotism," I mean devotion to a particular place and a particular way of life which one believes to be the best in the world but has no wish to force upon people ... nationalism, on the other hand, is inseparable from the desire for power. The abiding purpose of every nationalist is to secure more power and more prestige, *not* for himself but for the nation.[64]

In the words of the German sociologist and political economist Max Weber, nationalism is based upon "'sentiments of prestige,' rooted deep in notions of common descent and essential cultural/ethnic homogeneity. The prestige of a nation is directly linked to the foundational idea ... of that nation's 'mission' in the

63. Ibid., 446.
64. Maurizio Viroli, *For Love of Country: An Essay on Patriotism and Nationalism* (Oxford: Oxford University Press, 1995), 3.

world."[65] This is this form of nationalism that Pope Benedict was fighting against, a nationalism that, in the case of France, was hiding behind the concept of *mission civilisatrice*, the foundation of French colonial politics.

A couple of years after the promulgation of *Maximum Illud*, in an additional effort to restructure the world of missions, Pope Benedict recommended the Society for the Propagation of the Faith to the attention of Propaganda Fide. Founded in 1822 in Lyons, France, by a laywoman, Pauline Jaricot, the Society for the Propagation of the Faith had as its core mission to pray for missionaries and collect alms intended for the missions worldwide. As the society had made substantial headway since its founding, Pope Benedict planned to transfer its headquarters from Lyons to Rome for the sake of closer clerical control and release from French political pressure. On January 1922, on the occasion of the preparation for the celebration of the centenary of the society, the *Osservatore Romano*, the official organ of the Vatican, published an article announcing the transfer of the society to Rome.[66] There is no doubt that, had he not died a month later, Pope Benedict would have made official the measures announced by the newspaper. The transfer was effected a few months later by Pope Benedict's successor, Pius XI, in his motu proprio *Romanorum Pontificum* of May 3, 1922.[67] In this document, the new pope raised the society to the status of Pontifical Society for the Propagation of the Faith.

With these measures, the papacy concentrated in Rome the control and distribution of missionary resources. By centralizing the collection of international alms, the Holy See was breaking away from France in an attempt to remove accusations of na-

---

65. Stephen Backhouse, *Kierkegaard's Critique of Christian Nationalism* (Oxford: Oxford University Press, 2011), 5.

66. "Editorial Notes: Centenary of the Society for the Propagation of the Faith," *Catholic Missions*, May 1922, 118.

67. Pius XI, "Motu Proprio *Romanorum Pontificum* [May 3, 1922]," *AAS* 14 (1922): 321–30.

tionalism leveled against missionaries. This financial emancipation was to be understood as the Holy See's dissociation from the colonial powers, so that the populations of territories under mandate rule "would not confuse with the same distrust the priest, the soldier, and the merchant, so that the day the latter two would be pushed away, the priest could at least stay."[68]

A Regional Reality: Catholic Missions in Syria and Palestine

Maximum Illud was promulgated in November 1919, almost two years after the fall of Palestine and Syria into British hands. During this period, Catholic missions strove to ensure the reopening of their buildings and to enroll missionaries in order to relaunch their activities and quickly return to their prewar glory. They took initiatives, independently from the Vatican, that immediately brought them to the attention of the pontiff. A joint meeting of cardinals from various Roman congregations took place to discuss the situation. A series of resolutions, approved by the pope, were issued in June 1919.

Anticipating *Maximum Illud* and its denunciation of missionary nationalism, Propaganda Fide, the Congregation for the Oriental Church, and the Congregation for Extraordinary Ecclesiastical Affairs, in a joint address, clarified the dispositions that had to be taken in order to ensure the survival and renaissance of the Eastern Catholic missions and dioceses in a redesigned postwar world.[69]

---

68. "Ne confondissent dans la même défiance le prêtre, le soldat et le marchand, afin que le jour où ces deux derniers seraient repoussés, le prêtre du moins put rester"; Msgr. Eugène Beaupin, "Introduction," in *L'apostolat missionnaire de la France*, Conférences données à l'Institut Catholique de Paris, Série 1924–25 (Paris: Téqui, 1924–26) (my translation).

69. Adunanza Mista delle Sacre Congregazioni "de Propaganda Fide," "Pro Ecclesia Orientali," e degli Affari Ecclesiastici Straordinari, "Relazione sulle disposizioni da prendersi per provvedere al risarcimento dei Danni subiti dale Missioni e dale Diocesi Orientali," June 1919, ACCO, fasc. 4/7 bis. In addition to cardinals Gasparri, van Rossum, and

The issue at stake was a cause of great concern. European superiors of Oriental missions, impatient to obtain compensation for the damage their missions had suffered during the war, were sending their demand *"directly* [to] the government of their own country,"[70] without informing the Holy See. The controversy revolved around whether or not the missionaries receiving financial support from their native country would be legally bound by this act to the contributing nation as well as how that would affect both the missions and the Holy See.

The cardinals worried that the allocation of funds by a foreign government to restore Catholic buildings and churches would create a precedent, as the benefactors would, without any doubt claim a right of protection if not of direct control over these establishments. As many missionaries without much discernment would accept financial support from their native country, the patrimony of the Holy See in the region would eventually end up in foreign secular hands, not only suppressing the autonomy of the Holy See but also shifting the role of missionaries as one of conquering the territory for their own nation's interests rather than taking care of the supernatural interests of souls.[71] This affirmation was a direct forerunner of Pope Benedict's guiding principles, which would be enunciated in *Maximum Illud* a few months later.

The final answer to this problem was complicated, as the Holy See had to find a way that would ensure the independence of the church while accepting donations to rebuild the missions. At this time, the Holy See was penniless. On June 6, 1919, the mixed congregation published official guidelines that stipulated that the missionaries were allowed to accept compensation from

---

Marini, cardinals DeLai, Vico, Merry del Val, Frühwirth, Scapinelli, Lega, and Gasquet were present at the meeting.

70. Ibid.

71. Ibid.

a foreign country in order to rebuild their institutions. Neverthe-less, they had to ensure that the indemnity provided as a mea-sure of justice and reparation would not give the nation a right that would constitute a constraint on the freedom of the church or be assimilated into a title of property of the Catholic estab-lishment. The Holy See was the final authority to accept or reject the offer from the donor.[72]

In the emerging postwar world, Pope Benedict articulated a threefold rationale underlying the Holy See's diplomatic ap-proach in Europe and the Middle East. The pontiff initiated a new policy that shifted away from its past Eurocentric vision of the world, embracing the role of the Catholic Church as a uni-versal and transnational institution. This approach was com-bined with an anticipation of the decolonization era and self-determination of national minorities. It is based on these two premises that Pope Benedict completed the principles guiding his diplomacy with a policy of emancipation of the missionary world from colonial powers. Benedict XV prepared the church for an active role in the modern world. In Syria and Palestine, the pontiff adjusted his diplomacy to the new setting imposed by the mandate system as he designed a prudent policy that would adapt to short-term developments without compromising his long-term goal of emancipation of the church from the colonial powers and the colonial mindset.

72. ACCO, fasc. 39/29, Segretaria—Orientali Missioni, June 10, 1919.

7

THE HOLY SEE AND SYRIA

The Significance of Syria

Syria has always been a pivotal gateway between the East and the West. It was of equal concern to France and to the Holy See, as it had historically sheltered the largest Christian community in the Middle East and the most significant of French interests. Furthermore, Great Britain had no pressing interest in the region. As an imperial power, it was essentially concerned about its strategic position in Palestine, south of Syria, and its takeover of oil fields in Mesopotamia. Therefore, at the end of the war, the British government's goal was to ensure that Syria would fall into the hands of a friendly power. Its policy on this matter evolved from supporting an Arab kingdom led by Prince Faisal, the son of Hussein, sharif of Mecca, to consenting reluctantly to a French mandate.

Syria had never been of great concern for French economic or financial development, leaving it on cultural and religious grounds that Paris claimed a right to a mandate. Historically, France had an undeniable privileged presence and moral involvement in the area. Since the sixteenth century, its Catholic religious protectorate had ensured the protection of Latin and Eastern Catholic communities. It is on this religious ground that the Holy See's interests over Syria converged with those of

193

France. The Holy See always had as its core mission the protection of the rights and interests of Catholic populations in the Middle East.

But times had changed. The First World War had sounded the death knell for the prewar international system, with France having lost its privileged position. During the war, France was politically weakened in the Middle East due to its minor military contribution. Conversely, Britain's military accomplishments made it the dominant power in the region, with troops stationed in all the previous Arab provinces of the Ottoman Empire.

In this context, Pope Benedict engaged the Holy See in a new universal policy of emancipation from the colonial powers, which meant, in the newly emerging Middle East, the implementation of a supple diplomacy that would adjust to any political environment as long as the independence of the Holy See and the protection of Catholic interests would be guaranteed. This novel policy explains why the pontiff responded with genuine interest to Prince Faisal's offer to discuss the future government of Syria. The son of the emir of Mecca was expecting, in accordance with the Hussein-McMahon Correspondence of wartime, to establish an independent united Arab kingdom that would stretch from Aleppo in Northern Syria to Aden in Yemen.[1] In September 1918, British General Allenby and his army entered into Syria. He was accompanied by Prince Faisal, whose troops had supported the British on the Arab front during the war. On October 3, as Allenby's troops were advancing toward Damascus, the British general stopped his own army and let Faisal enter victoriously into Damascus, accompanied by Colonel T. E. Lawrence. This episode "created the myth of an Arab Revolt, advancing in tri-

1. The Hussein-McMahon Correspondence was an exchange of eight letters, from July 14, 1915, to January 30, 1916, between Sherif Hussein of Mecca and Sir Henry McMahon, the British high commissioner in Egypt. It concerns the Ottoman lands that the British were ready to cede to the Arabs in exchange for the sherif's revolt against the Ottoman government.

THE HOLY SEE AND SYRIA

umph and crowning its progress with the capture of a great city, only to be cheated of victory by underhanded intrigues and sordid ambitions."[2]

At the regional level, the apostolic delegate of Syria, Giannini, was concerned that an Arab kingdom would become engulfed in Muslim fanaticism while thousands of miles away in Rome Pope Benedict was receiving Prince Faisal warmly and acquiescing to him becoming king of Syria, as long as religious freedom for the Latin and Eastern Catholics were enforced.

Prince Faisal Meets with Pope Benedict

For the first time in the history of the papacy, "the head of the Catholic Church received the son of the Commander of the Faithful,"[3] an extraordinary event in itself but one that, for the very few scholars who mention it, concretely meant nothing.[4] Although Pope Benedict did not directly influence the course of political events in Syria, such an encounter sheds light on the changes that had occurred on the diplomatic scene. That Faisal asked for a meeting with the pope was a sign of the international stature that both the pontiff and Prince Faisal had gained since the end of the conflict, allowing them to discuss the future of Syria without the mediation of France.

Faisal spent four months in Europe. On February 6, 1919, a few days after the opening of the Paris Peace Conference, invited by Great Britain, he was granted a hearing before the Council of Ten and defended the legitimacy of an independent and sover-

2. On these events, see Jan Karl Tanenbaum, "France and the Arab Middle East, 1914–1920," *Transactions of the American Philosophical Society* 68 (1978): 21.

3. "Moslem Prince at Vatican: Faisal Tells Pope of Arabia's Hope of Complete Independence," *New York Times*, Apr. 27, 1919, 26.

4. See Sami Moubayed, *Syria and the USA: Washington's Relations with Damascus from Wilson to Eisenhower* (New York: I. B. Tauris, 2011), 20. Robert de Caix, civil secretary-general of the high commissioner in Syria, gave attention to this encounter and elaborated on its meaning to Minister Stephen Pichon; Gérard Khoury, *Une tutelle coloniale: Le mandat français en Syrie et au Liban; Écrits politiques de Robert de Caix* (Paris: Belin, 2006), 167.

195

eign Arab kingdom.[5] The Arab world was in effervescence, hoping to build a kingdom but worried by the imperialistic ambitions of France and England. Faisal met with Pope Benedict on April 21, 1919. At this time, the Holy See knew that, in accordance with the Sykes-Picot agreement of 1916 as well as the Hussein-McMahon Correspondence, the British had reserved Palestine for themselves, promised Mount Lebanon to France, and given inner Syria to Faisal.[6] Rome was also aware that the negotiations between Faisal and Clemenceau, the head of the French government, regarding the establishment of a sherifian kingdom under French protectorate, had failed, as British troops were still occupying Syria and Lebanon, infuriating French officials.[7] Therefore, when Faisal met with Pope Benedict, no final de jure settlement had been devised and no mandate had been allotted yet, leading to speculation about who would eventually govern the country.

On May 20, 1919, Gasparri sent a report of the meeting to Cardinal Marini, the secretary of the Congregation for the Oriental Church. He informed Marini that Faisal had confirmed in a written document that the Syrian government, under his leadership, would guarantee complete freedom to all Catholics, respecting the rights of the church and ensuring the protection of monasteries and other religious institutions.[8] There would be no return

5. The Council of Ten consisted of the heads of state and foreign ministers of Great Britain, France, Italy, the United States, and Japan. Its main task was to draft the peace treaty. The council was too large to be efficient. Eventually, the negotiations were handled by the "Big Three" (Great Britain, the United States, and France).

6. A secret agreement was concluded in May 1916 between the French and British governments that partitioned the Arab possessions of the Ottoman Empire between France and Britain in the expectation of the collapse of the Ottoman Empire. The terms of the agreement conflicted with McMahon's promises to Sherif Hussein.

7. Peter Sluglett, "The Mandates: Some Reflections on the Nature of the British Presence in Iraq (1914–1932) and the French Presence in Syria (1918–1946)," in *The British and French Mandates in Comparative Perspectives/Les mandats français et anglais dans une perspective comparative*, ed. Nadine Méouchy and Peter Sluglett, 120 (Leiden: Brill, 2004).

8. Gasparri to Marini, May 20, 1919, ACCO, fasc. 614/32—Oriente: L'Emiro Faisal: Udienza del S. Padre (1919).

THE HOLY SEE AND SYRIA

to the *millet* system, rendering any French interests to restore the Catholic protectorate obsolete. In the letter forwarded to Marini, it is not clear if it is Gasparri on his own account or Pope Benedict who asked Abbot Ubaid, a Maronite priest and Faisal's interpreter, to construe the terms of the meeting and explain what the prince concretely meant by "to facilitate the union between the Christian and Muslim populations of Syria and Palestine, therefore facilitating the establishment of an independent Arab state in the region."[9] The abbot responded that in his understanding, Prince Faisal was encouraging the Holy See to comfort the Eastern Catholic patriarchs and reassure them that the Holy See was aware of the emir's intentions and was satisfied with the guarantees they had received in respect to the absolute safeguard of liberty and religious independence of Catholics, churches, and pious foundations.[10] Then he emphasized how delicate but greatly important it was to inform Msgr. Giannini and the Latin patriarch in Jerusalem, Msgr. Camassei, about the guarantees of complete religious freedom given by Prince Faisal to the pontiff and thus avoid subjecting them to any political friction. Pope Benedict approved Abbot Ubaid's suggestions. Cardinal Marini was invited to address a formal letter to Giannini, Msgr. Cadi, Melkite patriarch, and Msgr. Huyaek, Maronite patriarch. They received the missive on June 13, and the patriarch of Jerusalem, in Rome at the time, was directly informed.

Pope Benedict's response was pragmatic and shed light on his diplomatic approach to the thorny Syrian question. He clearly perceived the benefits Faisal could gain from establishing good relations with the Holy See. Since the end of the war, the papacy had been enjoying a sudden resurgence of moral authority. As a universal institution with strong interests in Syria, it could be-

9. "Vedere agevolata l'unione tra l'elemento cristiano e quello mussulmano della Siria e della Palestina e facilitata in tal modo la costituzione di uno stato arabo indipendente nelle región suddette"; ACCO, May 20, 1919, ibid. (my translation).
10. Ibid.

come a precious and unique ally to Prince Faisal, assuming that his provisional government was meant to stay. In the long run, both parties could also envision the establishment of official diplomatic ties, an opportunity declined by the Holy See with the Ottoman Empire during the war. In the newly emerging world order, Pope Benedict was in a position to seize this unique opportunity to engage in direct diplomatic exchanges with a Muslim leader. It was a bold path to choose, as the Holy See was at the same time planning to resume diplomatic relations with France. As had already been done in the past, Paris would vehemently oppose the Holy See's attempt at emancipation.

Benedict's global and regional foreign policy shows that he had chosen a diplomatic route that would establish a clear line of demarcation between the colonial and semi-colonial possessions of France and the *Métropole*. He was anticipating the soon-to-come era of decolonization and was seeing in Arab nationalism a potential anti-imperialistic weapon against France. The visit of Prince Faisal was a positive sign of his will to assume, with the blessing of the British, the role of protector of Catholics in Syria, therefore replacing the French.[11] In April 1919 at the time of the meeting, the pontiff was preparing his groundbreaking apostolic letter *Maximum Illud*, which would initiate a policy of emancipation of the Holy See from the colonial powers, especially France.

Pope Benedict's diplomacy toward Prince Faisal's Syrian administration was also in line with Pope Leo XIII's policy regarding the Holy See's approval of different forms of governments. In his encyclical *Diuturnum* of 1881, on the origin of civil power, Pope Leo stated:

There is no reason why the Church should not approve of the chief power being held by one man or by more, provided only it be just, and

---

11. Letter of Robert de Caix of April 22, 1919, to Stephen Pichon, quoted in Gérard Khoury, *Tutelle coloniale*, 167.

that it tend to the common advantage. Wherefore, so long as justice be respected, the people are not hindered from choosing for themselves that form of government which suits best either their own disposition, or the institutions and customs of their ancestors.[12]

As long as Catholic communities were protected, Pope Benedict would be satisfied with a Syrian kingdom insofar as religious freedom and independence from colonial enterprise were guaranteed.

Pope Benedict's global and conceptual foresight was completed by an analysis of the practical situation in Syria. At the regional level, the pontiff's policy conflicted with the apostolic delegate's immediate focus on Catholic life in a Muslim and nationalist environment. Giannini, living at the center of the Syrian turmoil, wrote three important letters to Cardinal Gasparri to defend his position.

His first letter was written on May 7, 1919, before he was made aware of the content of the meeting between Pope Benedict and Faisal. Giannini understood the danger of an Arab sovereignty in Syria and, although cognizant of the imperialist rivalry between France and England, opted for a French protectorate as the least damaging solution for Catholic interests.[13] He warned that

the prospect of a sherifian dominion completely independent would be very serious.... In this case... our poor Christian minority would surely be increasingly reduced to the minimum and possibly condemned to fade away... faced with the inevitable invasion of the Islamic element of Arabia attracted to Syria because of the many material advantages that it offers in contrast with their native country.[14]

---

12. Leo XIII, "Encyclical Letter *Diuturnum*, on the Origin of Civil Power [June 29, 1881]," *ASS* 14 (1881): 3–14.

13. Giannini to Gasparri, May 7, 1919, ASV, AES Stati Ecclesiastici, pos. 1418, fasc. 564.

14. "Molto grave sarebbe...la eventualita di un dominio sceriffiano tutt'affatto indipendente....In questo caso...la nostra povera minoranza Cristiana si vedrebbe sicuramente sempre piu ridotta a minimi termini e forse condannata a sparire, di fronte all'inevitable invasione dell'elemento islamico del Arabia attirato in Siria dai molti vantaggi materiali che questa offerta rimpetto al native paese"; ibid. (my translation).

Although he mentioned Arabia exclusively, Giannini's remark came after the new anti-Iraqi slogan of "Syria for the Syrians" had started to make headlines in the press. The rising Arab nationalism was lacking in cohesion. When Syrian officers who had fought in the Ottoman armies returned home, they found their previous position occupied by Iraqis who had entered Damascus with Faisal's troops in October 1918. The Syrians complained that they "had become strangers in their own country."[15] The Syrian National Party, among other new associations, was founded to protect Syrian rights against what it saw as an Iraqi invasion. Arab nationalism was at its beginnings dominated by "a form of parochialism"[16] that weakened its organization and made any political arrangement with Faisal uncertain.[17] For that reason, Giannini had no confidence in Faisal's ability to guarantee the protection of Christians in Syria, not so much because he could not be trusted, but because in the context previously described, he would not have the authority or power to prevent violent Muslim outbursts against Catholic minorities. The apostolic delegate encouraged the Holy See to lobby in favor of a French protectorate. However, if a French protectorate were not politically possible, a British protectorate would still be better than the Arab government of Faisal.

France was the obvious choice, as it had been the age-old protector of Catholic interests in the Middle East. Although Giannini accused British agents in Syria of fueling an aggressive anti-Catholic propaganda led by Muslims as well as Orthodox and Protestants,[18] he believed a British protectorate would be more amenable to Catholics than a fanatic sherifian government.

15. Eliezer Tauber, *The Formation of Modern Syria and Iraq* (London: Frank Cass, 1995), 174.

16. Adeed Dawisha, *Arab Nationalism in the Twentieth Century: From Triumph to Despair* (Princeton, N.J.: Princeton University Press, 2003), 46–47.

17. Tauber, *Formation of Modern Syria*, 175.

18. Giannini to Gasparri, May 7, 1919, ASV, AES Stati Ecclesiastici, pos. 1418, fasc. 564.

He noticed a fact that could not have been missed by Pope Benedict. Faisal came back to Syria on a French warship, a sign of the advancement of the negotiations between him and the French government. However, he neglected to visit Catholic establishments, most of them French, but instead visited the Protestant American University of Beirut.[19] Three interpretations of this event are possible. Perhaps Faisal was not inclined to publicly demonstrate specific attention toward Catholic missions, a fact that weakened the promise he had made to Pope Benedict. It is also likely that with British troops being installed in Syria, a visit to Catholic establishments would have been discouraged or even forbidden by the British. Furthermore, visiting the American University could be interpreted as a signal to the U.S. government that Faisal was eager to obtain American protection in Syria and would be accommodating to both Catholics and Protestants.

Giannini was especially worried by the prospect of a British mandate in Lebanon, recalling that before the war, Great Britain had exercised a destructive anti-Catholic influence and instead favored the Druses, who after the Catholic Maronites were the most numerous religious group. The apostolic delegate concluded:

If the sovereignty of Emir Faisal is unavoidable, I would like it detached from the Hejjaz, under French protectorate and with constitutional guarantees well defined from the beginning, regarding the freedom of Syria in general, as well as the special privilege of Lebanon to remain autonomous as far as possible.[20]

His conclusion was a very perceptive anticipation of the political future of the region. On May 24, a couple of weeks after

19. Ibid.
20. "Se la sovranita dell'Emir Feisal e inevitabile, io la vorrei del tutto staccato dal Heggiaz, sotto protettorato francese e con garanzie costituzionali ben fissate sin dal principio, si per le liberta in generale di tutta la Siria, come per gli speciali privilege del Libano, da conservarsi, per quanto e possibile, autonomo"; Giannini to Gasparri, May 7, 1919, ASV, AES Stati Ecclesiastici, pos. 1418, fasc. 564 (my translation).

sending this letter to Gasparri, Giannini addressed another missive to the secretary of state, reinforcing his previous argument regarding the danger of a sherifian sovereignty over Lebanon. He mentioned widespread agitation in Lebanon, especially among the Maronites, who were forcefully resisting the most hated yoke of Islamism, which had often meant to them a life of exploitation and persecution.[21] Patriarch Huayek was planning to travel to Paris to defend the Lebanese Catholic identity at the Peace Conference and lobby in favor of independence.

The anti-sherifian tone used by Giannini in those two letters did not change after he received notice of the content of the meeting between Pope Benedict and Prince Faisal. He became even more insistent. In a note of July 13 adressed to Marini in response to the cardinal's letter of June 13, the apostolic delegate emphasized that Christians in general, Catholics and non-Catholics alike, vehemently rejected the prospect of a sherifian sovereignty. He noted:

The emir Faisal [is considered] a simple general of a division of the army of occupation. . . . It would be difficult to demonstrate that his promises have any weight. Therefore a potential disclosure of such promises, in these moments of excitement, [would] be badly interpreted. I would not be able reasonably to hope for anything but the most disadvantageous results for the prestige of the Holy See. . . . And for my part, I will abstain to publish [the note].[22]

What Giannini meant was that a written document by Faisal served as a bona fide intention but had no official value. Giannini was directly challenging the diplomatic course chosen

21. Giannini to Gasparri, May 24, 1919, ASV, AES Austria, 1919, pos. 1304, fasc. 516.

22. "L'Emir Faisal...un semplice generale di divisione dell'armata occupatrice....Sarebbe difficile il dimostrare che le sue promesse abbiano un qualche peso. Percio da un'eventuale divulgazione di siffatte promesse,...in questi momenti di effervescenza, ad essere molto male interpretate, io non potrei ragionevolmente aspettarmi che effetti piuttosto svantaggiosi al prestigio della Santa Sede. E dal canto moi mi guardero bene dal divulgarle"; Giannini to Marini, July 13, 1919, ACCO, fasc. 614/32, Oriente, Varie: L'Emiro Faisal: Udienza del S. Padre (1919) (my translation).

by Pope Benedict, as he was right to remind Rome that Faisal's assurances regarding religious freedom were not likely to be implemented. Without the physical and political protection of France or Britain, Catholics and Maronites would be at the mercy of their local governors. During Faisal's trip to Europe, Arab extremist nationalists had become empowered in Damascus.[23]

In the fall of 1919, the British government, until then the standard bearer of Arab nationalist ideology, abruptly changed its policy in the Middle East. Forsaking its previous support of Faisal's dream of an Arab kingdom in Syria, British officials let French troops enter Beirut on October 8 and withdrew from Damascus on November 26, 1919.

Pope Benedict followed closely the evolution of the new political situation. On one hand, considering the extremism of many of the Arab nationalists in Damascus who had brought the country to the verge of anarchy, the pontiff could not but be satisfied by the military and political presence of France in both Syria and Lebanon. On the other hand, Benedict's policy of emancipation was in jeopardy, as France was ready to reinstate its religious protectorate in the region. On November 21, 1919, General Gouraud was appointed the first French high commissioner in Syria. Well-known for his devotion to the church, he was also respected among French Catholics for his determination in dealing with Muslims.[24] He was accompanied by Robert de Caix, his civil collaborator and one of the main architects of the Quai d'Orsay's Syrian politics.

After a short interlude that saw Faisal crowned, France took the upper hand. Comforted by the conclusions of the conference at San Remo in April 1920, Gouraud sent an ultimatum to Faisal,

23. Howard M. Sachar, *The Emergence of the Middle East, 1914–1924* (New York: Knopf, 1969), 273.

24. Ibid., 276. Gouraud had a prewar experience as a colonial administrator in Morocco and Mauritania.

ordering him to resign and accept the French mandate in Syria as legitimate. Faisal refused and fled. He was later enthroned king of Iraq by the British.

Although times had changed, the political situation in the Middle East was still not ripe for any form of independence. Pope Benedict adjusted his policy to the new mandate system without losing sight of his ultimate goal of emancipation. He was paving the way for his successors.

THE HOLY SEE, FRANCE, AND SYRIA'S
STRUGGLE FOR INDEPENDENCE

Benedict XV, Robert de Caix, and Louis Massignon

On January 6, 1920, Prince Faisal and French prime minister Clemenceau signed a provisional agreement in which France "confirms its recognition of the rights of Arabic people of all faiths, settled in Syria, to unite in order to govern themselves as an independent nation."[25] The agreement also mentioned that France was to help the new kingdom to organize civil as well as military administrations; most importantly, Faisal would recognize the integrity and independence of Lebanon under French mandate.[26] But the French political map changed at the end of the month when Clemenceau lost the presidential elections and was replaced by Prime Minister Alexandre Millerand. The newly elected president was eager to maintain the provisions of the Faisal-Clemenceau agreement as long as Faisal was able to show proof of his authority.[27] His disappointment at the ability of the

25. "Confirme sa reconnaissance du droit des peuples de langue arabe, fixés sur le territoire syrien, de toutes confessions, à se réunir pour se gouverner elles-mêmes à titre de nation indépendente"; quoted in Gérard Khoury, "Robert de Caix et Louis Massignon: Deux visions de la politique française au Levant en 1920," in British and French Mandates, 180 (my translation).

26. Gérard Khoury, "Robert de Caix et Louis Massignon," 182; see also Carol Hakim, The Origins of the Lebanese National Idea: 1840–1920 (Berkeley, Calif.: California University Press, 2013), 250.

27. Hakim, Origins of the Lebanese National Idea, 253.

prince to federate the different Arab factions and ensure peace was soon palpable. The agreement was never executed, as Faisal joined the nationalists against the French government and was proclaimed king of Syria on March 6, 1920, only to flee the country a few months later.

The famous agreement was negotiated by Robert de Caix and Louis Massignon. The unfolding of the negotiations highlighted two opposite approaches regarding the future organization of the Levant in 1920.[28] Clemenceau, a notorious anti-colonialist, was eager to find a balance between the unification of the Arab populations, a position defended by Massignon, and the imperious necessity to satisfy French colonial interests, an approach favored by Robert de Caix.[29] From January 1920 until the battle of Maysalun on July 23, 1920, that signified the end of the sherifian dream and the implementation of the French mandate in Syria, the two visions were expounded. Eventually, it is Robert de Caix's vision that was implemented after the fall of the sherifian government and was enabled through Clemenceau's loss in the general elections of January 1920.

To the author's knowledge, there are no documents in the archives of the Vatican that can shed light on Benedict's direct evaluation of de Caix and Massignon's perspectives regarding the future of Syria, but his inclination toward Massignon's approach can be inferred. Conversely, in the letters sent by Giannini to the Holy See, one can discern an analogy of thought with Robert de Caix. The divergence of viewpoints between Pope Benedict and Giannini mirrored the opposition existing between the two French strategists. The Holy See had an immediate and long-term interest in the future of Syria and was following closely the grand politics at work between France, Britain, and Faisal.

Louis Massignon, a renowned French scholar of Islam, was

28. Gérard Khoury, "Robert de Caix et Louis Massignon," 165.
29. Ibid., 169.

appointed in 1917 the liaison officer attached to Faisal.[30] He had a global and idealistic vision of the Arab world and believed in the future of "a form of unitary Arab nationalism."[31] Massignon was thinking with a long-term perspective. In a letter of July 17, 1920, written to Gabriel Boulad, one of his friends, he revealed his strategy and its underlying philosophy.[32] As a negotiator, he acted as a Catholic who loved and knew the Muslim world. In his view, one cannot dissociate the political from the spiritual and human realms. To his friend, he wrote that "the current crisis in Syria, we want to live it 'hic et nunc' with our Lord Jesus. It is the only way to live it *bien et juste*," adding a few lines later that "it is not a waste of time, neither for 'political action' nor for the 'acute sense of social realities' to visit the Holy Sacrament."[33] Keeping in sight the protection of the Eastern Christians as a main goal, he explained that this protection would be best assured by a united Arab kingdom that would defend religious freedom for all confessions. He resented the emigration movement that saw Christian Syrians fleeing their country, accusing them of not acting in a Christian way and of lacking a good *political* education.[34]

Massignon sought to enhance the Arab cultural heritage of Syria while maintaining a French presence in the background. It was a position that was fiercely opposed by Robert de Caix because it weakened the prestige and the potential future of France in the region. De Caix, a journalist who entered the diplomatic

30. See the biography by Christian Destremau and Jean Moncelon: *Louis Massignon* (Paris: Plon, 1994).

31. Gérard Khoury, "Robert de Caix et Louis Massignon," 165.

32. Massignon to Gabriel Boulad, July 17, 1920, quoted in Gérard Khoury, "Robert de Caix et Louis Massignon," 170.

33. "La crise actuelle en Syrie, nous voulons la vivre 'hic et nunc' avec NS Jésus. C'est le seul moyen de la vivre bien et juste…ce n'est pas du temps perdu, pour 'l'action politique' ni pour le 'sens aigu des réalités sociales' qu'une visite au Très St. Sacrement"; quoted in Gérard Khoury, "Robert de Caix et Louis Massignon," 178 (my translation).

34. "Cette émigration navrante…n'est pas un acte chrétien, c'est une déception qui prouve combien l'éducation *politique* des chrétiens de Syrie se ressent de l'esclavage ancien"; ibid., 172 and 178.

world late in his life, became the secretary-general of the high commissioner in Syria, a position he held from November 1919 until 1925. Editor-in-chief of the *Bulletin de l'Asie française*, he was also a member of the Colonial Party and therefore a forceful advocate of a French mandate in Syria. A realist in politics, he envisioned a Middle East founded upon a federal system made of confessional communities under the protection of a great power. This approach, which favored the Christian minority, was adopted after Faisal fled from Damascus in July 1920. In a letter of April 11, 1920, to an official at the Quai d'Orsay, Mr. Bargeton, Robert de Caix rejected the eventuality of a sherifian kingdom that would not support French interests. He was opposed to the united kingdom favored by Massignon, an idea that led to the future balkanization of the region. According to him,

the peace of the world would be better served if there were in the Orient a number of small states, with relations under the control of France or England, that would be administered with the fullest domestic autonomy and would not have the aggressive tendencies of the big national unitary states.[35]

France's objective was to divide Syria in order to contain Arab nationalism.[36] De Caix's vision planted the seeds for future regional instability. By favoring the Christian and Shi'a Muslim minorities against the Sunni small majority, he destroyed the balance that had been in existence for centuries. His goal was to maintain the prestige of French culture in the Levant through the generalized use of French language and French institutions. This went against the sherifian dream of Syrian nationalism an-

35. "La paix du monde serait en somme mieux assurée s'il y avait en Orient un certain nombre de petits États dont les relations seraient controlées ici par la France et là par l'Angleterre, qui s'administreraient avec le maximum d'autonomie intérieure, et qui n'auraient pas les tendances agressives des grands États nationaux unitaires"; de Caix to M. Bargeton at the Quai d'Orsay, April 11, 1920, quoted in Gérard Khoury, "Robert de Caix et Louis Massignon," 169 (my translation).

36. Philip S. Khoury, *Syria and the French Mandate: The Politics of Arab Nationalism, 1920–1945* (Princeton, N.J.: Princeton University Press, 1987), 57.

chored in a united nation with the Arabic language as official cement.

While Louis Massignon's vision of postwar Syria has been put under the scholarly microscope, nothing similar had been done for Benedict XV, even though they were contemporary and shared a common vision. Both believed in the interdependence of the spiritual and political world, which led them to a shared vision of the universal dimension and centrality of man. Benedict, like Massignon, resented nationalist tendencies and wanted to see peoples of the Middle East, Christian, Muslim, Jew, or otherwise, embracing their own common destiny. In 1920, they reacted as men of their time, although very much in advance with this time. None of them took an anti-colonial stance, but they were anticipating the era of decolonization. Instead, in their areas, they advocated a new approach to colonialism. Benedict fully developed his philosophy in *Maximum Illud* in November 1919, emphasizing the need to train an indigenous clergy and respect indigenous cultures while paving the way for future inculturation.

The comparison stops here. While Pope Benedict lamented that non-Christians were "pitiable creatures living under a cloud of eternal damnation,"[37] therefore seeking their conversion, Massignon sought in place of conversion, which he found an "unnecessary and inhospitable condition to lay upon the friendship between two peoples...rather the...inculturation of the vision of Jesus Christ as the son of God within the religious discourse of Islam."[38] The similarity of views between Pope Benedict and Massignon can serve as a means to surmise Benedict's personal opinion of Prince Faisal's dream of a united Arab kingdom.

Massignon's approach was opposed by Robert de Caix who

37. Benedict XV, "Apostolic Letter *Maximum Illud* [Nov. 30, 1919]," *AAS* 11 (1919): 440–55.

38. Cleo McNelly Kearns, "Mary, Maternity, and Abrahamic Hospitality in Derrida's Reading of Massignon," in *Derrida and Religion: Other Testaments*, ed. Yvonne Sherwood and Kevin Hart, 86 (New York: Routledge, 2005).

demonstrated a short-term understanding and interest in the affairs of Syria. However, he was genuinely convinced that he was working in favor of a peaceful future. De Caix did not trust the Arab people and envisioned a federal structure governed by France. Maintaining the cultural prestige and political influence of France was essential to him. Giannini, in his correspondence with Cardinal Dubois, the archbishop of Rouen, who had started a journey to the Middle East in December 1919, emphasized this need for a strong colonial power like France to assuage the fears of the Christian minorities in Syria and Lebanon.

Cardinal Dubois's Mission to the Near East

The new world order, although more amenable to the Holy See's independent diplomatic action, was still guided by a colonial impulse that disrupted the chain of command from the pontiff to both the apostolic delegate in Syria and the bishops and citizens of the victorious powers. Three bishops visited Palestine and Syria after the war, but none of them was officially sent by the pope. They were on a mission planned by their own government but needed papal assent before embarking in their journey.

Cardinal Dubois, the archbishop of Rouen, was following in the steps of Cardinal Bourne of England and Cardinal Giustini of Italy. He is the only one who left a detailed relation of his visit to Lebanon.[39] The travels that took him to the Balkans, Constantinople, Lebanon, Palestine, and Egypt lasted one hundred days, from December 14, 1919, to March 24, 1920. The cardinal did not travel through inner Syria because of the unresolved political situation.[40]

39. Cardinal Bourne and Cardinal Giustini's missions were essentially directed toward Palestine.

40. Dominique Trimbur, "Une appropriation française du Levant: La mission en Orient du cardinal Dubois, 1919–1920," in *Une France en Méditerranée: écoles, langue et culture françaises, XIXe–XXe siècles*, ed. Patrick Cabanel (Paris: Créaphis, 2006), 115.

In a conference given after returning from his trip, Dubois expressed his state of mind on the eve of his departure. "For this crusade of a new kind [he said] we were going to bring together, during three months and a half, our prayers, our goodwill, our patriotism, our efforts—and also our hopes."[41] In the same breath, he mentioned prayers and patriotism, church and homeland. The question worth asking is how Cardinal Dubois understood patriotism.

Pope Benedict would have agreed with political theorists who contend that nationalism and patriotism "undermine human flourishing by prioritizing the unstable, abstract notion of the 'compatriot' over the concrete reality of the 'neighbor.'"[42] Likewise, he would have endorsed Viroli's position that "nationalism is not to be confused with patriotism," as "a particular place and a particular way of life which one believes to be the best in the world but has no wish to force upon other people."[43] If we follow Viroli's definition, we can argue that although Cardinal Dubois may have been genuinely patriotic-minded, the French government had a clear nationalistic goal that was embodied by Dubois.

Benedict XV's groundbreaking apostolic letter on missions, *Maximum Illud*, had been published a few months earlier, urging clergy members to put the interests of the church before those of one's country. One can assume that Cardinal Dubois was establishing a distinction between patriotism and nationalism, but he did not express it plainly and found himself in a quandary over his primary allegiance.

41. "Pour cette croisade d'un nouveau genre, nous allions mettre en commun, pendant trois mois et demi, nos prières, notre bonne volonté, notre patriotisme, nos efforts—et aussi nos espérances"; Une mission en Orient, Conférence faite à la société normande de géographie, le 28 mai 1920, par son Éminence le Cardinal Dubois, archevêque de Rouen, Rouen, 1920, 7, quoted in Trimbur, "Appropriation française du Levant," 115 (my translation).

42. Stephen Backhouse, *Kierkegaard's Critique of Christian Nationalism* (Oxford: Oxford University Press, 2011), 2.

43. Maurizio Viroli, *For Love of Country: An Essay on Patriotism and Nationalism* (Oxford: Oxford University Press, 1995), 3.

The French government was eager, with Cardinal Dubois's compliance, to associate in Arab minds France and Catholicism, perpetuating the prewar model founded on the French Catholic protectorate. Father Lobry, a Lazarist who escorted Dubois on his trip, clearly stated that the French cardinal was traveling in the Orient in the name of his native country. In lands where religion was not distinct from nationality, Lobry claimed that Cardinal Dubois would emerge from his trip as both a great representative of France and a much-respected religious leader.[44]

Pope Benedict, whose immediate goal was to reestablish diplomatic ties with Paris, did not interfere. Cardinal Dubois was one of three cardinals who had traveled in the Middle East in those immediate postwar years. Benedict was especially satisfied with Cardinal Bourne's visit of Palestine. Dubois's journey was seen by the Holy See as almost anecdotal. While in Beirut, the French cardinal complained to Giannini about the cold reception he had received in Lebanon. In a memo of February 26, 1920, Giannini bluntly exposed why, considering the French tradition in Syria, the French mission did not receive the welcome it expected in Beirut, a reception less friendly than in Palestine or Egypt. He accused the French government of pursuing a timid diplomacy that was overshadowed by the British and that favored the Muslim population of Syria and Lebanon.

The behavior of Colonel de Piedpape[45] [wrote Giannini], although a Christian, clearly gave the impression that France was above all...a Muslim power. His visit to the great mosque, his attitude that ignores the work of Catholic missionaries, his project of neutral schools in Lebanon have already produced a profound uneasiness.[46]

44. Annales de la Congrégation de la Mission, 85:217–63—Asie, Syrie, Journal de M. Lobry, Mission de S. Em. le Cardinal Dubois en Orient, 221, quoted in Trimbur, "Appropriation française du Levant," 116.

45. The first French troops landed in Lebanon on October 24, 1918, under Major de Piedpape's commandment.

46. "L'attitude du Colonel de Piedpape, un chrétien cependant, a donné nettement l'impression que la France était surtout...une puissance musulmane. Sa visite à la grande

He concluded ominously that the pan-Islamic peril was not a myth anymore. Only a strong France protecting Catholic rights and interests could reverse the trend.[47] At the end of 1919 under Clemenceau's government, France, a colonial power with strong interests in Muslim countries—among them Morocco and Algeria—was leading a dual diplomacy to assuage the risk of Muslim outbursts in its colonies while satisfying its Catholic population in the *Métropole* and preparing for a resumption of its diplomatic ties with the Holy See.

The reaction of the apostolic delegate to Cardinal Dubois's complaints highlights the gap existing between Pope Benedict's global vision of emancipation from colonial ties and Giannini's practical reasoning, which favors a natural return to a prewar model. Giannini was not able to think in other terms than those resulting from passé imperialist and colonial paradigms. Pope Benedict had the advantage of being far removed from the direct center of action in Syria and therefore was able not only to design a long-term policy but also to demonstrate his quality as a global thinker and visionary whose strategy seemed counterintuitive but recognizant of the end of an epoch, with its old-fashioned protectorates.

A CHRISTIAN STATE: GREATER LEBANON

Catholic Maronites and the Confessional State

In order to weaken Arab nationalism in Syria, France applied the principle of "divide and rule."[48] General Gouraud, the newly appointed high commissioner, divided the territory of Syria under mandate into six states: the states of Damascus and Aleppo (1920),

---

mosquée, sa manière d'ignorer l'œuvre des missionnaires catholiques, son projet d'écoles neutres dans le Liban ont produit un malaise déjà profond"; Giannini to Cardinal Dubois, Feb. 26, 1920, ASV, AES Stati Ecclesiastici, 1916–22, pos. 1418, fasc. 565 (my translation).

47. Ibid.

48. William L. Cleveland and Martin P. Bunton, *A History of the Modern Middle East* (Boulder, Colo.: Westview Press, 2009), 218.

the Alawite (1920) and Jabal Druse (1921) states, the autonomous Sanjak of Alexandretta (1921), and the state of Greater Lebanon established on September 1, 1920.[49] To make the latter economically viable, the coastal cities of Beirut, Sidon, Tyre, and Tripoli, as well as the Bekaa Valley and the regions of South Lebanon, were added to the predominantly Christian *mutasarrifiyyah* of Mount Lebanon, a governorate that had been created in 1861.[50] Those newly added cities were predominantly Sunni Muslim except for Beirut, the capital, which had a population evenly mixed between Christians and Muslims. Meanwhile, the Bekaa Valley and the southern area were Shiite Muslim, tipping the religious scales against the once majority Christian population. The prewar administrative district (*sanjak*) of Mount Lebanon was 76 percent Christian and 24 percent Druse.[51] In 1920, Greater Lebanon was the home of Christian and Muslim sects that were all minorities. The Maronites and other Christians represented 58 percent of the population. The Maronites, once representing 54 percent of all Christians, were now the largest minority group, barely reaching the 30 percent mark.[52] This redistribution in favor of the Muslim population was accelerated by the exodus of an estimated 100,000 Christian Lebanese, who between 1900 and 1914 had left Mount Lebanon for Egypt and the Americas, leaving behind them a territory that at that time was too small and economically not viable.[53]

49. The reference work on the history of Lebanon remains Edmond Rabbath's *Essai de synthèse*, which analyzes "le phénomène communautaire"; Rabbath, *La formation historique du Liban politique et constitutionnel: Essai de synthèse* (Beirut: Librairie orientale, 1973).
50. The Règlement organique for Mount Lebanon was signed on June 9, 1861. It stipulated that the *mutasarrifiyyah* would be administered by a Christian governor appointed by Constantinople.
51. Eugene Rogan, *The Arabs: A History* (New York: Basic Books, 2009), 216. The Druses are members of a religious sect that descends from the Shiite branch of Islam in Egypt. The split occurred in the eleventh century.
52. Cleveland and Bunton, *History of the Modern Middle East*, 225; see also William W. Harris, *The New Face of Lebanon: History's Revenge* (Princeton, N.J.: Markus Wiener, 2005), 42, and Gérard Khoury, *La France et l'Orient arabe: Naissance du Liban moderne (1914–1920)* (Paris: Armand Colin, 1993).
53. Rogan, *Arabs*, 212.

The history of the Maronites goes back to the fifth century and the person of St. Maroon, the first patriarch of the Maronite Church. Originally settled in Northern Syria, they fled to the Lebanese mountains during the Islamic conquest of the seventh century. The Crusades of the late eleventh century were a turning point that opened the community to the French crusaders and the Holy See. Since then, the Maronite Church has boasted of its unbroken ties with the papacy and of being the only Eastern Catholic Church without an Orthodox counterpart. It entered into full union with Rome in 1736, retaining its own Syriac liturgy.

The Maronites also enjoyed a close cultural and political relationship with France. In 1860, after the massacre of Maronites by the Druses, France, as the protector of the Christians in the Ottoman Empire, had sent troops to rescue them. An international agreement followed that made the sanjak of Mount Lebanon independent and governed by a non-Lebanese Christian appointed by the sultan with the approval of the Western powers. As a result, Lebanon became exclusively associated with the Maronites, converting their church into a supporter of Lebanese nationalism.[54]

With the advent of Greater Lebanon on September 1, 1920, the relation between France and the new state did not go without some inconsistencies from the perspective of French international politics. Although the French government had supported Maronite claims in favor of an independent confessional state, it also gave proof of its goodwill to the Muslim constituency of Syria in order to satisfy their coreligionists in the French empire of North Africa. Thus, the French reinforced their ties with the Muslim minorities of Lebanon and Syria. This new Muslim

---

54. Laura Zitrain Eisenberg, *My Enemy's Enemy: Lebanon in the Early Zionist Imagination, 1900–1948* (Detroit, Mich.: Wayne State University Press, 1994), 47; see also Hakim, *Origins of the Lebanese National Idea*.

policy was also an answer to the new demographic realities that showed a growth of the Muslim population in territories under French mandate combined with a decrease of the Christian communities.[55] Conversely, in Greater Lebanon, disregarding the demographic data, France gave the Maronites disproportionate representation in the new governing body. Ten members represented the Christian population, while only four Sunni Muslims, two Shiite Muslims, and one Druse represented the other confessions.[56]

The bastion of French influence, the new state of Greater Lebanon (although a creation with no historical boundaries) became the national home that most Maronites were longing for. Lebanon had always been more attuned to European culture than the rest of Syria. Most Maronites, although of Arabic descent, were more attracted to French culture than to their own. Robert de Caix repeated in a letter to the Quai d'Orsay what a young Maronite from Beirut had told him:

A century ago, everyone in the [Lebanese] mountains spoke Syriac and this was the national language of my grandfather; the Arabic language, it is the tongue of the conqueror; I rather speak French.[57]

Some Maronites even wanted the French language to become the official language of Greater Lebanon.

In 1919, the Maronite patriarch Huayek, endowed with both spiritual and temporal power, made the trip to the Paris Peace Conference to reassert the historical connection between the Lebanese people and France. He opposed them to the non-Christian populations of Greater Syria, supporters of Prince Faisal, stressing that

55. Vincent Cloarec, *La France et la question de Syrie, 1914–1918* (Paris: CNRS, 1998), 39.
56. Rogan, *Arabs*, 217.
57. "Toute la montagne parlait syriaque il y a encore un siècle et c'était la langue nationale de mon grand-père; l'arabe, c'est la langue du conquérant; j'aime autant parler le français"; quoted in Gérard Khoury, *Tutelle coloniale*, 315 (my translation).

a sedentary people, prolific, civilized, able to direct its own domestic affairs, and able to develop in the future its progress and enrichment, should not be compelled to work under the suzerainty and for the benefit of wandering and poor populations, or populations who are idle, uncultivated and without traditions.[58]

Patriarch Huayek had strong patriotic beliefs that he expressed through communiqués to the Maronite faithful. His most debated topics were the Maronite union with Catholicism, patriotism, and education.[59] He interpreted patriotism as a way to express his religion through the love of his nation. The Maronite Catholic identity served as the link with both France and the Holy See, transforming the confessional identity into a national one. The patriarch was fully supported by the Holy See. The creation of Greater Lebanon was clearly the victory of Huyaek and the religious element over secular Lebanon.

Although it may seem to be common sense, few Maronites realized the incompatibility between Christian Lebanon and Greater Lebanon. Few had taken the measure of the demographic change that had occurred in the transition from Mount Lebanon to Greater Lebanon. The Christians and the Druses were the only communities to have suffered "both proportionate and absolute decline."[60] Huyaek was warned by Robert de Caix that "the Christians' 'megalomania' would sow the seeds of disintegration for the state they were trying to create,"[61] to no avail.

Patriarch Huyaek was well respected and loved. During the

58. "Un peuple sédentaire, prolifique, civilisé, en mesure déjà de diriger ses propres affaires intérieures, et capable de développer dans l'avenir son progrès et son enrichissement, ne saurait être contraint à travailler sous la suzeraineté et pour le bénéfice de populations errantes et pauvres, ou bien oisives, incultes et sans traditions"; *Pro-Memoria* prepared by Maronite Patriarch Huayek, attached to letter from Giannini to Gasparri, June 2, 1919, ASV, AES Austria, 1919, pos. 1304, fasc. 516 (my translation).

59. Asher Kaufman, *Reviving Phoenicia: In Search of Identity in Lebanon* (New York: I. B. Tauris, 2004), 38.

60. William W. Harris, *Lebanon: A History, 600–2011* (New York: Oxford University Press, 2012), 178.

61. Eisenberg, *My Enemy's Enemy*, 48.

war, he had suffered physically and morally under the rule of Djemal Pasha, the Ottoman commander of Syria, a trauma that necessitated a long time of recuperation. His semi-retreat left a vacuum in the Maronite Church that weakened it at a crucial time. This void opened an opportunity for the Holy See to intensify its involvement in the affairs of the Maronite Church, an instance of Pope Benedict's resolve to strengthen the relations between the Roman and Eastern Catholics. Consequently, the apostolic delegate Giannini strengthened his already existing friendship with the patriarchal vicar, Bishop Abdallah al-Khuri, supporting his efforts to take over the Maronite patriarchate.[62] Al-Khuri, a dominant force in Lebanese politics, was a friend to look after.

The creation of Greater Lebanon, although under a mostly Christian governing body, gave the French the power to establish a new religious legislation that would satisfy equally Christians and Muslims. It was Pope Benedict's main concern to see that the Catholics would not lose their old civil and religious privileges. In April 1921, Giannini forwarded to Gasparri a *pro-memoria* he had prepared upon the request of General Gouraud regarding the new legislation in civil and religious matters that would affect the Catholic communities.[63] In civil matters, Giannini asked Gouraud to grant the Catholic clergy and religious institutions the same privileges and exemptions they enjoyed before the war. In religious matters, he asked the high commissioner to ensure that religious freedom would be recognized for all communities. It concretely meant freedom from governmental encroachment in matters like recruitment of secular and religious clergy.

62. Meir Zamir, *Lebanon's Quest: The Road to Statehood, 1926–1939* (London: I. B. Tauris, 2000), 43.

63. Giannini to Gasparri, Apr. 19, 1921, ASV, AES Stati Ecclesiastici, 1916–22, pos. 1418, fasc. 566.

The Holy See, France, and
Protestant Propaganda

The growth of the Muslim population in Syria and Lebanon was not the only challenge encountered by Catholic authorities. American Protestant propaganda, sometimes fueled by French authorities, was a major competitor to Catholic presence in Greater Lebanon. Catholic missions were hard-pressed to efficiently fight the proselytism of American missionaries, lacking the financial means to be successful.

American Protestantism had a long history in Lebanon. In 1823, when the first American Presbyterian missionaries landed on its shores, the Maronite patriarch was outraged. The Presbyterians had come to the Ottoman Empire to rescue its inhabitants from eternal damnation—that is, to fight both Islam and Catholicism. In 1847, the Ottoman government authorized the Protestants to have their own *millet*, therefore being legalized under British consular protection. But it was the establishment of the Syrian Protestant College in Beirut in 1866—it changed its name to American University of Beirut in 1920—that confirmed the ascendancy of Protestant missionaries in Lebanon and the Ottoman Empire and opened Catholic eyes to the need to react to this organized and powerful competition.[64] After being officially suppressed by Pope Clement XIV in 1773,[65] the Jesuits returned to Lebanon in 1831, the Holy See's answer to American Protestant proselytizing in geographical Syria. St. Joseph University opened in Beirut in 1875 under Jesuit patronage, a response to the Syrian Protestant College. Consequently, Beirut became the intellectual center of Syria.

64. Charles A. Frazee, *Catholics and Sultans: The Church and the Ottoman Empire (1453–1923)* (Cambridge: Cambridge University Press, 1983), 276 and 282.

65. Clément XIV, "Brief *Dominus ac Redemptor* [July 21, 1773]," Bref de N.S.P. le Pape Clément XIV en date du 21 Juillet 1773 portant suppression de l'Ordre régulier dit Société de Jésus.

It is worth mentioning that the literature about the Ottoman Empire and the newly emerging Middle East almost reluctantly acknowledged the role of Catholic missions and their influence in education. George Antonius, in his seminal book *The Arab Awakening*, recognized the influence of Catholic missions and schools in the late nineteenth-century Ottoman Empire but saw them as a pale imitator of Protestant schools. Although recent historians have reversed Antonius's interpretation, most of the time they dismiss the role the missions played in the cultural and religious development of the populations of the empire.[66] This is an odd omission in the view of the actual contribution of French religious orders in Syria, especially the Jesuits. They maintained schools, a seminary, and St. Joseph University in Beirut.[67] Their reputation was such that they were able to lobby at the Paris Peace Conference in favor of a French mandate in Syria and Lebanon. They were especially vindicated after General Gouraud was appointed high commissioner of Syria and Lebanon. A devout Catholic, he was also the brother of a Jesuit.[68] Jesuits were especially active in the field of education, offering a high-quality education to the cultured families from Lebanon.

The Protestant competition was fierce. Giannini complained to Gasparri and Admiral Mornet, the head of the Syrian division of the French navy, that it was evident that the Protestants were launching an anti-French propaganda. It was quite understandable, Giannini noted, as "in Syria, France and Catholicism have been synonyms for centuries."[69]

He protested against a religious propaganda funded in part

66. Elizabeth Thompson, "Neither Conspiracy nor Hypocrisy: The Jesuits and the French Mandate in Syria and Lebanon," in *Altruism and Imperialism: Western Cultural and Religious Missions in the Middle East*, ed. Eleanor H. Tejirian and Reeva Spector Simon, 67 (New York: Middle East Institute, Columbia University, 2002).

67. Stephen Hemsley Longrigg, *Syria and Lebanon under French Mandate* (New York: Octagon, 1972), 43.

68. Thompson, "Neither Conspiracy nor Hypocrisy," 74.

69. Giannini to Gasparri, Mar. 23, 1920, AP, N.S., vol. 755 (1922), rub. 126.

by American Catholics, unaware that their contribution was helping Protestant proselytizing. In addition, France, which was keen to associate itself with Catholicism in order to keep its prestige in Greater Lebanon intact, was oddly promoting Protestant activities in Syria by granting their agents the administration of French charities. Giannini also lamented the choice of a lay Protestant, "a violent man under a pleasing appearence," as director of public instruction.[70]

Pope Benedict was closely monitoring the Protestant activities in the Middle East, as they were directly affecting his Oriental policy of strengthening ties with the Catholic Eastern churches and rapprochement with the separated brethren. Launching a "second spring of the Eastern Church,"[71] his most visible and applauded decision in this matter was his naming St. Ephrem, the Syrian deacon and patriarch of the ancient Syriac Church, doctor of the church. As Sidney Griffith, puts it:

Of all the writers of the Syriac-speaking churches in the patristic period, it is undoubtedly Ephraem, the deacon of Nisibis and Edessa, whose name is the most immediately recognized today among those who treasure the thought of the teachers of the east in the formative centuries of Christian thought. His lifetime spanned the first three quarters of the fourth century, arguably one of the most significant periods in the formulation of the classic statements of orthodox doctrine.[72]

Pope Benedict recognized in St. Ephrem a theologian, a musician, and a poet, a man so outstanding that he was hailed the "lyre of the Holy Spirit."[73] His music and poetry united Catholics of different rites. The Maronite Church's prayers and musical

70. Ibid.

71. J. Gorayeb, SJ, "St. Ephrem, The New Doctor of the Universal Church," *Catholic Historical Review* 7 (Oct. 1921): 303–15.

72. Sidney H. Griffith, *"Faith Adoring the Mystery": Reading the Bible with St. Ephraem the Syrian*, Père Marquette Lecture in Theology 1997 (Milwaukee, Wisc.: Marquette University Press, 1997), 1.

73. Benedict XV, "Encyclical Letter *Principi Apostolorum Petro* [Oct. 5, 1920]," On St. Ephrem the Syrian. *AAS* 12 (1920): 463.

traditions were greatly influenced by St. Ephrem's poetry and music. Therefore, his becoming the first doctor of the church among the Eastern Catholic saints was interpreted by the Maronites as a clear sign of Pope Benedict's esteem and protection of their community.

What Pope Benedict could not do in the political realm, he accomplished in the spiritual sphere. Naming St. Ephrem doctor of the church was not only a sign of his resolve to work toward the unity of the church but also a way to recognize the role of the Roman Catholic Church in the Middle East since the time of early Christianity.

The question of the future and the protection of Catholic communities in Syria and Lebanon in the view of a growing Muslim population was paralleled in neighboring Palestine with the question of what effect the new Jewish home would have on the welfare of Catholics in the Holy Land. Two emerging nationalisms, Arab and Jewish, were fighting in the area that would affect the Christians population and further its demographic plummeting.

8

THE HOLY SEE AND

PALESTINE

WHO SHALL CONTROL PALESTINE?

The Significance of Palestine

In an article published in the Jesuit review *Études* in September 1921, Father Joseph Huby argued that the Palestinian question was not an issue of colonial politics between Britain and France but rather, quoting the distinguished Belgian orientalist Father Henri Lammens, "an ecumenical question."[1] Actually, it was both.

Palestine, the historical Holy Land, which for the purpose of this study corresponds to the territory that stretches from the Mediterranean Sea to the Jordan River, south of mandatory Syria, lived under Muslim Ottoman rule from its conquest in 1516 until its capture by British troops in December 1917.[2] It was of little economic and political interest to the Ottoman government, as the land was underdeveloped and not extensively settled.

On the eve of the Great War, Palestine was home to Muslim,

---

1. Joseph Huby, "Le problème juif," *Études* (Sept. 1921): 520. The heading, "Who shall control Palestine?," is from Doreen Ingrams, *Palestine Papers, 1917–1922: Seeds of Conflict* (London: John Murray, 1972), 36.

2. Originally, the British mandate over Palestine encompassed today's Jordan, Israel, and the West Bank. In 1923, the British divided mandatory Palestine into two distinct administrative units: Palestine, west of the Jordan River, and Trans-Jordan, east of the Jordan River.

Christian, and Jewish communities that amounted to 700,000 Arabs, both Muslim and Christian, and 85,000 Jews, most of them living in Jerusalem and its surroundings. The majority of the Jewish population had Ottoman citizenship. Among the Arabs, the great majority was Sunni Muslim. Only about 16 percent were Christian Arabs, concentrated in Jerusalem, Bethlehem, Jaffa, Nazareth, and Haifa.[3] Those Christians were overwhelmingly Greek and Armenian Orthodox. The Latin rite Catholics numbered about 20,000 in 1914.[4]

For centuries, the city of Jerusalem, the heart of the Holy Land, has held a special place in the hearts and minds of those living in Palestine, which has always been the source of strong religious sentiments and manifestations. To Muslims, it is one of the three holy cities of Islam, along with Mecca and Medina. It is the city where, according to Muslim tradition, Mohammed ascended to heaven. To the Jewish people, it is the holiest city, going back to Abraham, the father of Judaism, whose obedience was tested by God on Mount Moriah, the site where stood the Temple Mount at the heart of the Old City.[5] As for the Christians, Jerusalem is directly associated with the life of Jesus who ministered, suffered death, and was resurrected in the Holy City.

It is the conflictual relationship among the three monotheistic faiths—Judaism, Christianity, and Islam—that gave to the Pales-

---

3. See Neville J. Mandel, *Arabs and Zionism Before World War I* (Berkeley, Calif.: University of California Press, 1977), xxi; Tom Segev, *One Palestine Complete: Jews and Arabs under the British Mandate* (New York: Henry Holt, 2000), 22; David K. Fieldhouse, *Western Imperialism in the Middle East, 1914–1958* (Oxford: Oxford University Press, 2006), 123.

4. Francis M. Perko, "Toward a 'Sound and Lasting Basis': Relations between the Holy See, the Zionist Movement, and Israel, 1896–1996," *Israel Studies* 2 (Spring 1997): 3; see also Justin McCarthy, *The Population of Palestine: Population History and Statistics of the Late Ottoman Period and the Mandate* (New York: Columbia University Press, 1990). A report presented by Fr. Robinson to the Holy See in May 1921 put this number at 14,000; ACCO, rub. 19/10, fol. 5663, May 9, 1921. The discrepancy is due to the lack of reliable sources.

5. See Gn 22:2 (NASB): "He said, 'Take now your son, your only son, whom you love, Isaac, and go to the land of Moriah, and offer him there as a burnt offering on one of the mountains of which I will tell you.'"

tinian question its ecumenical dimension. A novel interest of the Great Powers—Britain, France, and Russia—for the Holy Land developed in the 1830s, adding a new political and geostrategic level of involvement intimately tied to the religious element. Each nation expanded its influence through the protection of religious minorities, supporting the missionary activities of its citizens.[6]

Russia, the unofficial protector of Greek Orthodox populations, was using the protectorate to put a foot in Palestine and eventually gain preeminence and political presence there. But with the outbreak of the Bolshevik Revolution in October 1917, the Russian threat to French and British interests in the region faded away. The destruction of the Russian Empire and the collateral weakening of its church drove Russia out of Palestine and threw the Greek Orthodox communities into confusion.[7]

At the end of the war, France and Britain, the two major victorious colonial powers, were left facing each other in Palestine. The role and influence of wartime allies like Italy were real but politically minor. The Holy Land had become the *chasse gardée* of the British, the "strategic bulwark of Egypt," a situation dictated by geopolitical realities.[8] But Palestine's future was not to be determined by geopolitical and colonial rationale only. A British official commented in the early 1920s that "Palestine for most of us was an emotion rather than a reality,"[9] which explained, in

---

6. Alexander Scholch, "Britain in Palestine, 1838–1882: The Roots of the Balfour Policy," *Journal of Palestine Studies* 22 (Autumn 1992): 40.

7. See chapter 3 regarding the role of the prewar Russian protectorate over the Orthodox communities of the Ottoman Empire.

8. Palestine became the "indispensable geo-political link between Mesopotamia and Egypt." As Friedman explains, "The more firmly entrenched the British position in Egypt (since 1882) the deeper grew the estrangement from Turkey in the prewar period, the more compelling became the need to change British policy. In contrast to the nineteenth century, it was now Egypt, not the Ottoman Empire that required British protection. Henceforth, the urge to widen the *cordon sanitaire* off the Suez Canal zone became almost irresistible"; Isaiah Friedman, *The Question of Palestine, 1914–1918: British-Jewish-Arab Relations* (New York: Schocken Books, 1973), 1–2.

9. C. R. Ashbee, *Palestine Notebook, 1918–1923* (London: Heinemann, 1923), 276.

part, that Britain consolidated its role as protector of the Protestant communities and expanded it to the Jewish people under
the chiliastic concept of restoration of the Jews.[10] British and Zionist aspirations became closely interrelated in the Holy Land.

As for France, Palestine was the land where it had the most
significant religious responsibility. In addition to the long-
privileged tradition of protecting the Latin and Eastern Catholic
populations, the French, as chief representatives of Catholicism,
held a special position in the protection of the Holy Places of
Palestine. With the liberation of the land by Christian troops,
this protectorate had no more reason to exist.[11] Nevertheless,
the French were adamant and kept their colonial aspirations
alive. Ronald Storrs, the British military governor of Jerusalem,
recalled a conversation he had with François Georges-Picot,
the French high commissioner, who with some grandiloquence
justified French interest in postwar Palestine, commenting that
"C'était dans leur sang—plus fort qu'eux mêmes (sic)'—and would
have to be reckoned with."[12]

The Holy See's interest over Palestine is unique and prior to
the war was closely tied to France's policy in the region. Rome's
main diplomatic concern had always been the protection of the
Holy Places and of the Latin and Eastern Catholic communities
in the Holy Land. This had been the task of the French since the
sixteenth century. A Copernican change, with tremendous consequences for the Holy See's influence in the region, occurred
on December 9, 1917, with the capture of Jerusalem by British
troops led by General Allenby. The Holy See's diplomatic role
took a sharp turn as the papacy became a direct interlocutor in
the Palestinian question. The time was ripe for Benedict XV to

10. Scholch, "Britain in Palestine," 40.
11. See chapter 2 for a discussion regarding the Catholic French protectorate in the
prewar Ottoman Empire. The main Christian Holy Places in the Holy Land are situated
in Jerusalem, Bethlehem, and Nazareth.
12. Ronald Storrs, *Orientations* (London: Nicholson and Watson, 1945), 279.

contemplate the emancipation of the Holy See from French colonial politics, a simultaneous policy in Palestine and Syria, and
reshape its past diplomacy, now putting the British factor at the
core. In this new context, he embraced the Palestinian question
and developed an independent and state-like diplomacy that addressed its political and interreligious aspects.

The Control of Palestine:
Benedict XV's Assessment

The fall of Jerusalem was hailed by the Holy See with great
rejoicing. After centuries of Muslim domination, Palestine had
returned into the hands of Christianity. While in Rome, the bells
of St. Peter's Basilica remained silent in accordance with the pontiff's vow of impartiality in the conflict, a *Te Deum* was sung in the
Church of Santa Croce in Jerusalem.[13] A unique opportunity was
laid at Pope Benedict's feet to increase the influence of Catholicism in Palestine, claiming a direct role in the administration
and the future of Jerusalem and the Holy Places. The peace conference did not meet until a year after the fall of the Holy City,
in January 1919, leaving the final status of Palestine, and specifically Jerusalem, officially undecided during this critical period.
Although an occasion for the pontiff to affirm the power of the
Holy See, any error of appreciation or wrong anticipation of the
diplomatic situation by Pope Benedict would have long-lasting
negative effects on the life and future of Catholicism in Palestine. Rarely in history had decisions been so crucial.

The main concerns for many popes prior to Benedict XV had
been to ensure the protection of Catholic *dhimmis*, regrouped in
millets, and to maintain Catholic influence in the administration
of the Holy Places, most of which were under Catholic and Or-

13. Thomas E. Hachey, ed., *Great Britain Legation: Anglo-Vatican Relations, 1914–1939;*
Confidential Annual Reports of the British Ministers to the Holy See (London and Boston:
G. K. Hall, 1972), 20.

thodox guardianship. Conversely, Pope Benedict faced a totally new and exciting situation. First, Palestine was back in Christian hands for the first time in seven hundred years. Second, Moscow, which had claimed the title of "Third Rome," had withdrawn from world politics in the wake of the Bolshevik Revolution, leaving the Orthodox churches, which had been under Russian protection for centuries, in disarray. For an unprecedented situation, Pope Benedict had to offer an unprecedented response.

The foundational questions facing the pontiff were: Who should control Palestine in order to fully answer Rome's claims over the Holy Places? And how would the Holy See be affected by the final outcome? Both the Arabs under the leadership of Prince Faisal and the Zionists led by Chaim Weizmann had expectations of dominion over the Holy Land in accordance with British wartime promises. Arabism and Zionism had emerged at the same time, both stimulated by repression, one by the policy of the Young Turks in the Ottoman Empire, the other by the Russian pogroms against the Jewish population.[14]

On December 5, 1918, during a meeting of the British Eastern Committee, Lord Curzon summed up the available options concerning the future administration of the Holy Land.[15] Palestine had been conquered by Britain, stressed Curzon, with a "very insignificant aide from small French and Italian contingents,"[16] and was since then administered by the British, a statement that signified the British rebuff to any request from Paris regarding French administration of the Holy Land. The committee was also opposed to the institution of an international administration but favored Great Britain or the United States as potential

14. Albert Hourani, *Syria and Lebanon: A Political Essay* (Oxford: Oxford University Press, 1946), 106.

15. Lord Curzon (1859–1925), a shrewd analyst of foreign policy, joined the British War Cabinet in 1916 as lord president of the Council. He became British foreign secretary in 1919.

16. Ingrams, *Palestine Papers*, 48.

mandatory powers. However, the thought of an American mandate over Palestine, although attractive to many, was quickly dropped.[17]

The administration of the Holy Land was a decisive matter for the future of Catholicism. In an allocution delivered at the secret consistory of March 10, 1919, about the future of Palestine and the Holy Places, the pontiff deliberately omitted mentioning France, the centuries-long protector of Catholic interests in the Holy Land.[18] This omission was noticed by the French and the English-language press and can be explained by the pope's resolve to conciliate two complementary diplomatic goals.[19] On one hand, Benedict XV anticipated the assignment of the Palestine mandate to the British and consequently adopted a prudent wait-and-see policy regarding the future of the French protectorate. From this perspective, the omission was a signal sent to the British that the Holy See intended to have a say in Palestinian affairs without any French interference; but it was also a message to the French that Rome was keeping its options open in the Holy Land, inciting Paris to reconsider the state of its severed diplomatic relations with the Holy See. However, that Pope Benedict took for granted a future British mandate did not mean that he was satisfied with this outcome or that he had definitely relinquished any support from the French in the sensitive subject of the guardianship of the Holy Places.

In June 1919, Duke Tommaso Gallarati Scotti, an Italian writer, went on a mission to Paris on behalf of the Italian government.[20] His report, the result of unofficial encounters with prominent French Catholics like the poet-diplomat Paul Claudel, sheds light

17. Ibid., 51.

18. Benedict XV, "Consistorial Allocution *Antequam Ordinem* [Mar. 10, 1919]," *AAS* 11 (1919): 97–101.

19. "Vatican Anxious to Conciliate France," *New York Times*, Mar. 18, 1919, 2.

20. Tommaso Gallarati Scotti, an influential Italian Catholic writer, became ambassador to England and Spain after World War II.

on how Pope Benedict's response to the prospect of a British mandate and its Zionist corollary was interpreted at the time.[21] According to Gallarati Scotti's interlocutors, "the future government of Palestine was not a major concern of the papacy,"[22] as the Holy See was mostly interested in resuming diplomatic relations with France and assuring a seat at the newly founded League of Nations, a mission entrusted to Msgr. Cerretti.

Although there is no reason to doubt the claims made by Gallarati Scotti's French interlocutors, the rationale behind the pope's position needs further examination. Assuming that one of Benedict's main diplomatic goals was to secure a seat at the League of Nations, it would then be logical that the pontiff would not react directly, either in favor of or against a British mandate. He would be expected to shift the diplomatic debate from bilateral talks to the new multilateral setting of the league, which Benedict envisioned as a universal body entrusted with the monitoring of the future French and British mandates and a place where the Holy See could benefit from the support of other Catholic nations.

Two facts contradict, or at least weaken, the likelihood of this scenario. First, as discussed earlier,[23] there is no solid evidence that Pope Benedict was eyeing a seat at the League of Nations, as he became quickly disenchanted with its failure to lay down solid foundations to secure world peace and collective security. As Sir Alec Randall, the British second secretary to the Holy See, noted in his book *Vatican Assignment*, "The Holy See, . . . when the war was over, showed no sign of wishing to join the League of Nations and, as regards the peace treaties, merely tried to ensure, by unofficial contacts, that the religious rights of the Church and the Holy See were safeguarded as far as possible."[24]

21. Frank E. Manuel, "The Palestine Question in Italian Diplomacy, 1917–1920," *Journal of Modern History* 27 (Sept. 1955): 278.

22. Ibid., 279.

23. See chapter 6, "The Holy See and the Postwar World Order."

24. Alec Randall, *Vatican Assignment* (London: Heinemann, 1956), 127.

Second, the assumption that Pope Benedict was not concerned with the future administration of Palestine because he trusted that England would protect Catholic communities and preserve the custodianship of the sanctuaries, in accordance with their historic rights, does not stand.[25] The words of the pontiff, pronounced in his allocution to the consistory, highlight it.

Pope Benedict worried:

[I]t would be...a bitter grief if unbelievers in Palestine were put in a superior or more privileged position, still more so if the august monuments of the Christian religion were assigned to those who were not Christians. We know, furthermore, that non-Catholic foreigners endowed with ample means are taking advantage of the unspeakable misery and ruin produced by the war to disseminate their own doctrines. It is unbearable that so many souls, losing the Catholic faith, should go to perdition there in the very place where our Lord Jesus Christ won for them eternal salvation.[26]

In this stern statement, Pope Benedict was accusing Britain of favoring the new Jewish settlers as well as the wealthy Protestant missions. This declaration clearly contradicts Gallarati Scotti's conjecture that the future government of Palestine was not a source of concern to Pope Benedict. Although it could be argued with Sergio Minerbi that, in 1917 and early 1918, "it was not clear [to anyone] whether Palestine should be internationalized, be placed under an Anglo-French condominium, or come under exclusive British control,"[27] by the time of the papal allocution of March 1919, the situation was settled in the public arena, though still unofficially, in favor of the British.

Pope Benedict did foresee the benefits that the Holy See could gain in the long run from British rule over Palestine, with the

25. Manuel, "Palestine Question," 279.

26. Benedict XV, *Antequam Ordinem*, quoted and translated in *The Times* (London), "Pope and the Holy Places: Appeal to Peace Conference," Mar. 12, 1919, 9.

27. Sergio I. Minerbi, *The Vatican and Zionism: Conflict in the Holy Land, 1895–1925* (Oxford: Oxford University Press, 1990), 15.

unique opportunity for the Holy See to seize its independence from France, a policy simultaneously enforced in other areas of the emerging Middle East. However, Pope Benedict was not naive and knew that British rule also meant the advance of Zionist and Protestant influence in the Holy Land. The pontiff chose to support a scenario that was not ideal but gave the Holy See a new freedom that would have many opportunities to bear fruit in the future.

The consternation of prominent clergy members at Pope Benedict's apparent naivety was shortsighted. Benedict was shaping his diplomacy for the decades to come, enhancing the Holy See's ability to respond to any new and unexpected situation with the most ammunition. Cardinal Amette, archbishop of Paris, visited the Vatican in March 1919 and expressed his concern to the pontiff regarding the political and religious conditions in Palestine. He also met with Gallarati Scotti in Paris. The cardinal's judgment conflicted with the pontiff's appreciation of the situation. One day after the occupation of Jerusalem by General Allenby's troops, the British foreign minister Lord Balfour instructed Count de Salis to make sure that the Holy See receive formal assurance that order would be kept at the Holy Places in Jerusalem,[28] which assurance in no way meant that the influence of the Catholic Church would be maintained or enhanced. The archbishop argued that British guarantees had no long-term value. Amette rightly foresaw a Protestant offensive meant to weaken the moral influence of Catholicism in the Holy Land and abate its historical rights in the custodianship of the Holy Places.[29] His concerns were legitimate and shared by the pontiff, but Benedict knew that the Holy See's diplomatic prestige, although greatly enhanced since the end of the war, was not sufficient to conclusively affect the decisions of the Great Powers.

28. Minerbi, *Vatican and Zionism*, 18.
29. Manuel, "Palestine Question," 279.

Cardinal Amette's worry coincided with Cardinal Bourne's concern regarding the danger of the Protestant offensive in the Holy Land.[30] Cardinal Bourne, archbishop of Westminster, visited Palestine between December 1918 and March 1919. Minerbi argues that it was his report, fiercely decrying the influence that Protestants had gained among Catholic educational institutions in Palestine, that convinced Pope Benedict to openly attack the Protestant propaganda in his allocution of March 10, 1919.[31]

Pope Benedict chose a diplomatic course entrenched in realism. He did not have a pro-British diplomacy per se but was amenable to the British mandate in Palestine and to the French mandate in Syria. In the Anglo-French verbal agreement of December 1918 between French premier Clemenceau and David Lloyd George, the French unequivocally ceded Palestine to the British in exchange for a mandate in Syria. When the question of Palestine came up again at the Conference of San Remo in April 1920, the new French premier, Alexandre Millerand, maintained that in the settlement of December 1918 the French had agreed to a British mandate in place of international control of Palestine provided that the question of the Holy Places would be settled in favor of France. Lloyd George and Italian premier Nitti rejected the French claim.[32] It can be successfully argued that in early 1919, the time of Gallarati Scotti's visit to prominent French Catholics and of Pope Benedict's allocution to the consistory, the pontiff was confident that, although the British would control Palestine, Catholic rights would still be protected either by France or by an international commission.

According to Gallarati Scotti, the British assurance that, anticipating the end of the French protectorate, an international

30. See Joseph Grabill, *Protestant Diplomacy and the Near East: Missionary Influence on American Policy, 1870–1927* (Minneapolis: University of Minnesota Press, 1971).

31. Minerbi, *Vatican and Zionism*, 30.

32. H. Eugene Bovis, *The Jerusalem Question, 1917–1968* (Stanford, Calif.: Hoover Institution Press, 1971), 7.

commission would eventually be appointed to protect the rights of the Catholic Church in the guardianship of the Holy Places satisfied Pope Benedict, whose main interest was to secure universal recognition of the Holy See as an independent power and had therefore no intention to challenge Britain over the Palestine question.[33] Although it is hard to reconcile these statements with the harsh words of Pope Benedict's address of March 1919, a more in-depth examination underlines two facets of the Holy See's diplomacy in 1919. First, at the international level, it highlights the high-profile approach of the diplomatic dialogue between the Holy See and Britain and the renewed influence exercised by the Holy See in the diplomatic game. Second, at the level of regional negotiation, it reinforces the assumption that the reshaping of the Middle East encouraged Pope Benedict to put his trust in the British.

The situation escalated dramatically in 1920 with the increased power granted to both Protestants and Zionists at the expense of Catholic influence, an evolution that would force the pontiff to readjust his diplomacy in the Holy Land.

BENEDICT XV AND ZIONISM: BREAK
OR CONTINUITY?

Since its inception in the late nineteenth century, the relations between the Holy See and the Zionist movement have been the topic of a multitude of studies. Most of these cover a broad span, from Theodor Herzl's meeting with Agliardi, the papal nuncio in Vienna, on May 19, 1896, to the Fundamental Agreement between the Holy See and the State of Israel of December 30, 1993. With the notable exception of Andrej Kreutz's *Vatican Policy on the Palestinian-Israeli Conflict*,[34] most of these studies dwell upon

33. Manuel, "Palestine Question," 279.

34. Andrek Kreutz, *Vatican Policy on the Palestinian-Israeli Conflict: The Struggle for the Holy Land* (Westport, Conn.: Greenwood Press, 1990).

the same well-known issues, often oversimplifying them or adopting a partisan position regarding the policy of the Holy See over the years.[35] The received narrative by Sergio Minerbi, *The Vatican and Zionism*, although thoroughly researched and widely influential, is an example of partiality in the treatment of the relationship between the Holy See and the Zionist movement. In this book, as in most other studies, Pope Benedict XV's stand on the Zionist question is described as definitely anti-Zionist in continuity with the position of his predecessors, especially Pope Pius X. There is no attempt to shed light on the motivating forces behind Pope Benedict's personal understanding of the long-term impact that the Zionist movement had on the Catholic Church in the Holy Land in view of the pontiff's appreciation of the future of the Holy See's participation in international relations. Eugene J. Fisher and George E. Irani are among the few scholars to have challenged two of the author's main hypotheses.[36] Fisher argued against Minerbi's identifying the hostility of the Catholic Church against Zionism as the result of immutable doctrinal positions, while Irani criticized Minerbi's "interpretation of the Holy See's opposition to Zionism since its inception as an ideology."[37]

Thorough research of the rich material found in the Vatican Archives provides a basis for revisiting and questioning Miner-

35. See Minerbi, *Vatican and Zionism*; Livia Rokach, *The Catholic Church and the Question of Palestine* (London: Saqi Books, 1987). Different articles also address the issue; see, for example, Richard P. Stevens, "The Vatican, the Catholic Church, and Jerusalem," *Journal of Palestine Studies* 10 (Spring 1981): 100–10; see also Adriano Ercole Ciani, "The Vatican, American Catholics and the Struggle for Palestine, 1917–1958: A Study of Cold War Roman Catholic Transnationalism" (PhD diss., University of Western Ontario, Canada, 2011).

36. Eugene Fisher is the executive secretary of the Secretariat for Catholic-Jewish Relations of the National Conference of Catholic Bishops since 1977. George Emile Irani is the author of *The Papacy and the Middle East: The Role of the Holy See in the Arab-Israeli Conflict, 1962–1984* (Notre Dame, Ind.: University of Notre Dame Press, 1986); see also Eugene J. Fisher, "The Vatican and the State of Israel," *First Things* (Apr. 1991) and George E. Irani, review of *Vatican and Zionism*, by Sergio I. Minerbi, *Catholic Historical Review* 78 (Jan. 1992): 135–36.

37. Irani, review of *Vatican and Zionism*.

bi's reasoning regarding the rationale behind Benedict's diplomacy and the outcome of his undertakings in Palestine. We can argue that Pope Benedict's policy in Palestine was looking favorably at Zionist aspirations, breaking with his predecessors' stance, a reflection of Pope Benedict's understanding of the role and influence of the church in the international community.[38] The Zionist issue was, in the pontiff's view, neither solely religious nor ideological, but also the British strategic response to new regional realities in the Middle East.

Benedict's position did not suggest, however, that he was relinquishing the church's rights on the Holy Places of Palestine. On the contrary, the pontiff's well-publicized demonstrations against infringement on Catholic rights have to be analyzed in the context of support of a Jewish Home in Palestine and anticipation of its future after the British mandate's eventual termination.

Benedict XV and Zionist Aspirations

The Zionist leaders had few opportunities to meet with popes and officials of the Curia until the publication of the Balfour Declaration on November 2, 1917. The first encounter took place on May 19, 1896, when Theodor Herzl, the "spiritual father of the [Zionist] movement,"[39] met with Antonio Agliardi, the papal nuncio in Vienna. Herzl's goal was to assuage the fears of the Christian world, and particularly those of the Vatican, that the Jews represented a threat to them.[40] Adopting a resolute secular position, Herzl promised Agliardi that in the event of the creation of a Jewish state in Palestine, Jerusalem and its Holy Places, as well as Bethlehem and Nazareth, would be excluded from the

---

38. Andrej Kreutz also contends that "the Vatican's embroilment in the Palestinian problem and the reasons underlying it have undergone a constant evolution that is a reflection of transformations within the Church and in its relations with the international community"; Kreutz, *Vatican Policy*, x.

39. Kreutz, *Vatican Policy*, 32.

40. Minerbi, *Vatican and Zionism*, 95.

Jewish territory. He promised to support the principle of extra-territoriality of those sites under the protectorate of the Holy See.[41] The nuncio and the Curia remained unfazed.

Eight years later, Herzl received the same treatment when he met, on January 25, 1904, with Pope Pius X. The pontiff's dismissal of the Zionist demands was rooted in doctrinal grounds.[42] Although the pope himself was not personally prejudiced against the Jews, the famous words he uttered as pope had a definite anti-Zionist tone:

We cannot encourage this movement. We cannot prevent the Jews from going to Jerusalem—but we could never sanction it. The ground of Jerusalem, even if it were not always sacred, has been sanctified by the life of Jesus Christ. As the head of the church, I cannot tell you otherwise. The Jews have not recognized our Lord, therefore we cannot recognize the Jewish people.[43]

Benedict XV had a different understanding of the role of the church in the international community. He belonged to a new epoch and witnessed the emergence of a new world order in the Middle East and in Europe. The pontiff had been deeply involved in the humanitarian assistance provided to the populations of Palestine during the war. He had been in contact with various Jewish religious leaders, especially from the United States, who had reached out to him to ensure the protection of their people in Europe and in Syria and Palestine.[44] He was also well aware that Palestine was not "empty"—that in the words of two rabbis visiting the land in 1898, "the bride is beautiful, but she is married to another man."[45]

41. Theodor Herzl, *The Complete Diaries of Theodor Herzl* (New York: Herzl Press, 1960), 1:353–54; see also Shlomo Avineri, *Herzl's Vision: Theodor Herzl and the Foundation of the Jewish State*, trans. Haim Watzman (Katonah, N.Y.: BlueBridge, 2014).

42. Kreutz, *Vatican Policy*, 33.

43. Herzl, *Complete Diaries*, 4:1603.

44. See chapter 5, "Benedict XV's Humanitarian Assistance."

45. Shalom Goldman, *Zeal for Zion: Christians, Jews, and the Idea of the Promised Land* (Chapel Hill: University of North Carolina Press, 2009), 23.

Few scholarly sources address "the hidden question" of the Arab presence in Palestine from a Vatican perspective.[46] To Pope Benedict, the recognition of the Arab population had a double meaning. It was first and foremost a sign of his paying particular attention to the fate of the Christian Arabs, especially to the Eastern Catholics and to the potential rapprochement with the Greek Orthodox communities. It also followed the principles expounded by Wilson in his Fourteen Points, an issue tied to the self-determination of minorities and a principle supported by Pope Benedict.[47]

The literature covering the May 1917 meetings between Pope Benedict, Cardinal Gasparri, and the Zionist envoy Nahum Sokolow is abundant and restates Minerbi's thesis that the pontiff, initially holding a positive appreciation for the Zionist cause, later changed his mind. However, Pope Benedict's stand, not pro-Zionist but sympathetic to the cause, did not change but simply adjusted to the new situation while keeping in mind that his primary goal was the protection of Christian minorities and sites of Palestine.

When Pope Benedict and Sokolow met, in a long private audience, on May 4, 1917, the war was at a stalemate, although it was well-known in Vatican quarters that an Allied victory would mean the carving up of the Ottoman Empire in favor of Britain and France. Sokolow was confident that Pope Benedict viewed the establishment of a Jewish national home in Palestine with goodwill. The pontiff's position was evidence that the Holy See did not base its pro or anti-Zionist stand on "immutable theological positions."[48] Benedict broke with the anti-Zionist line of his predecessors. Under his pontificate the anti-Zionist campaign led by *L'Osservatore Romano* and the Jesuit journal *Civiltà*

46. Ibid.
47. See chapter 6, "The Holy See and the Postwar World Order."
48. Minerbi, *Vatican and Zionism*, xxx.

Cattolica was contained.[49] Interpreting the famous words uttered by the pontiff during the meeting, "Yes, yes, I think we shall be good neighbors,"[50] Minerbi and Friedman conjecture that "the pope's assurances of good neighborliness to Sokolow must...be read not in the spiritual but in the geographical context,"[51] of a Catholic presence in an internationalized area, as planned by the Sykes-Picot Agreement.

The situation drastically changed at the end of 1917 with two related events: the Balfour Declaration of November 2, 1917, and the capture of Jerusalem by British troops one month later. From that day onward, the future of Palestine and Zionism remained in British hands. On November 2, 1917, the British foreign secretary, Lord Arthur Balfour, issued the "British Declaration of Sympathy with Zionist Aspirations," known as the Balfour Declaration. It was a document whose main motive was to make sure that no other country could control Palestine, therefore ensuring strategic and political control of the region.[52] The declaration promised British support "for the establishment in Palestine of a national home for the Jewish people," adding that "nothing shall be done which may prejudice the civil and religious rights of the existing non-Jewish communities in Palestine."[53] The fall of Jerusalem a month later and the establishment of a military (then civil) British government in Palestine turned the declaration of intent into a practical reality.[54]

Pope Benedict entertained no illusion about the long-term existence and development of the Jewish home. He did not change

---

49. Frank J. Coppa, *The Papacy, the Jews, and the Holocaust* (Washington, D.C.: The Catholic University of America Press, 2006), 133.

50. Minerbi, *Vatican and Zionism*, 112.

51. Friedman, *Question of Palestine*, 155.

52. Fieldhouse, *Western Imperialism*, 147.

53. J. C. Hurewitz, *Diplomacy in the Near and Middle East: A Documentary Record, 1914–1956* (Princeton, N.J.: Van Nostrand, 1956), 2:26.

54. See Jonathan Schneer, *The Balfour Declaration: The Origins of the Arab-Israeli Conflict* (New York: Random House, 2010).

his mind, as Minerbi asserts, returning to the anti-Zionism of his predecessors but adjusted his diplomacy to the presence of the Zionists, a presence meant to last. Like most of his contemporaries, he understood the Balfour Declaration as a promise eventually to establish a Jewish state. His main concern remained the control of the Holy Places by Christians.

A dispatch sent by Giannini to Gasparri on November 7, 1918, described the project of a Jewish national home as "fiercely preposterous."[55] It shows how few people shared Benedict's insight and long-term understanding of the future of Palestine. Contrary to Giannini, Benedict believed in the future of the Jewish national home, and his new diplomacy in Palestine reflected the reasons justifying the awarding of Palestine to the Jews.

In an article published in 1989, "The Surrogate Colonization of Palestine," the anthropologist Scott Atran argued in favor of a threefold rationale behind the British support of a Jewish national home: geopolitical strategy, the civilizing mission of "enlightened imperialism," and religion.[56] According to the author, "from the outset, Weizmann [the president of the Zionist Organization] stressed the strategic value of surrogate colonization."[57]

If Great Britain does not wish anyone else to have Palestine…it will have to watch it…that involves as much responsibility as would be involved by a British protectorate over Palestine….I therefore thought that the middle course could be adopted…the Jews take over the country; the whole burden of organization falls on them, but for the next ten or fifteen years they work under a temporary British protectorate.[58]

55. "Ferocemente grottesco"; Giannini to Gasparri, Nov. 7, 1918, ASV, AES Stati Ecclesiastici, 1916–22, pos. 1418, fasc. 563 (my translation).

56. Scott Atran, "The Surrogate Colonization of Palestine, 1917–1939," *American Ethnologist* 16 (Nov. 1989): 721.

57. Ibid.

58. Chaim Weizmann, *Trial and Error: The Autobiography of Chaim Weizmann* (Philadelphia: Jewish Publication Society of America, 1949), 177, quoted in Atran, "Surrogate Colonization," 721.

Pope Benedict could not but have thought along the same lines, attentive to the strategic importance of Palestine for the British as the bulwark of Egypt, with the Zionists as an ally and vital support to the British Empire.

The Jewish colonization would also follow "enlightened imperialist principles,"[59] developing into a sophisticated nation that would serve as a very efficient and active safeguard for the Suez Canal.[60] As the result of the immigration of the Jewish population of Eastern Europe to Palestine, up to 125,000 Jews populated the region in 1914, a sharp rise from the 24,000 present in 1882.[61] The volume of this flow had steadily increased as the war intensified the sufferings and oppression of the Jewish populations of Ukraine and Poland. Pope Benedict was aware of the power of attraction that the return of the Chosen People to their promised land had on the evangelicalism of British leaders like Prime Minister Lloyd George, Lord Balfour, and Churchill. It went back to the 1840s, when the British minister Lord Palmerston started to entertain the idea of a Jewish settlement in the Ottoman Empire in the context of his evangelical faith, expecting the restoration of the Jews to their land and their possible conversion to Christianity.[62] Most Anglo-Saxon Protestants regarded the Old Testament with "almost mystical veneration" and carried a sense of debt to the Jews for the treatment reserved to them by Christianity throughout the centuries.[63] Weizmann himself emphasized the enormous respect the Anglo-Saxon Protestants were showing to the Zionists as the representatives of a great tradition.[64]

Contrary to the short-term vision of men like Giannini, Pope Benedict anticipated that the Jewish national home was there

59. Ibid.
60. Ibid.
61. Mandel, *Arabs and Zionism*, xxiv. Other authors mention 85,000 Jewish souls.
62. Leonard Stein, *The Balfour Declaration* (New York: Simon and Schuster, 1961), 3.
63. Howard M. Sachar, *The Emergence of the Middle East, 1914–1924* (New York: Knopf, 1969), 197; Fieldhouse, *Western Imperialism*, 118, 131.
64. Weizmann, *Trial and Error*, 157, quoted in Atran, "Surrogate Colonization," 721.

to stay and grow under the auspices of Britain. His personal positive appreciation of Zionism ran against the pervasive anti-Zionism of the Christian and Muslim population of Palestine. In his dispatches, Giannini did not hide his anti-Zionism. In a letter of February 13, 1920, the apostolic delegate speculated about the "hated Jewish Zionism warmly favored by the British colonial agents, sometimes with dubious means, and against which the Muslims and Christians have come together."[65] Giannini was not the only member of the Catholic clergy complaining about the Zionists and their new national home. The lack of clarity of the Balfour Declaration left room for interpretation, encouraging anti-Zionist church officials to ask for its abrogation.[66]

Prominent Christians and Muslims from Palestine joined rank with Giannini and other anti-Zionist clergy members, opposing Jewish immigration. They established diverse political and cultural associations to that effect. The first official Muslim-Christian Association (MCA) was founded in Jaffa in March 1918. Its goal was to obstruct the purchase of land by the Jews,[67] but also to showcase their alliance and refute the British contention that Palestinian Arabs' newly founded associations lacked homogeneity because of a religious divide. There was indeed a religious divide, as Muslims stressed the Islamic character of Palestine, encouraging their new Christian allies to convert to Islam. Still, they were currently united against the Zionist threat.[68]

65. "Odiato sionismo ebraico calorosamente favorite dagli agenti coloniali inglesi, con mezzi talvolta perfino poco puliti, e contro del quale si sono collegati gl'indigeni musulmani e cristiani"; Giannini to Gasparri, Feb. 13, 1920, ASV, AES Francia, 1919–20, pos. 1333, fasc. 697 (my translation).

66. See James Renton, "Flawed Foundations: The Balfour Declaration and the Palestine Mandate," in Britain, Palestine and Empire: The Mandate Years, ed. Rory Miller, 15–38 (Farnham, UK: Ashgate, 2010).

67. Anthony O'Mahony ed., The Christian Communities of Jerusalem and the Holy Land: Studies in History, Religion, and Politics (Cardiff: University of Wales Press, 2003), 19; see also Martin Bunton, Colonial Lands Policies in Palestine, 1917–1936 (Oxford: Oxford University Press, 2007).

68. Roberto Mazza, Jerusalem: From the Ottomans to the British (London: I. B. Tauris, 2009), 70.

The burgeoning associations started to coordinate their activities in November 1919 when they established an umbrella organization to represent them. On the eve of the peace conference, the Supreme Committee of the Arab Societies in Palestine contacted Pope Benedict, begging him to intervene in their favor and condemn Zionism.[69] The committee, in a note directed to the participants at the peace conference but also sent to the Holy See, did not hesitate to use the Christian argument: "the transformation of Palestine into a National Home for the Jews is a source of great troubles... in the land... where Jesus Christ was born and crucified." They warned them that "the responsibility of this is yours.... History shall blame you for your deed."[70]

One of the most fervent anti-Zionist clergymen was the newly appointed Latin patriarch of Jerusalem, Luigi Barlassina. In a letter addressed to Cardinal van Rossum on May 8, 1921, Barlassina wrote rather candidly that

if the Holy See succeeded in obtaining the cessation of the Zionist program, such an event would create a solid pedestal to our institutions against potential Muslim fanaticism. On the other hand, remaining silent would be surely interpreted as indifference, or as a lack of interest from the Holy See for the cause of Palestine and its inhabitants.[71]

As with any well-seasoned diplomat, Pope Benedict looked beyond the immediate local consequences of the implementation of the Balfour Declaration and had no intention of lobbying in favor of its abrogation. As the government of a universal and

---

69. Christian-Muslim Association to Vatican, Oct. 21, 1919, ASV, Segr. Stato, Affari Eccl. Asia-Africa-Oceania, pos. 53, fasc. 40; see also Mazza, *Jerusalem*, 71.

70. Arab Committee, Jerusalem, May 17, 1920, ASV, Segr. Stato, Affari Eccl. Asia-Africa-Oceania, pos. 53, fasc. 40; see also Mazza, *Jerusalem*, 72.

71. "Se la S. Sede riuscisse a ottenere la cessazione del programma sionista, certo sarebbe il trionfo della Chiesa Cattolica in Oriente, e tale avvenimento formerebbe un solidi piedestallo alle nostre istituzioni contro ogni eventuale fanatismo musulmana. Il silenzio invece verrebbe certamente interpretate o come indifferenza, o come insufficienza della Santa Sede per la causa della Palestina, e dei suoi abitanti"; Barlassina to van Rossum, May 8, 1921, AP, N.S., vol. 694 (1921), rub. 126, fol. 69–94 (my translation).

transnational institution, the Holy See was in a delicate position. Pope Benedict was taking into account the powerful worldwide influence of the Jewish diaspora. Any hostile attitude of the Holy See would stir up an anti-Catholic backlash and reinforce the anti-Zionist reputation of the Catholic Church. Moreover, the Holy See had a huge responsibility toward the Jews. Any anti-Semitic discourse or action could stimulate dangerous anti-Semitic reactions in areas where the Jewish people had suffered tremendously during the war.

Pope Benedict did not address the Zionist question publicly until the opening of the Paris Peace Conference in January 1919 and after receiving disquieting reports from Palestine. British cardinal Bourne had embarked in a tour including the Middle East that lasted from December 1918 to March 1919. He arrived in Jerusalem on January 18, 1919, where he encountered a situation that he later described as "distinctly menacing."[72] He added that the danger came from some Jewish immigrants who were claiming a political Zionist domination that went much further than the terms of the Balfour Declaration.[73] Bourne's reports to the British government and to Pope Benedict mentioned "a loud and emphatic protest against Mr. Balfour's promises and against the projects of the Zionists."[74] He begged Lloyd George and Balfour to clarify the meaning of the declaration. If by "Jewish National Home" Balfour meant "Jewish State," then, in Cardinal Bourne's reasoning, Pope Benedict could only withdraw his support to the Zionist cause and plans of development in Palestine.

The situation was serious enough that the pontiff decided to address the issue publicly, in the consistory of March 10, 1919, when he declared:

---

72. Ernest Oldmeadow, *Francis Cardinal Bourne* (London: Burne, Oates, and Washburn, 1943), 148.

73. Ibid.; statement made in 1925 about the 1919 visit.

74. Ibid., 173.

Our anxiety is most keen as to the decision which the Peace Congress at Paris is soon to take...for surely it would be...a bitter grief if unbelievers in Palestine were put in a superior or more privileged position, still more so if the august monuments of the Christian religion were assigned to those who were not Christians.[75]

The confirmation of the British mandate on Palestine at the Conference of San Remo in April 1920 did not improve the status of the Christians in Palestine. For the second time, in June 1921, Pope Benedict overcame his reservation and addressed the College of Cardinals at the Secret Consistory of June 13, 1921, in rare nondiplomatic terms:

Our fears have been only too well realized. It is known that the position of the Christians in Palestine has not only not been improved, but it has become worse under the new civil regime which has been established and which tends—if not in the intentions of its founders, certainly in its effects—to deprive Christianity of the position which it has hitherto held and to substitute for it the Jews.[76]

Worried by the impact the allocution would have on restive Christian Arab populations in Palestine, Colonel Storrs, the British governor, forbade the publication of Pope Benedict's talk in Palestine. The anti-Zionist and anti-British patriarch of Jerusalem, Luigi Barlassina, complained to Storrs that the censor had refused the publication of the text of the Holy Father's allocution of June 13 in *Rakib Sahyoun*, the organ of the patriarchate for the diocese of Palestine. Storrs justified the censorship, claiming that it was an unofficial text, which compared to the official version was obviously a false rendering of the pope's allocution. Barlassina, who replied that the article was a textual extract of the official document, accused the British of launching an "injurious and slanderous attack against the pope, with the view

75. Benedict XV, *Antequam Ordinem*, 97–101.
76. Benedict XV, "Consistorial Allocution *Causa Nobis* [June 13, 1921]," *AAS* 13 (1921): 281–84.

of lessening His prestige and authority."[77] Beyond the veracity of comments on both sides, the censorship was evidence of the tension reigning in Palestine and the importance given to papal declarations.

In the allocution, it was actually the way the British were handling their mandate in Palestine that was the subject of Pope Benedict's indignation more than the Zionists' presence per se. The pontiff affirmed:

We do not indeed wish that the rights of the Jewish element should be infringed upon but that the just rights of Christianity should not be subordinated to them.[78]

This comment, akin to an official recognition of Jewish presence and rights in Palestine,[79] evidences Pope Benedict's sympathetic stance toward Zionism but even goes further in recognizing an early form of potential dialogue.

Minerbi concludes that the Vatican was strongly opposed to Zionism, an assertion that needs further examination. First and foremost, the voice of the pope did not always coincide with the voice of other Catholic members of the higher clergy, at the Curia or elsewhere. After Cardinal Bourne's personal comments to the press that Zionism was "quite contrary to Christian sensitivity and tradition"[80] came the condemnation of Zionism uttered by the archbishop of Milan, Cardinal Ratti. His words are especially important, as he became pope after Benedict XV's death, under the name of Pius XI. In the October 7, 1921, issue of the newspaper *Palestine Weekly*, published in Jerusalem, an interview of Cardinal Ratti by the Italian *Il Secolo* was printed, in which he stated in unusual nondiplomatic terms that

77. Barlassina to Colonel R. Storrs, Aug. 12, 1921, AP, N.S., vol. 694 (1921), rub. 126, fol. 140.

78. Benedict XV, *Causa Nobis*, 281–84.

79. Jean-Dominique Montoisy, "Israël-Vatican: Le nouveau dialogue," *Studia Diplomatica* 34, no. 6 (1981): 755.

80. Ingrams, *Palestine Papers*, 60.

the followers of His Excellency Sir Herbert Samuel with their disguised form of concessional protectionism neither can nor ought to aspire to make Palestine a Jewish monopoly, a condition which will only offend the most deeply rooted feelings of the Christian masses. England, who covers with her prestige and power the acts of the High Commissioner in Palestine, should not forget that the Holy See has in its hands certain weapons of reprisal.[81]

Uttering such an unveiled threat is startling—assuming that *Il Secolo* reproduced the exact words of Cardinal Ratti—and a rare occurrence in diplomatic circles. It never got Pope Benedict's approval.

Armed with a large dose of patience, Benedict XV was a visionary, a long-term thinker, and a seasoned diplomat. The pontiff, attentive to the rising anti-Semitism in Europe, was well aware that the Jewish immigration to Palestine would increase and that the British mandate, by definition, would eventually leave room to self-government. What Pope Benedict could not have envisioned was that the British were to rule Palestine in a most autocratic manner until the mandate was over in 1948.[82] As a realist and a pragmatist, Pope Benedict did not directly challenge the Balfour Declaration or the British mandate, as he had no direct negotiating power, but he acted in order to protect his own interests—namely, the protection of the Holy Places and the Catholic minorities in the Holy Land.[83]

81. "The Vatican and Palestine," published in *Palestine Weekly*, Jerusalem, Oct. 7, 1921, AP, N.S., vol. 694 (1921), rub. 126, fol. 309.

82. Fieldhouse, *Western Imperialism*, 151; see also the authoritative work of Bernard Wasserstein, *The British in Palestine: The Mandatory Government and Arab-Jewish Conflict, 1917–1929* (London: Royal Historical Society, 1978).

83. See Silvio Ferrari, *Vaticano e Israele: Dal secondo conflitto mondiale alla Guerra del golfo* (Florence, Italy: Sansoni Editore, 1991), 41.

The Question of Jerusalem and the
Protection of the Holy Places

With the question of the protection of the Catholic communities and the Holy Places came the issue of the future of the French protectorate. The situation was delicate. On one hand, Pope Benedict's main diplomatic goal was the emancipation of the Holy See from the French Catholic protectorate. The capture of Jerusalem by General Allenby and the assignment of a British mandate over Palestine at the Conference of San Remo in April 1920 was a unique opportunity to end the protectorate. On the other hand, Palestine was becoming the national home of the Jews, a situation that brought about heated discussions regarding the ownership and protection of the Holy Places. From this perspective, it was in Benedict's interest to devise a policy that without confirming the French protectorate would not dismiss it, as long as a satisfactory solution would not be found and implemented. France had one negotiating card in hand that the Holy See could not and would not dismiss. The French government could use the long sought-after resumption of diplomatic relations between the Holy See and Paris as a strategic advantage, as it gave France leverage to obtain satisfaction regarding the Catholic protectorate.

The French protectorate had been established to protect the church interests in a land governed by a non-Christian government. With the establishment of the British mandate in Palestine, the protectorate had ceased to exist, a fact that was confirmed by France, Britain, and Italy at the San Remo Conference.[84] To compensate for the official loss of their protectorate, the French looked with favor on the Holy See's attempt to transfer the protectorate to Belgium, a policy akin to the establish-

---

84. Hachey, ed., *Great Britain Legation*, 22.

ment of a surrogate protectorate over the Holy Places. Belgium was a Catholic country, without special interests in Palestine, but with close relations with Paris and the Vatican. A Belgian protectorate would have allowed France to remain the (albeit hidden) dominant power in the Holy Land. Belgian nationalists were also dreaming of territorial expansion and set their eyes on the Holy Places of Palestine. Therefore, Cardinal Mercier, archbishop of Mechelen and primate of Belgium, wrote to Balfour offering Belgium as a candidate for the Catholic protectorate in Palestine as a compensation for not having been selected to host the League of Nations.[85] Gasparri supported Mercier's demand.[86] According to the late church historian Roger Aubert, Cardinal Mercier's plan was driven by anti-Zionist motives and the fear that the Jewish immigration to the Holy Land was importing communist influence, detrimental to the Christian fabric of the country.[87] The Belgian efforts ended in failure.

The eventual solution to the protection of the rights of the different religious communities of Palestine and their claims over the Holy Places came in the form of an international commission whose rules were sketched by Sir Herbert Samuel, the high commissioner, in November 1920. He proposed a commission of thirty-one members with three Catholics recommended by the Holy See.[88] The details concerning the status of the Holy Places and of this international commission were submitted on December 6, 1920, to the League of Nations in two articles of the draft for the British mandate. Article 13 placed the responsibility for the Holy Places on Britain, which was accountable to the league.

85. Sebastiano Nicotra, nuncio to Belgium, to Gasparri, June 16, 1919, ASV, Segr. Stato, Guerra (1914–18), fasc. 112.

86. Gasparri to Nicotra, July 9, 1919, ibid.

87. Roger Aubert, "Les démarches du Cardinal Mercier en vue de l'octroi à la Belgique d'un mandat sur la Palestine," *Bulletin de la Classe des Lettres et des Sciences Morales et Politiques* 5 (1979): 204.

88. Minerbi, *Vatican and Zionism*, 48.

The Holy See was flatly ignored. As for article 14, it originally called for an international commission specifying that only the Council of the League of Nations would nominate the chairman of the commission.

The Holy See's response to those articles was fierce, as Pope Benedict understood these two articles as evidence that Britain was taking over responsibility of the Holy Places, a situation that would not have created serious problems were it not for the pro-Zionist and Protestant policy of the British government.

Pope Benedict died in January 1922, before a final agreement was reached. The text of the British mandate for Palestine was eventually accepted on July 22, 1922. Pius XI, Pope Benedict's successor, kept Cardinal Gasparri as his secretary of state, ensuring continuity with Benedict's diplomacy regarding the protection of the Holy Places. On June 4, 1922, the Holy See prepared an *aide-mémoire* presenting its claims. After praising "the spirit of justice and impartiality" of Great Britain, the Holy See complained that according to the draft of the mandate, "the Jews would have in Palestine a privileged and predominant position over Catholics [and that] the rights of Christians—and especially those of Catholics—would not be sufficiently safeguarded."[89] The Holy See focused its attacks on the mandate's article 14, which established "a special Commission to study and settle all questions and complaints concerning the different religious confessions" in the Holy Places. Rome made clear that they could and would never approve that the commission had on its agenda the discussion of the ownership of the sanctuaries, as the great majority of them had been in Catholic hands for centuries, even under Ottoman domination.[90] The official text of July 24, 1922, gave satisfaction to the Holy See, as it declared that "the method

89. *Aide-mémoire*, June 4, 1922, ASV, Arch. Nunz. Parigi, b. 395, fasc. 316.
90. Ibid.

of nomination, the composition and the functions of this Commission shall be submitted to the Council of the League for its approval, and the Commission shall not be appointed or enter upon its functions without the approval of the Council."[91]

The approval of the British mandate by the Council of the League of Nations had been delayed by the Holy See's objections, relayed by the representatives at the league of a number of Catholic countries. Balfour complained to Maurice Hankey, secretary to the cabinet, that the reluctance of most of the world Catholic countries—France, Poland, Spain, Brazil, and even Italy—to discuss the Palestine mandate at the council was the result of papal pressure through the nuncios.[92]

At the close of Pope Benedict's pontificate, the British were rightly under the impression that the Holy See had warmed to their administration in Palestine but kept following attentively the Zionist and Protestant developments.[93]

THE PROTESTANT CONQUEST
OF PALESTINE: A MIGHTY DANGER
TO CATHOLIC FUTURE

The Protestant Danger

As the universal leader of the Catholic Church, Pope Benedict acknowledged the Protestant ecumenical movement that had started in 1910 with the World Missionary Conference at Edinburgh, Scotland. However, he refrained from sending delegates to any of the meetings and forbade Catholics to participate.[94] In December 1921 the first Malines Conversation, a series of five

---

91. Walter Laqueur and Barry M. Rubin, eds., *The Israel-Arab Reader: A Documentary History of the Middle East Conflict* (New York: Penguin, 2001), 30–36.

92. PRO CAB, 24/136, quoted in Ingrams, *Palestine Papers*, 168.

93. Minerbi, *Vatican and Zionism*, 57.

94. James M. Oliver, *Ecumenical Associations: Their Canonical Status with Particular Reference to the United States of America* (Rome: Editrice Pontificia Universita Gregoriana, 1999), 18, 31.

unofficial encounters between Anglicans and Roman Catholics at Malines, Belgium, started with the approbation of the pontiff. This was as far as the Holy See was ready to move in the debate over the unity of the church.

In the meantime, in Palestine, at the regional diplomatic and ecclesiastical level, the tension between Protestants and Roman Catholics was palpable. Britain, as the mandatory power of Palestine, sheltered two groups of protégés in the Holy Land: the Jews and the Protestants.

The Protestants were under the unofficial protection of the British since the establishment of the Protestant bishopric in Jerusalem. In October 1841, in a letter to his friend John Kelbe, John Henry Newman had commented on the political will of his government to develop a religious influence in Jerusalem through the presence of Protestants, such as the Greek Church had for Russia and the Latin Catholic Church had for France.[95] The future Catholic convert cardinal was referring to the King of Prussia's suggestion to the British government to set up a joint Protestant bishopric in Jerusalem to minister to Anglicans and German Protestants and to respond to the need to give Protestantism an institutional base in the Holy Land. The maintenance of the bishopric was to be organized by the two powers.[96] The Prussian-British bishopric was established in late 1841 against the recommendations of the Prussian ambassador in Constantinople, who found the plan "to be inopportune, ill-informed, and visionary."[97] Many in the Anglican Church also met its creation with reservation. For Newman, it was the coup de grâce that led him to eventually abandon his Anglican faith and enter the Roman Catholic Church.

95. John Henry Newman, *Correspondence of John Henry Newman with John Kelbe and Others, 1839–45* (London: Birmingham Oratory, 1917), 148, quoted in R. W. Greaves, "The Jerusalem Bishopric, 1841," *English Historical Review* 64 (July 1949): 328–52.

96. Greaves, "Jerusalem Bishopric," 328.

97. Ibid., 340.

The Protestant bishopric became a disappointment both politically and religiously. Forty years later, in 1881, Chancellor Otto von Bismarck denounced the ecclesiastical organization of the bishopric as favoring the Anglicans.[98] Consequently, the joint bishopric was dissolved in 1885, leaving the ecclesiastical structure exclusively under an Anglican bishop. While the German Protestants had freed themselves from the Anglicans, the American missionaries welcomed maintaining an Anglican patriarchate, as their growing numbers were necessitating the presence of a friendly power to protect them efficiently.

In the postwar era, with the British administration of Palestine, following the liberation of the land, American Protestant missions intensified their activities. A report compiling questions raised by Barlassina, Latin patriarch of Jerusalem, and the Custody of the Holy Land was sent to Propaganda Fide on January 11, 1920. It highlighted the danger represented by Protestant proselytizing in Palestine, especially in Jerusalem. The author of the note specifically mentioned the danger that the American missions represented, pointing out that until then and unlike the American missionaries, the Anglicans had not been active or well-organized because their appointed bishop, Dr. McInnis, was not "a man of action."[99] The Spanish consul at Jerusalem, Count de Ballobar, had an opposite opinion. To him, the Protestant bishop was "the one who runs everything in Jerusalem." According to the same consul, McInnis was also the one directing, "behind the scenes," the humanitarian assistance for Syria and Palestine, "the most efficient instrument of the policy of English influence."[100] However, the situation was to change soon, as he

---

98. Ibid., 352.

99. Report to Propaganda Fide, January 11, 1920, AP, N.S., vol. 755 (1922), rub. 126, fol. 135.

100. Eduardo Moreno and Roberto Mazza, eds., *Jerusalem in World War I: The Palestine Diary of a European Diplomat, Conde de Ballobar* (London: I. B. Tauris, 2011), 200; see also chapter 5 of this book.

was going to be replaced by Dr. Waggett, "a man of great influence, energetic and able to organize a redoubtable protestant movement."[101]

The same report noted that the Protestant missions benefited from unlimited funds and an efficient organization. Ominously, it foresaw the complete ruin of Catholic schools and institutions and their takeover by the American missions. A striking example was that, in Beit Djallah, a suburb of Jerusalem, half of the fifty children who attended the local Catholic school had transferred to the American school, whose headmaster was a Protestant pastor.[102]

The situation was worrisome, as schools had always been the most efficient instrument to establish Catholic influence among Palestinian families. In a report sent to Rome in January 1919, Msgr. Camassei, who was soon replaced by Barlassina as Latin patriarch, explained that families wanted their sons to study English and Arabic, as Palestine was under British control, and stressed how the American Red Cross and other Protestant establishments were able to offer, in addition to an excellent education, free food and clothes.[103] It was obvious that parents were not sending their children to the American mission schools for the sake of Protestantism but rather were attracted by the numerous concrete and practical advantages that the wealthy missions were able to provide.

Reestablishing Harmony in the Church

Sweeping changes were necessary and pressing to respond to Protestant propaganda and reassert Catholic influence in Palestine. The remedies were twofold: modernize and financially sup-

101. Report to Propaganda Fide, Jan. 11, 1920, AP, N.S., vol. 755 (1922), rub. 126, fol. 135.
102. Ibid., fol. 137.
103. Report from Camassei, "Stato delle missioni patriarcali," Jan. 27, 1919, AP, N.S., vol. 629 (1919), rub. 126, fol. 173–77.

port the Catholic educational network and, more importantly, bring about *une entente cordiale* between the different Catholic factions in Palestine to present a united stand against the Protestant danger.

Fr. Paschal Robinson, a Franciscan professor at the Catholic University of America in Washington, D.C., was sent to Palestine by Pope Benedict in 1919 to investigate the situation of Catholic education. He suggested the establishment of English-speaking Catholic schools in order to prevent the identification of everything English with Protestantism, in the same way everything French had been associated to Catholicism for centuries. The eventual decision to reject this suggestion was directly tied to Benedict's call to missionaries to forego nationalistic attitudes, a theme he developed in his apostolic letter *Maximum Illud* on missions and promulgated in November 1919, the year Robinson traveled to Palestine. The suggestion that English-speaking Catholic ministers should be introduced to answer families' demands to have their children taught in English was also opposed because of the fear that it would arouse susceptibilities and jealousy on the part of congregations of other nationalities, as it would create a new "national center of interest." Robinson strongly rejected the idea of a "multiplicity of national centers of influence," which, according to him, had always prevented the unity of the different Catholic communities living in Palestine.[104]

In October 1920, Fr. Robinson was called back as apostolic visitor to Palestine to settle the dispute between the Latin patriarchate and the Custody of the Holy Land, a dispute that created a rift among Catholics and was impeding the church's ability to present a much-needed united front and a successful approach to the Protestant threat. As was stated frankly in the earlier report,

104. Documenti circa le varie questioni tra Mons. Barlassina e la Custodia di Terra Santa, Jan. 11, 1920, AP, N.S., vol. 755 (1922), rub. 126, fol. 139.

it remains obvious that, as of today, the first and main duty rests in the union of all the Catholic forces in Palestine against the common danger that threatens us because of the American propaganda and of other movements opposed to the Church. Consequently, the measure that is most needed is undeniably une *entente cordiale*, or if you wish more cordial than in the past between the patriarchate of Jerusalem and the orders and religious congregations in Palestine.[105]

From the perspective of the British administration in Palestine, Robinson's mission was very successful, as it improved relations between the British administration and Patriarch Barlassina, famous for his anti-British and anti-Zionist stand. The relationship between the patriarchate and the Custody remained edgy and highlighted the tension existing between Propaganda Fide and the secretary of state, an issue of domestic policy that bore direct influence on diplomatic relations between the Holy See and Britain. Cardinal Gasparri extended his support to Barlassina, who had difficult relations with Propaganda Fide, a supporter of the Franciscan Custody. The relationship between the Custody and the patriarchate had been unfriendly since the reinstauration of the latter in 1847, to the point that the Custody directly and bluntly accused the Holy See of bearing responsibility for the tense situation. Barlassina had a reputation for lacking diplomatic tact but, however, of being honest and obedient. The Holy See never considered responding to pressure from either Britain, as the mandatory power, or the Custody to recall the energetic patriarch.

On October 4, 1918, in the brief *Inclytum Fratrum Minorum*

---

105. "Il demeure évident qu'à l'heure actuelle, le premier et le principal devoir consiste dans l'union de toutes les forces catholiques en Palestine contre le péril commun qui nous menace du fait de la propagande américaine et des autres mouvements opposés à l'Église. Par conséquent, la mesure la plus nécessaire est incontestablement une *entente cordiale*, ou si l'on veut plus cordiale que par le passé entre le patriarcat de Jérusalem et tous les ordres et Congrégations religieuses en Palestine"; Documenti circa le varie questioni tra Mons. Barlassina e la Custodia di Terra Santa, Jan. 11, 1920, AP, N.S., vol. 755 (1922), rub. 126, fol. 140 (my translation).

Conditorem,[106] on the occasion of the celebration of the seven-hundredth anniversary of the Custody of the Holy Land, Pope Benedict confirmed the centuries-old position held by the papacy that the Franciscans will "guard, manage and govern" the Custody of the Holy Places.[107] Conversely, on June 14, 1920, regarding the question of the responsibilities of both the Custody and the patriarchate over the Holy Places of Palestine, Propaganda Fide declared that "the Custody of the Holy Land cannot do any alteration or restoration...of the Sanctuaries of Palestine without the explicit consent of the Patriarch [because he] represents the Church."[108]

The statement by Propaganda Fide directly opposed the pontiff's brief of October 1918, a fact immediately noticed by the head of the Custody of the Holy Land, Fr. Ferdinando Diotallevi, who bitterly complained about the Latin patriarchate in a dispatch of July 3, 1921, sent to Gasparri and van Rossum.[109] Diotallevi started his report reminding the Holy See that the Ottoman government had always looked at the Custody as the "incarnation of Catholicism in the Orient."[110] The reestablishment of the Latin patriarchate created an ambiguity that damaged both the Catholic fabric and the administration of the Holy Places. To avoid tension and to restore the peace and harmony that were desperately missing in Palestine, Diotallevi asked the pontiff to reassert the power of the Custody against the patriarchate. The issue endured after the pontiff's death in January 1922.

106. Benedict XV, "Brief *Inclytum Fratrum Minorum Conditorem* [Oct. 4, 1918]," *AAS* 10 (1918): 437–39.

107. "Custodire, reggere e governare"; Pro-Memoria sui francescani e I Luoghi di Terra Santa to van Rossum, 1920, AP, N.S., vol. 755 (1922), rub. 126, fol. 69–112 (my translation).

108. "Il Custode di Terra Santa possono fare alcuna innovazione o restaurazione...nei Santuari della Palestina senza l'esplicito consenso del Patriarca...il Patriarca rappresenta la Chiesa"; Relazione Circa il progetto di un Modus Vivendi, Nov. 1922, AP, N.S., vol. 755 (1922), rub. 126, fol. 852 (my translation).

109. Pro memoria per determinare le relazioni fra il Patr. di Gerusalemme e la Custodia di Terra Santa, July 3, 1921, AP, N.S., vol. 755 (1922), rub. 126, fol. 691–706.

110. Ibid.

While the palpable tension between Latin Catholic factions hindered a much-needed harmony, the Eastern rite Catholic churches of Palestine also needed improvement. Diotallevi warned that these churches, regardless of their rite, should be strengthened and developed spiritually, morally, and economically. This was the necessary condition for any attempt at a future rapprochement with the separated Oriental churches.[111] Pope Benedict entrusted this mission to the Congregation for the Oriental Church and the Pontifical Oriental Institute. Three years after its establishment in 1917, there were few encouraging results. The derelict condition of most Eastern Catholic churches was a hindrance to their ability to attract dissidents who were content with their own churches.[112] The Latin Church did not provide a credible alternative to the Orthodox, as they were still under the old belief that the Latin Church sought only to Latinize them so as to more easily absorb them.[113] Their misgivings were reinforced by an aggressive anti-Catholic campaign mounted by the Protestants, who benefited from the diplomatic support of Protestant Britain.

Baron Carlo Monti expressed his worry after the visit of the Anglican bishop of Gibraltar to Smirna in March 1920. In his report Monti stressed that the danger of a rapprochement between the Anglican and the Greek Orthodox churches had to be closely watched. He added that an official banquet had been the occasion of a joint intervention of the Greek and British authorities to vote in favor of the union between the Protestant and Greek churches and to build the most intimate relations between Eng-

111. Ferdinando Dotallevi, Custode di Terra Santa, Memoriale alla S. Congregazione Pro Ecclesia Orientali per l'Unione delle Chiese, Rome, May 1921, ACCO, 1920, rub. 40, rito greci, fasc. 6050.

112. Ibid.

113. N. Anad, Maronita Assistente Onorario della Bibl. Vaticana, to Isaia Papadopoulos, Assessore della translation), S. Congregazione per la Chiesa Orientale, January 9, 1919, ACCO, 1920, rub. 40, rito greci, fasc. 4956.

land and Greece.[114] Pope Benedict's effort to set up an environment conducive to a rapprochement with the Orthodox Church ran up against the British government's endeavors to take over the Greek Orthodox Church by providing ample financial means to a bankrupt church.[115]

Pope Benedict had little time left to tackle the issue of the reorganization of the Latin and Eastern Catholic churches in the Middle East and devise a policy that would secure the protection of the Holy Places. He passed away before the British mandate to Palestine was officially sanctioned on July 24, 1922. His legacy lived on as his successor Pius XI retained Cardinal Gasparri as his secretary of state, a signal to the rest of the world, especially to the British and the French, that the new pontiff's foreign policy would follow in the path of his predecessor, Benedict XV.

114. Monti to van Rossum, no date, AP, N.S., vol. 693 (1921), rub. 126, fol. 544 rv.
115. ACCO, rub 19/10. With revenues from Russian pilgrims drying up after the Bolshevik Revolution, the Greek Orthodox Church was on the verge of bankruptcy.

CONCLUSION

Those who witnessed the Great War often described it in apocalyptic terms, "predicated on divine justice."[1] It was a total war in which all were expecting Benedict XV, the world supreme moral authority, to take sides. He was vilified for resisting the general public's and governments' pressure as he chose to put the church's diplomacy at the service of peace and keep an impartial stance. His original hope was to return to the prewar status quo, maintain the integrity of the Austro-Hungarian Catholic Empire, and keep Italy out of the hostilities. His greatest diplomatic attempt to end the war and prepare for peace, the Peace Note of August 1, 1917, when not received with contempt, was rebuffed by all governments.

Pope Benedict's wartime European diplomacy ended in failure, but, in an apparent paradox, the pontiff's moral authority and the prestige of the church were restored and enhanced in the few months that followed the armistice. Civil governments rushed to establish diplomatic ties with the Holy See. In the defunct Ottoman Empire, Turkish Muslim, Jewish, and Christian dignitaries paid a special tribute to Benedict XV as they funded a statue of the pontiff that still stands today, welcoming visitors in the courtyard of the Cathedral of the Holy Spirit in Istanbul. The pontiff, scorned during the war, was then praised, and through him the role of the church as an active force in world politics was recognized.

1. Jay Winter, *Sites of Memory, Sites of Mourning: The Great War in European Cultural History* (Cambridge: Cambridge University Press, 1996), 178.

Benedict XV's ecclesiastical and foreign policy bore the mark of a visionary whose response to the immediate needs and demands of his contemporaries was often overshadowed by the misunderstanding surrounding his international policies. A systematic analysis of his diplomacy in the emerging Middle East allowed us to gauge the pontiff's statesmanship and to shed light on the long-term repercussions of his diplomacy at the regional and international levels. With the abolition of the capitulations by the Ottoman government in 1914 and the end of the French Catholic protectorate, a unique opportunity arose for the pontiff to release the Holy See from France's encroachment in its foreign policy. During the war, the pontiff was prudent, and his supple diplomacy reflected a wait-and-see position.

He combined two policies at the political and ecclesiastical levels, distinguishing between short- and long-term diplomatic endeavors. At the political level, Benedict XV's diplomacy was designed to ensure the daily protection of Catholic communities and properties. Much energy was spent responding to the persecution suffered by higher members of the Catholic clergy, a persecution that was akin to a direct attack on the Catholic Church and the pope, at the hand of Djemal Pasha, the governor of Syria. The pontiff also devoted time and personal wealth to offer relief to starving populations without regard to religion or nationality. At the ecclesiastical level, Benedict institutionalized the unionist ecclesiology implemented by his predecessor, Leo XIII, and created a new ecclesial structure to strengthen the Eastern Catholic churches and prepare a conducive environment for an anticipated rapprochement with the dissident Orthodox churches. The creation in 1917 of a special Congregation for the Oriental Church supported by a Pontifical Oriental Institute responded to these needs.

The Holy See gained its diplomatic freedom from France following the abrogation of the French protectorate only to be caught in a diplomatic tussle with the Ottoman government, which was hoping to enter into diplomatic ties with the Holy See. The contempt and disparagement with which the pontiff's diplomacy was received in Europe had no influence on the Ottoman government, as it recognized the head of the Catholic Church as a moral authority to be reckoned with.

In the postwar era, the geopolitical and religious situations became more complex as the region was redesigned and new powerful actors emerged. The Arab provinces of the defunct Ottoman Empire were partitioned and assigned as mandates to France and Britain. During this period, Benedict XV became preoccupied with reestablishing diplomatic ties with France. The pontiff was not satisfied with the new prestige and moral influence the papacy was exerting on a wounded world as long as he was not able to resume formal relations with France, a central piece on the ecclesio-political chessboard of the Holy See, in Europe as in the Middle East. In this matter, Benedict XV initiated a two-speed diplomacy that established a clear distinction between the French colonial empire and metropolitan France. This was an astute and far-seeing policy. Although the French Catholic protectorate was eventually abandoned, in people's minds, Catholicism was still associated with France. The pontiff anticipated the decolonization movement and was aware that if Catholicism were still linked with France, Catholic interests, communities, and missions would be in great danger when the independence movements sprang into action, especially in the turbulent Muslim world. The mandates received by France and Britain on Syria and Palestine were just that. They were temporary tutelages on behalf of the League of Nations, representing non-self-governing societies that would need supervision for a short period of time before gaining independence.

The Holy See's policy of emancipation was integrated into a universal vision of the world, detached from the old Eurocentric vision. When in *Maximum Illud*, the apostolic letter on mission-ary work,[2] Benedict XV asked missionaries to resist nationalistic tendencies, he was asking them to cut ties with their homeland and put their trust in the Catholic Church to support and pro-tect them physically and financially. Benedict XV prepared the church for this task.

Benedict XV's pontificate was solitary on all fronts. The war had confined the pontiff to isolation. Italy, as a result of the lin-gering Roman Question, succeeded in excluding the Holy See from the peace negotiations. The pontiff's diplomacy was mis-understood by the European and American governments. In the Middle East, even clergy members who were closely associated with crafting and implementing the Holy See's foreign policy misunderstood it. A consistent pattern can be traced back to the early days of Benedict's pontificate. There are examples of collaborators challenging the pontiff's diplomatic decisions, as these did not respond in their view to the immediate issue at stake. The apostolic delegates in Constantinople and Beirut, Dol-ci and Giannini, sent strongly worded reports to the secretary of state that highlighted two levels of diplomatic negotiations: that in Rome and those at the local and regional level. When Msgr. Giannini respectfully complained about the naivety of Rome, he misread Benedict's diplomacy, for the apostolic delegate was still thinking in a prewar and short-term frame while Benedict was projecting the church in the twentieth century and was thinking in universal terms.

Throughout a pontificate that lasted less than eight years, Benedict XV navigated Peter's barque through a war of unknown scope. He created a structure to strengthen the Eastern church-es and prepared them for a rapprochement with the Orthodox churches. He was hailed for his humanitarian assistance. Once

2. Benedict XV, "Apostolic Letter *Maximum Illud* [Nov. 30, 1919]," *AAS* 11 (1919): 440–55.

the war ended, he acquired a new prestige and moral authority. He was the first pontiff to demonstrate an understanding of Zionism and understood that the Jewish National Home was there to stay. He witnessed events whose consequences still reverberate in today's politics.

Therefore, one question is worth asking: why did Benedict XV's pontificate have to wait until the end of the twentieth century to benefit from a scholarly reappraisal of his reign, a reign that took place one hundred years ago? Although far from being a comprehensive reappraisal, the work initiated by a small group of scholars, making use of different archival resources, sheds light on different unexplored aspects of the pontiff's life and reign. The first study was undertaken by John Pollard in 1999 and served as an informative framework and inspiration for further work on the role of the papacy in the modern world.

Four circumstances motivate this new interest in Pope Benedict. First and foremost, Benedict XV benefited from a renewed interest in his name as Cardinal Ratzinger chose the name of Benedict when he ascended the throne of Peter in April 2005.[3] In his first message for the celebration of the World Day of Peace in 2006, the newly elected Benedict XVI declared:

The very name Benedict, which I chose on the day of my election to the Chair of Peter, is a sign of my personal commitment to peace. In taking this name, I wanted to evoke both the Patron Saint of Europe, who inspired a civilization of peace on the whole continent, and Pope Benedict XV, who condemned the First World War as a "useless slaughter" and worked for a universal acknowledgment of the lofty demands of peace.[4]

3. Francesca Aran Murphy, "Globalization from Benedict XV to Benedict XVI: The 'Astonishing Optimism' of *Gaudium et Spes* in a Missionary Context," *Nova et Vetera*, English edition, 8, no. 2 (Spring 2010): 395–424.

4. Benedict XVI, "Message of His Holiness Pope Benedict XVI for the Celebration of the World Day of Peace," January 1, 2006, Vatican official website, http://www.vatican.va/holy_father/benedict_xvi/messages/peace/documents/hf_ben-xvi_mes_20051213_xxxix-world-day-peace_en.html.

It is also through the recent scholarly interest in the pontificate of Pius XII during the Second World War that Benedict XV's
reign is reappraised. Historians compared the two pontificates
and their roles during the two wars.[5] Their interest was galva-
nized by the ties uniting the two pontiffs, as Eugenio Pacelli, the
future Pius XII, served as Benedict XV's secretary of the Congregation for Extraordinary Ecclesiastical Affairs in 1914, before
becoming nuncio to Bavaria in 1917.

Two other simultaneous events are drawing attention to
Benedict XV's pontificate as the one-hundredth anniversary of
the outbreak of World War I, commemorated in 2014, coincides
with the one-hundredth anniversary of the beginning of Pope
Benedict's pontificate.

This work is the first to focus on Benedict's diplomacy at the
regional level. It is to be hoped that this new field will be further investigated. A timely study could delve deeper into Benedict XV's diplomacy in Syria and Lebanon and the role played by
France, the mandatory power, in the formative years of the state.
A similar reasoning could be applied to the study of Benedict
XV's diplomacy in Palestine, although the Zionist movement
and the creation of a Jewish National Home already benefit from
a vast literature that presents the role of Britain and the position
of the Vatican. Other regional studies are much needed regarding the role of Benedict XV in other parts of the world, especially
in Eastern Europe.

At the international diplomatic level, a study is needed that
would investigate the long-term legacy of Benedict XV's policy
in its ecclesiastical and political dimensions, especially on the
role of the church in the modern world under the light of *Gaudi-*

5. John F. Pollard, "The Papacy in Two World Wars: Benedict XV and Pius XII Compared," in *Totalitarian Movements and Political Religions* (London: Routledge, 2001): 83–96;
see also Pollard, *The Papacy in the Age of Totalitarianism, 1914–1958* (Oxford: Oxford University Press, 2014).

um et Spes, the Constitution on the church in the modern world, promulgated by Paul VI in December 1965 at the Second Vatican Council.

Pope Benedict XV's pontificate was the catalyst for all future pontificates throughout the twentieth century:

out of his pontificate came the great Church diplomats who would become his successors—Pius XI, Pius XII, indirectly John XXIII, and Paul VI. They were men who were either schooled by him or by his associates and who helped shape the twentieth-century world and the Church in which they lived.[6]

6. Michael P. Riccards, *Vicars of Christ: Popes, Power, and Politics in the Modern World* (New York: Crossroad, 1998), 85.

BIBLIOGRAPHY

ARCHIVES

Archivio della Sacra Congregazione
per le Chiese Orientali (ACCO)

Fasc. 4/7bis, 19/10, 115/5

Fasc. 39/29, Orientali Missioni

Fasc. 115/5

Fasc. 541/28, Bizantini-Melchiti

Fasc. 614/32, Oriente

Rub. 19/10, fol. 5663.

Rub. 40, rito greci, fasc. 6050, 4956

Archivio Segreto Vaticano (ASV)

AES Austria, 1913–15, pos. 1047, fasc. 445

AES Austria, 1915, pos. 1055, fasc. 448; pos. 1057, fasc. 458; pos. 1061.

AES Austria, 1915–16, pos. 1071, fasc. 465

AES Austria, 1916, pos. 1104, fasc. 470; pos. 1099, fasc. 469; pos. 1123, fasc. 476.

AES Austria, 1917, pos. 1211, fasc. 496

AES Austria, 1918–19, pos. 1314, fasc. 517

AES Austria, 1918, 1920, pos. 1337, fasc. 529

AES Austria, 1919, pos. 1304, fasc. 516

AES Francia, 1917, pos. 1295–96, fasc. 686

AES Francia, 1919–1920, pos. 1333, fasc. 697

AES Stati Ecclesiastici, 1916–22, pos. 1418, fasc. 562, 563, 564, 565, 566

AES Stati Ecclesiastici, pos. 1429, fasc. 572

Arch. Deleg. Turchia, Dolci I, II, III

Arch. Nunz. Libano, 1913–16, Registry Propaganda Fide, 68.

Arch. Nunz. Parigi, b. 392, fasc. 304

Arch. Nunz. Parigi, b. 395, fasc. 316

Segr. Stato, Guerra (1914–18), fasc. 1, 84, 305–1, 130–31

Segr. Stato, Guerra (1914–18), rubr. 244, fasc. 110, 111, 112

Segr. Stato, 1914, rubr. 257, fasc. 1
Segr. Stato, 1915, rubr. 257, fasc. 1, 3
Segr. Stato, 1917, rubr. 257, fasc.1
Segr. Stato, 1918, rubr. 244, fasc. 93, 111
Segr. Stato, 1919, pos.53, fasc. 40—Affari Eccl. Asia-Africa-Oceania.

Archivio Storico "De Propaganda Fide" (AP)

N.S., vol. 592 (1917), rub. 126
N.S., vol. 629–30 (1919), rub. 126
N.S., vol. 658 (1920), rub. 126
N.S., vol. 693–94 (1921), rub. 126
N.S., vol. 755 (1922), rub. 126

PAPAL DOCUMENTS
Benedict XIV

"Apostolic Letter *Allatae Sunt* on the Observance of Oriental Rites [July 26, 1755]." http://www.ewtn.com/library/encyc/b14allat.htm

Benedict XV

"Encyclical Letter *Ad Beatissimi Apostolorum Principis* [Nov. 1, 1914]." *AAS* 6 (1914): 585–99.
"Decretum *Preces Pro Pace Certis Diebus Dicendae Praescribuntur* [Jan. 10, 1915]." *AAS* 7 (1915): 13–14.
"Prayer for Peace Prescribed by Pope Benedict XV, to be said 21 March." *Ecclesiastical Review* 52 (Mar. 1915): 353.
"Apostolic Exhortation *To the Belligerent Peoples and Their Rulers* [July 28, 1915]." *AAS* 7 (1915): 365–68.
"Lenten Letter to Cardinal-Vicar Pompilj. *Al Tremendo Conflitto* [Mar. 4, 1916]." *AAS* 8 (1916): 58–60.
"Brief *Romanorum Pontificum* [Feb. 25, 1916]." *AAS* 9 I (1917): 61–62.
"Brief *Cum Catholicae Ecclesiae* [Apr. 15, 1916]." *AAS* 8 (1916): 137–38.
"Motu Proprio *Dei Providentis*, de Sacra Congregatione pro Ecclesia Oriental [May 1, 1917]." *AAS* 9 I (1917): 529–31.
"Apostolic Exhortation *Dès le début* [Aug. 1, 1917]." *AAS* 9 I (1917): 417–20.
"Motu Proprio *Orientis Catholici* [Oct. 15, 1917]." *AAS* 9 I (1917): 531–33.
"Brief *Inclytum Fratrum Minorum Conditorem* [Oct. 4, 1918]." *AAS* 10 (1918): 437–39.
"Consistorial Allocution *Antequam Ordinem* [Mar. 10, 1919]." *AAS* 11 (1919): 97–101.
"Apostolic Letter *Maximum Illud* [Nov. 30, 1919]." *AAS* 11 (1919): 440–55.

BIBLIOGRAPHY

"Encyclical Letter *Pacem, Dei Munus Pulcherrimum* [May 23, 1920]." *AAS* 12 (1920): 209–18.

"Encyclical Letter *Principi Apostolorum Petro* [Oct. 5, 1920]." On St. Ephrem the Syrian. *AAS* 12 (1920): 457–71.

"Encyclical Letter *Annus Iam Plenus* [Dec. 1, 1920]." *AAS* 12 (1920): 553–56.

"Consistorial Allocution *Causa Nobis* [June 13, 1921]." *AAS* 13 (1921): 281–84.

Actes de Benoît XV. vol. 1. Paris: Bonne Presse, 1924.

Benedict XVI

Message of His Holiness Pope Benedict XVI for the Celebration of the World Day of Peace, January 1, 2006. http://www.vatican.va/holy_father/benedict_xvi/messages/peace/documents/hf_ben-xvi_mes_20051213_xxxix-world-day-peace_en.html.

"Visit of His Holiness Benedict XVI to the Congregation for the Oriental Churches, 9 June 2007." http://www.vatican.va/holy_father/benedict_xvi/speeches/2007/june/documents/hf_ben-xvi_spe_20070609_congr-orientchurch_en.html.

Clement XIV

"Brief *Dominus ac Redemptor* [July 21, 1773]." Bref de N.S.P. le Pape Clément XIV en date du 21 Juillet 1773 portant suppression de l'Ordre régulier dit Société de Jésus.

John XXIII

"Encyclical *Pacem in Terris* [Apr. 11, 1963]." *AAS* 55 (1963): 257–304.

John Paul II

"Apostolic Letter *Orientale Lumen,* to mark the Centenary of Orientalium Dignitas of Pope Leo XIII [May 2, 1995]." *AAS* 87 (1995): 745–74.

Leo XIII

"Encyclical Letter *Diuturnum,* on the Origin of Civil Power [June 29, 1881]." *ASS* 14 (1881): 3–14.

"Apostolic Letter *Praeclara Gratulationis Publicae.*" [On the Reunion of Christendom] [June 20, 1894]." *Leonis XIII Acta* 14 (1894): 195–214.

"Apostolic Letter *Orientalium Dignitas* [On the Churches of the East] [Nov. 30, 1894]." *Leonis XIII Acta,* 14 (1894).

"Apostolic Letter *Maximo cum Animi* [Aug. 20, 1898]." *ASS* 31 (1898–99): 193–95.

Pius IX
"Apostolic Letter *Nulla Celebrior* [July 23, 1847]." *Acta Pius IX*. Vol.1.

Pius XI
"Motu Proprio *Romanorum Pontificum* [May 3, 1922]." *AAS* 14 (1922): 321–30.

Second Vatican Council
"Constitutio pastoralis de Ecclesia in mundo huius tempris" [Pastoral Constitution on the Church in the Modern World] (*Gaudium et Spes*) [Dec. 7, 1965]. *AAS* 58 (1966): 1025–1120.

Suprema Sacra Congregatio S. Officii
"De Participatione Catholicorum [July 4, 1919]." *AAS* 11 (1919): 312–16.

SECONDARY SOURCES

Aksakal, Mustafa. *The Ottoman Road to War in 1914: The Ottoman Empire and the First World War*. Cambridge: Cambridge University Press, 2010.

Albrecht-Carrié, René. *A Diplomatic History of Europe since the Congress of Vienna*. London: Harper and Row, 1958.

American Jewish Committee. "10th Annual Report of the American Jewish Committee, 12 November 1916." In *American Jewish Year Book* 19 (1916).

Antonius, George. "Syria and the French Mandate." *International Affairs* 13 (July 1934): 523–39.

———. *The Arab Awakening: The Story of the Arab National Movement*. London: Hamish Hamilton, 1945.

Araujo, Robert John, and John A. Lucal. *Papal Diplomacy and the Quest for Peace: The Vatican and International Organizations from the Early Years to the League of Nations*. Ann Arbor, Mich.: Sapientia Press of Ave Maria University, 2004.

Artinian, Vartan. "The Formation of Catholic and Protestant Millets in the Ottoman Empire." *Armenian Review* 28, no. 1 (spring 1975): 3–15.

Ashbee, C. R. *Palestine Notebook, 1918–1923*. London: Heinemann, 1923.

Asquith, Herbert Henry. *Letters to Venetia Stanley*. Edited by Michael Brock and Eleanor Brock. Oxford: Oxford University Press, 1982.

Atran, Scott. "The Surrogate Colonization of Palestine, 1917–1939." *American Ethnologist* 16 (Nov. 1989): 719–44.

Aubert, Roger. "Les démarches du cardinal Mercier en vue de l'octroi à la Belgique d'un mandat sur la Palestine." *Bulletin de la Classe des Lettres et des Sciences Morales et Politiques* 5 (1979).

Avineri, Shlomo. *Herzl's Vision: Theodor Herzl and the Foundation of the Jewish State.* Translated by Haim Watzman. Katonah, N.Y.: Blue-Bridge, 2014.

Azoury, Negib. *Le réveil de la nation arabe dans l'Asie turque.* Paris: Plon, 1905.

Backhouse, Stephen. *Kierkegaard's Critique of Christian Nationalism.* Oxford: Oxford University Press, 2011.

Barton, James L. *Story of Near East Relief (1915–1930): An Interpretation.* New York: Macmillan, 1930.

Bass, Gary J. *Freedom's Battle: The Origins of Humanitarian Intervention.* New York: Knopf, 2008.

Batiffol, Pierre. "Pope Benedict and the Restoration of Unity," *Constructive Quarterly* 6 (1918): 209–25.

Baudrillart, Alfred. *Les carnets du Cardinal Baudrillart, 1er août 1914–31 décembre 1918.* Paris: Editions du Cerf, 1994.

Beales, A. C. F. *The Catholic Church and International Order.* Hardmondsworth, UK: Penguin, 1941.

Beaupin, Eugène. "Introduction." In *L'apostolat missionnaire de la France.* Conférences données à l'Institut Catholique de Paris, Série 1924–25. Paris: Téqui, 1924–26.

Bell, Lady Francis, ed. *The Letters of Gertrude Bell.* 2 vols. New York: Boni and Liveright, 1927.

Bentwich, Norman. "The Abrogation of the Turkish Capitulations." *Journal of Comparative Legislation and International Law* 5 (1923): 182–88.

Berridge, G. R., Maurice Keens-Soper, and Thomas G. Otte. *Diplomacy Theory from Machiavelli to Kissinger.* New York: Palgrave, 2001.

Binchy, D. A. "The Vatican and International Diplomacy." *International Affairs* 22 (Jan. 1946): 47–56.

Boemeke, Manfred Franz, Gerald D. Feldman, and Elisabeth Gläser, eds. *The Treaty of Versailles: A Reassessment after 75 Years.* Cambridge: Cambridge University Press, 1998.

Bovis, H. Eugene. *The Jerusalem Question, 1917–1968.* Stanford, Calif.: Hoover Institution Press, 1971.

Braude, Benjamin, and Bernard Lewis, eds. *Christians and Jews in the Ottoman Empire: The Functioning of a Plural Society.* New York: Holmes and Meier, 1982.

Bryson, Thomas A. "A Note on Near East Relief: Walter George Smith, Cardinal Gibbons, and the Question of Discrimination against Catholics." *Muslim World* 61 (July 1971): 202–9.

———. *American Diplomatic Relations with the Middle East, 1784–1975: A Survey.* Metuchen, N.J.: Scarecrow Press, 1977.

Buell, Raymond L. "The Vatican and the New World." *Current History* 16 (Sept. 1922): 981.

Bunton, Martin. *Colonial Land Policies in Palestine, 1917–1936.* Oxford: Oxford University Press, 2007.

Burg, David F., and L. Edward Purcell. *Almanac of World War I.* Lexington: University Press of Kentucky, 1998.

Burleigh, Michael. *Sacred Causes: The Clash of Religion and Politics from the Great War to the War on Terror.* New York: HarperCollins, 2007.

Burrows, Matthew. "'Mission Civilisatrice': French Cultural Policy in the Middle East, 1860–1914." *Historical Journal* 29 (1986): 109–35.

Cabanes, Bruno. *The Great War and the Origins of Humanitarianism, 1918–1924.* Cambridge: Cambridge University Press, 2014.

Campos, Michelle U. *Ottoman Brothers: Muslims, Christians, and Jews in Early Twentieth-Century Palestine.* Stanford, Calif.: Stanford University Press, 2011.

Cecil, Algernon. "Vatican Policy in the Twentieth Century." *Journal of the British Institute of International Affairs* 4 (Jan. 1925): 1–29.

Chickering, Roger, and Stig Förster, eds. *The Shadows of Total War: Europe, East Asia, and the United States, 1919–1939.* Cambridge: Cambridge University Press; London: German Historical Institute, 2003.

Ciani, Adriano Ercole. "The Vatican, American Catholics, and the Struggle for Palestine, 1917–1958: A Study of Cold War Roman Catholic Transnationalism." Ph.D. diss., University of Western Ontario, Canada, 2011.

Çiçek, M. Talha. *War and State Formation in Syria: Cemal Pasha's Governorate During World War I, 1914–1917.* New York: Routledge Studies in Middle Eastern History, 2014.

Cleveland, William L., and Martin P. Bunton. *A History of the Modern Middle East.* Boulder, Colo.: Westview Press, 2009.

Cloarec, Vincent. *La France et la question de la Syrie, 1914–1918.* Paris: CNRS, 1998.

Compston, Christine, and Rachel F. Seidman, eds. *Our Documents: 100 Milestone Documents from the National Archives.* New York: Oxford University Press, 2003.

Coppa, Frank J. *The Papacy, the Jews, and the Holocaust.* Washington, D.C.: The Catholic University of America Press, 2006.

———. *The Papacy in the Modern World: A Political History.* London: Reaktion Books, 2014.

Courbage, Youssef, and Phillipe Fargues. *Chrétiens et juifs dans l'Islam arabe et turc.* Paris: Fayard, 1992.

Cragg, Kenneth. *The Arab Christian: A History in the Middle East.* London: Mowbray, 1992.

Croce, Giuseppe M. "Alle origini della Congregazione Orientale e del Pontificio Istituto Orientale: Il contributo di Mons. Louis Petit." In *The Pontifical Oriental Institute: The First Seventy-Five Years; 1917–1992,* edited by Edward G. Farrugia, 257–333. Rome: Orientalia Christiana, 1993.

Cumming, Henry H. *Franco-British Rivalry in the Post-War Near East: The Decline of French Influence.* London: Oxford University Press, 1938.

Davison, Roderic H. "Turkish Attitudes concerning Christian-Muslim Equality in the Nineteenth Century." *American Historical Review* 59 (July 1954): 844–64.

Dawisha, Adeed. *Arab Nationalism in the Twentieth Century: From Triumph to Despair.* Princeton, N.J.: Princeton University Press, 2003.

De la Brière, Yves. "Le règne pontifical de Benoît XV." *Études* (Feb. 5, 1922): 257–74.

DeNovo, John A. *American Interests and Policies in the Middle East, 1900–1939.* Minneapolis: University of Minnesota Press, 1963.

Destani, B., ed. *Minorities in the Middle East: Religious Communities in Jerusalem, 1843–1974, and Minorities in Israel.* Chippenham, UK: Archive Editions, 2005.

Destremau, Christian, and Jean Moncelon. *Louis Massignon.* Paris: Plon, 1994.

Djemal Pasha. *Memories of a Turkish Statesman, 1913–1919.* New York : George H. Doran, 1922.

Documents diplomatiques français. Edited by the Commission de publication des documents diplomatiques français. Série 1920–1932. Vol. 4 (16 Janvier–30 Juin 1921). Brussels: Peterlang, 2004.

Durand, Jean-Paul, OP. "Les accords de Mytilène de 1901 entre le gouvernement français et la Sublime Porte." In *Le pontificat de Léon XIII, renaissances du Saint-Siège?* edited by Philippe Levillain and Jean-Marc Ticchi, 185–202. Rome: École française de Rome, 2006.

Ecumenical Patriarchate of Constantinople. "Encyclical Letter *Unto the Churches of Christ Everywhere* [Jan. 1920]." *Ecumenical Review* 12, no. 1 (Oct. 1959): 79–82.

Eisenberg, Laura Zitrain. *My Enemy's Enemy: Lebanon in the Early Zionist Imagination, 1900–1948.* Detroit, Mich.: Wayne State University Press, 1994.

Ellis, John Tracy. *The Life of James Cardinal Gibbons, Archbishop of Baltimore, 1834–1921.* 2 vols. Milwaukee, Wisc.: Bruce, 1952.

El-Mudarris, Hussein I., and Olivier Salmon, eds. *Le Consulat de France à Alep au XVIIe siècle: Journal de Louis Gédoyn, vie de François Picquet, mémoires de Laurent d'Arvieux.* Alep: Ray, 2009.

Esterka, P. "Toward Union: The Congresses at Velehrad." *Journal of Ecumenical Studies* 8 (1971): 10–51.

BIBLIOGRAPHY

Evans, G. R. *Method in Ecumenical Theology: The Lessons So Far.* Cambridge: Cambridge University Press, 1996.

Evans, Malcolm D. *Religious Liberty and International Law in Europe.* Cambridge: Cambridge University Press, 1997.

Eyezo'o, Salvador, and Jean-François Zorn, eds. *Concurrences en mission: Propagandes, conflits, coexistences (XVIe–XXIe siècle).* Paris: Karthala, 2011.

Fabrizio, Daniela. "Il protettorato religioso sui Cattolici in Oriente: La questione delle relazioni diplomatiche dirette tra Santa Sede e Impero ottomano, 1901–1918." *Nuovo Rivista Storica* 3 (1998): 583–626.

Fargues, Philippe. "The Arab Christians of the Middle East: A Demographic Perspective." In *Christian Communities in the Arab Middle East: The Challenge of the Future,* edited by Andrea Pacini. Oxford: Oxford University Press, 1998.

———. "Demographic Islamization: Non-Muslims in Muslim Countries." *SAIS Review* 21, no. 2 (2001): 103–16.

Fattal, Antoine. *Le statut légal des non-musulmans en pays d'Islam.* Beirut: Imprimerie catholique, 1958.

Ferrari, Silvio. *Vaticano e Israele: Dal secondo conflitto mondiale alla Guerra del golfo.* Florence, Italy: Sansoni Editore, 1991.

Fieldhouse, David K. *Western Imperialism in the Middle East, 1914–1958.* Oxford: Oxford University Press, 2006.

Fisher, Eugene J. "The Vatican and the State of Israel." *First Things* (Apr. 1991): 11–12.

Florinsky, Michael T. "A Page of Diplomatic History: Russian Military Leaders and the Problem of Constantinople during the War." *Political Science Quarterly* 44 (Mar. 1929): 108–15.

Frary, Lucien J., and Mara Kozelsky, eds. *Russian-Ottoman Borderlands: The Eastern Question Reconsidered.* Madison, Wis.: University of Wisconsin Press, 2014.

Frazee, Charles A. *Catholics and Sultans: The Church and the Ottoman Empire, 1453–1923.* New York: Cambridge University Press, 1983.

Friedman, Isaiah. *The Question of Palestine, 1914–1918: British-Jewish-Arab Relations.* New York: Schocken Books, 1973.

———. *Palestine, a Twice-Promised Land? The British, the Arabs and Zionism (1915–1920).* New Brunswick, N.J.: Transaction Publishers, 2000.

Fromkin, David. *A Peace to End All Peace.* New York: Henry Holt, 1989.

Gasparri, Pietro. *Il Protetorato cattolico della Francia nell'Oriente e nell' estremo Oriente: Studio storico giuridoco di un prelate Romano.* N.p.: 1904

Gelvin, James. "The Ironic Legacy of the King-Crane Commission." In *The Middle East and the United States: A Historical and Political Reas-*

sessment, edited by David W. Lesch, 13–29. Boulder, Colo.: Westview Press, 2007.

Gilbert, Martin. *The First World War.* New York: Henry Holt, 1994.

Gill, Joseph. "Interessamento della S.C. Orientale per gli studi superiori." In *La Sacra Congregazione per le Chiese Orientali: Nel cinquantesimo della fondazione (1917–1967).* Rome: Tipografia Italo-Orientale "San Nilo," 1969.

Goldman, Shalom. *Zeal for Zion: Christians, Jews, and the Idea of the Promised Land.* Chapel Hill: University of North Carolina Press, 2009.

Gorayeb, Joseph, SJ. "St. Ephrem, the New Doctor of the Universal Church." *Catholic Historical Review* 7 (Oct. 1921): 303–15.

Goyau, Georges. *Papauté et chrétienté sous Benoît XV.* Paris: Perrin, 1922.

Grabill, Joseph. *Protestant Diplomacy and the Near East: Missionary Influence on American Policy, 1810–1927.* Minneapolis: University of Minnesota Press, 1971.

Graham, Robert. *Vatican Diplomacy: A Study of Church and State on the International Plane.* Princeton, N.J.: Princeton University Press, 1959.

Greaves, R. W. "The Jerusalem Bishopric, 1841." *English Historical Review* 64 (July 1949): 328–52.

Gregory, John Duncan. *On the Edge of Diplomacy: Rambles and Reflections, 1902–1928.* London: Hutchinson, 1929.

Grenville, J. A. S., ed. *The Major International Treaties, 1914–1973: A History and Guide with Texts.* London: Methuen, 1974.

Grief, Howard. *The Legal Foundation and Borders of Israel under International Law.* Jerusalem: Mazo, 2008.

Griffith, Sidney H. *"Faith Adoring the Mystery": Reading the Bible with St. Ephraem the Syrian.* Père Marquette Lecture in Theology 1997. Milwaukee, Wisc.: Marquette University Press, 1997.

———. *The Church in the Shadow of the Mosque: Christians and Muslims in the World of Islam.* Princeton, N.J.: Princeton University Press, 2008.

Hachey, Thomas E., ed. *Great Britain Legation: Anglo-Vatican Relations, 1914–1939; Confidential Annual Reports of the British Ministers to the Holy See.* London and Boston: G. K. Hall, 1972.

Hajjar, Joseph. *Les chrétiens uniates du Proche-Orient.* Paris: Éditions du Seuil, 1962.

———. *Le christianisme en Orient.* Beirut: Librairie du Liban, 1971.

———. *Le Vatican, la France et le catholicisme oriental (1878–1914).* Paris: Beauchesne, 1979.

———. *L'Europe et les destinées du Proche-Orient.* 5 vols. Damas: Dar Tlass, 1998.

Hakim, Carol. *The Origins of the Lebanese National Idea: 1840–1920.* Berkeley, Calif.: California University Press, 2013.

Harris, William W. *The New Face of Lebanon: History's Revenge*. Princeton, N.J.: Markus Wiener, 2005.

———. *Lebanon: A History, 600–2011*. New York: Oxford University Press, 2012.

Hehir, J. Bryan. "The Catholic Church and the Middle East, Policy and Diplomacy." In *The Vatican, Islam, and the Middle East*, edited by Kail C. Ellis, 109–24. Syracuse, N.Y.: Syracuse University Press, 1987.

Heinl, Robert, Jr. *Dictionary of Military and Naval Quotations*. Annapolis, Md.: United States Naval Institute, 1966.

Herzl, Theodor. *The Complete Diaries of Theodor Herzl*. Vol. 1. New York: Herzl Press, 1960.

Heston, Edward. "Papal Diplomacy: Its Organization and Way of Acting." In *The Catholic Church in World Affairs*, edited by Waldemar Gurian and Matthew A. Fitzsimmons, 33–42. Notre Dame, Ind.: University of Notre Dame Press, 1954.

Hitti, Philip K. *History of Syria including Lebanon and Palestine*. Vol. 1. Piscataway, N.J.: First Gorgias, 2002.

Hopwood, Derek. *The Russian Presence in Syria and Palestine, 1843–1914*. Oxford: Clarendon Press, 1969.

Hourani, Albert. *Syria and Lebanon: A Political Essay*. Oxford: Oxford University Press, 1946.

Huby, Joseph. "Le problème juif." *Études* (Sept. 1921): 513–42.

Hurewitz, J. C. *Diplomacy in the Near and Middle East: A Documentary Record, 1914–1956*. 2 vols. Princeton, N.J.: Van Nostrand, 1956.

Ingrams, Doreen. *Palestine Papers, 1917–1922: Seeds of Conflict*. London: John Murray, 1972.

Irani, George Emile. *The Papacy and the Middle East: The Role of the Holy See in the Arab-Israeli Conflict, 1962–1984*. Notre Dame, Ind.: University of Notre Dame Press, 1986.

———. Review of *The Vatican and Zionism: Conflict in the Holy Land, 1895–1925*, by Sergio Minerbi. *Catholic Historical Review* 78 (Jan. 1992): 135–36.

Jedin, Hubert. *History of the Church*. Vol. 10, *The Church in the Modern Age*. Edited by Hubert Jedin, Konrad Repgen, and John Dolan. New York: Crossroad, 1981.

Joint International Commission for the Theological Dialogue between the Roman Catholic Church and the Orthodox Church. "Uniatism, Method of Union of the Past, and the Present Search for Full Communion," 7th Plenary Session, Balamand School of Theology (Lebanon), June 17–24, 1993. Centro Pro Unione, *Information Service* 83 (1993/II): 96–99.

Karpat, Kemal H. "The Transformation of the Ottoman State, 1789–

1908." *International Journal of Middle East Studies* 3 (July 1972): 243–81.

———. "Ottoman Views and Policies towards the Orthodox Christian Church." In *Orthodox Christians and Muslims*, edited by N. M. Vaporis. Brookline, Mass.: Holy Cross Orthodox Press, 1986. Also published in *Greek Orthodox Theological Review* 31 (1986): 131–55.

———. *Studies on Ottoman Social and Political History.* Leiden: Brill, 2002.

Kaufman, Asher. *Reviving Phoenicia: In Search of Identity in Lebanon.* New York: I. B. Tauris, 2004.

Kearns, Cleo McNelly. "Mary, Maternity, and Abrahamic Hospitality in Derrida's Reading of Massignon." In *Derrida and Religion: Other Testaments*, edited by Yvonne Sherwood and Kevin Hart, 73–96. New York: Routledge, 2005.

Keegan, John. *The First World War.* New York: Knopf, 1999.

Kerner, Robert J. "Russia, the Straits, and Constantinople, 1914–1915." *Journal of Modern History* 1 (Sept. 1929): 400–15.

Khoury, Gérard. *La France et l'Orient arabe: Naissance du Liban moderne (1914–1920).* Paris: Armand Colin, 1993.

———. "Robert de Caix et Louis Massignon: Deux visions de la politique française au Levant en 1920." In *The British and French Mandates in Comparative Perspectives: Les mandats français et anglais dans une perspective comparative*, edited by Nadine Méouchy and Peter Sluglett, 165–84. Leiden: Brill, 2004.

———. *Une tutelle coloniale: Le mandat français en Syrie et au Liban; Écrits politiques de Robert de Caix.* Paris: Belin, 2006.

Khoury, Philip S. *Syria and the French Mandate: The Politics of Arab Nationalism, 1920–1945.* Princeton, N.J.: Princeton University Press, 1987.

Kohn, Hans. *Nationalism and Imperialism in the Hither East.* London: Routledge, 1932.

Kreutz, Andrej. *Vatican Policy on the Palestinian-Israeli Conflict: The Struggle for the Holy Land.* Westport, Conn.: Greenwood Press, 1990.

Kucherov, Samuel. "The Problem of Constantinople and the Straits." *Russian Review* 8, no. 3 (July 1949): 205–20.

La Piana, George F. "From Leo XIII to Benedict XV." *American Journal of Theology* 21 (Apr. 1917): 175–92.

Laqueur, Walter, and Barry M. Rubin, eds. *The Israel-Arab Reader: A Documentary History of the Middle East Conflict.* New York: Penguin, 2001.

Latour, Francis. *La papauté et les problèmes de la paix pendant la première guerre mondiale.* Paris: L'Harmattan, 1996.

Lauren, Paul Gordon. "Theories of Bargaining with Threats of Force: Deterrence and Coercive Diplomacy." In *Diplomacy: New Approaches in History, Theory, and Policy*, edited by Paul Gordon Lauren, 183–212. New York: Free Press, 1979.

Laurens, Henry. "Le Vatican et la question de la Palestine." In *Nations et Saint-Siège au XXe siècle*, Colloque sous la direction d'Hélène Carrère d'Encausse et de Philippe Levillain. Paris: Fayard, 2003.

Lawrence, T. E. *Seven Pillars of Wisdom: A Triumph*. Garden City, N.Y.: Doubleday, 1935.

Leclercq, Jacques. *Thunder in the Distance: The Life of Père Lebbe*. New York: Sheed and Ward, 1958.

Legrand, Hervé. "La fondation de l'Institut Pontifical Oriental en 1917, premier pas vers l'oecuménisme." Paper presented at the Pontifical Oriental Institute, Rome, Italy, Nov. 9, 2007.

Leslie, Shane. *Cardinal Gasquet*. London: Burns and Oates, 1953.

Lipman, Vivian D. "America-Holy Land Material in British Archives, 1820–1930." In *With Eyes toward Zion*. Vol. 2, *Themes and Sources in the Archives of the United States, Great Britain, Turkey and Israel*. Édited by Moshe Davis. New York: Praeger, 1986.

Loiseau, Charles. *Politique romaine et sentiment français*. Paris: Grasset, 1923.

Longrigg, Stephen Hemsley. *Syria and Lebanon under French Mandate*. New York: Octagon, 1972.

Macfie, A. L. *The End of the Ottoman Empire, 1908–1923*. London: Longman, 1998.

MacMillan, Margaret. *The War That Ended Peace: The Road to 1914*. New York: Random House, 2013.

MacNutt, Francis Augustus. *A Papal Chamberlain: The Personal Chronicle of Francis Augustus MacNutt*. London: Longmans, 1936.

Mahieu, Patrice, OSB. *Paul VI et les orthodoxes*. Paris: Éditions du Cerf, 2012.

Makdisi, Ussama. *Artillery of Heaven: American Missionaries and the Failed Conversion of the Middle East*. Ithaca, N.Y.: Cornell University Press, 2007.

Mandel, Neville J. *Arabs and Zionism Before World War I*. Berkeley: University of California Press, 1977.

Manela, Eres. *The Wilsonian Moment: Self-Determination and the International Origins of Anticolonial Nationalism*. Oxford: Oxford University Press, 2007.

Manuel, Frank E. "The Palestine Question in Italian Diplomacy, 1917–1920." *Journal of Modern History* 27 (Sept. 1955): 263–80.

Manzano, Moreno Eduardo, and Roberto Mazza, eds. *Jerusalem in World War I: The Palestine Diary of a European Diplomat*, by Conde de Ballobar. London: I.B. Tauris, 2011.

Matz, Nele. "Civilization and the Mandate System under the League of Nations as Origin of Trusteeship." In *Max Planck Yearbook of United*

Nations Law, edited by A. von Bogdandy and R. Wolfrum. Vol. 9. Leiden: Brill, 2005.

Mayer, Arno J. *Political Origins of the New Diplomacy, 1917–1918*. New Haven: Yale University Press, 1959.

Mayeur, Jean-Marie. "Les Églises et les relations internationales: L'Église Catholique." In *Histoire du Christianisme des origines à nos jours*, vol. 12, *Guerres mondiales et totalitarismes (1914–1958)*, edited by Jean-Marie Mayeur, Charles Pietri, André Vauchez, and Marc Venard, 297–345. Paris: Desclée, 1990.

Mazza, Roberto. "Church at War: The Impact of the First World War on the Christian Institutions of Jerusalem, 1914–20." *Middle Eastern Studies* 45, no. 2 (Mar. 2009): 207–27.

———. *Jerusalem: From the Ottomans to the British*. London: I. B. Tauris, 2009.

McCarthy, Justin. *The Population of Palestine: Population History and Statistics of the Late Ottoman Period and the Mandate*. New York: Columbia University Press, 1990.

McCormick, Anne O'Hare. *Vatican Journal, 1921–1954*. New York: Farrar, Straus, and Cudahy, 1957.

Méouchy, Nadine, and Peter Sluglett, eds. *The British and French Mandates in Comparative Perspectives*. Leiden: Brill, 2004.

Minerbi, Sergio I. *The Vatican and Zionism: Conflict in the Holy Land, 1895–1925*. Oxford: Oxford University Press, 1990.

Mombelli, Alexander. "Palestine: Catholics Affirm Principle of Their Rights." *Catholic News*, December 7, 1935. Jerusalem, N.C.W.C. http://www.catholicnews.sg/index.php?option=com_content&view=article&id=4266&Itemid=78.

Montoisy, Jean-Dominique. "Israël-Vatican: Le nouveau dialogue." *Studia Diplomatica* 34, no. 6 (1981): 753–70.

Morgenthau, Henry. *Ambassador Morgenthau's Story: A Personal Account of the Armenian Genocide*. Garden City, N.Y.: Doubleday, 1918.

Moubayed, Sami. *Syria and the USA: Washington's Relations with Damascus from Wilson to Eisenhower*. New York: I. B. Tauris, 2011.

Murphy, Francesca Aran. "Globalization from Benedict XV to Benedict XVI: The 'Astonishing Optimism' of *Gaudium et Spes* in a Missionary Context." *Nova et Vetera*, English Edition 8, no. 2 (Spring 2010): 395–424.

Murray, Robert. "Ephrem Syrus, St." In *Catholic Dictionary of Theology*. Vol. 2. London: Nelson, 1967, 220–23.

Nevakivi, Jukka. *Britain, France, and the Arab Middle East, 1914–1920*. London: Athlone, 1969.

Nicault, Catherine. "The End of the French Religious Protectorate in Jerusalem." *Bulletin du CRFJ* 4 (Spring 1999): 77–92.

Oldmeadow, Ernest. *Francis Cardinal Bourne*. London: Burne, Oates, and Washburn, 1943.

Oliver, James M. *Ecumenical Associations: Their Canonical Status with Particular Reference to the United States of America*. Rome: Editrice Pontificia Universita Gregoriana, 1999.

O'Mahony, Anthony, ed. *Palestinian Christians: Religion, Politics, and Society in the Holy Land*. London: Melisende, 1999.

———, ed. *The Christian Communities of Jerusalem and the Holy Land: Studies in History, Religion, and Politics*. Cardiff: University of Wales Press, 2003.

O'Mahony, Anthony, Goran Gunner, and Kevork Hintlian, eds. *Christian Heritage in the Holy Land*. London: Scorpion Cavendish, 1995.

Paterson, Thomas, J. Garry Clifford, and Shane J. Maddock. *American Foreign Relations: A History to 1920*. Vol. 1. Boston, Mass.: Wadsworth, 2010.

Pélissié du Rausas, Gérard. *Le régime des capitulations dans l'empire ottoman*. 2 vols. Paris: Arthur Rousseau, 1902.

Perko, Francis M. "Toward a 'Sound and Lasting Basis': Relations between the Holy See, the Zionist Movement, and Israel, 1896–1996." *Israel Studies* 2 (Spring 1997): 1–21.

Pernot, Maurice. *Le Saint-Siège, l'Église catholique et la politique mondiale*. Paris: Armand Colin, 1924.

Peters, F. E. *Jerusalem: The Holy City in the Eyes of Chroniclers, Visitors, Pilgrims, and Prophets from the Days of Abraham to the Beginnings of Modern Times*. Princeton, N.J.: Princeton University Press, 1985.

Peters, Walter H. *The Life of Benedict XV*. Milwaukee, Wisc.: Bruce, 1959.

Picaudou, Nadine. *La décennie qui ébranla le Moyen Orient, 1914–1923*. Paris: Éditions Complexe, 1992.

Poe, Marshall. "Moscow, the Third Rome: The Origins and Transformations of a 'Pivotal Moment.'" *Jahrbücher für Geschichte Osteuropas* 49, no. 3 (2001): 412–29.

Poetker, Joel S. *The Fourteen Points*. Colombus, Ohio: Charles E. Merrill, 1969.

Poggi, Vincenzo, SJ. "Il settantennio del Pontificio Istituto Orientale." In *The Pontifical Oriental Institute: The First Seventy-Five Years; 1917–1992*, edited by Edward G. Farrugia. Rome: Orientalia Christiana, 1993.

———. *Per la storia del Pontificio Istituto Orientale: Saggi sull'istituzione, i suoi uomini e l'Oriente Cristiano*. Rome: Orientalia Christiana Analecta, 2000.

Pollard, John F. *The Unknown Pope: Benedict XV (1914–1922) and the Pursuit of Peace*. London: Geoffrey Chapman, 1999.

———. "The Papacy in Two World Wars: Benedict XV and Pius XII Compared." In *Totalitarian Movements and Political Religions*. London: Routledge, 2001.

———. *The Papacy in the Age of Totalitarianism, 1914–1958*. Oxford: Oxford University Press, 2014.

Quilliam, Neil. *Syria and the New World Order*. Reading, UK: Garner, 1999.

Quinn, John R. "From a Moral Voice Raised in the International Dialogue." *Origins* 13 (May 3, 1984): 571.

Rabbath, Edmond. *La formation historique du Liban politique et constitutionnel: Essai de synthèse*. Beirut: Librairie orientale, 1973.

Randall, Alec. *Vatican Assignment*. London: Heinemann, 1956.

Renoton-Beine, Nathalie. *La colombe et les tranchées: Les tentatives de paix de Benoît XV pendant la Grande Guerre*. Paris: Éditions du Cerf, 2004.

Renton, James. "Flawed Foundations: The Balfour Declaration and the Palestine Mandate." In *Britain, Palestine and Empire: The Mandate Years*, edited by Rory Miller, 15–38. Farnham: Ashgate, 2010.

Renzi, William A. "The Entente and the Vatican during the Period of Italian Neutrality, August 1914–May 1915." *Historical Journal* 13 (Sept. 1970): 491–508.

Reynolds, Michael A. *Shattering Empires: The Clash and Collapse of the Ottoman and Russian Empires, 1908–1918*. Cambridge: Cambridge University Press, 2011.

Riccards, Michael P. *Vicars of Christ: Popes, Power, and Politics in the Modern World*. New York: Crossroad, 1998.

———. *Faith and Leadership: The Papacy and the Roman Catholic Church*. Lanham, Md.: Lexington Books, 2012.

Rieff, David. *A Bed for the Night: Humanitarianism in Crisis*. New York: Simon and Schuster, 2002.

Rivier, Alphonse. *Principes du droit des gens*. 2 vols. Paris: Arthur Rousseau, 1896.

Robson, Laura. *Colonialism and Christianity in Mandate Palestine*. Austin, Tex.: University of Texas Press, 2011.

Rodogno, Davide. *Against Massacre: Humanitarian Interventions in the Ottoman Empire, 1815–1914: The Emergence of a European Concept and International Practice*. Princeton, N.J.: Princeton University Press, 2012.

Rogan, Eugene. *The Arabs: A History*. New York: Basic Books, 2009.

———. *The Fall of the Ottomans: The Great War in the Middle East*. London: Basic Books, 2015.

Rokach, Livia. *The Catholic Church and the Question of Palestine*. London: Saqi Books, 1987.

Rolland, Romain. *Les précurseurs*. Paris: Éditions de l'Humanité, 1920.

Rothwell, V. H. *British War Aims and Peace Diplomacy, 1914–1918*. Oxford: Clarendon Press, 1971.

Ruether, Rosemary, and Herman Ruether. "The Vatican, Zionism, and the Israeli-Palestinian Conflict." In *Zionism and the Quest for Justice in the Holy Land*, edited by Donald E. Wagner and Walter T. Davis, 118–38. Eugene, Ore.: Pickwick Publications, 2014.

Sachar, Howard M. *The Emergence of the Middle East, 1914–1924*. New York: Knopf, 1969.

Sayegh, Maximos IV, ed. *The Eastern Churches and Catholic Unity*. New York: Herder and Herder, 1963.

Schneer, Jonathan. *The Balfour Declaration: The Origins of the Arab-Israeli Conflict*. New York: Random House, 2010.

Scholch, Alexander. "Britain in Palestine, 1838–1882: The Roots of the Balfour Policy." *Journal of Palestine Studies* 22 (Autumn 1992): 39–56.

Scotta, Antonio. *La conciliazione ufficiosa: Diario del barone Carlo Monti "incarito d'affari" del governo italiano presso la Santa Sede (1914–1922)*. 2 vols. Città del Vaticano: Libreria Editrice Vaticana, 1997.

Segev, Tom. *One Palestine Complete: Jews and Arabs under the British Mandate*. New York: Henry Holt, 2000.

Senturk, Recep. "Minority Rights in Islam." In *Islam and Human Rights: Advancing a U.S.–Muslim Dialogue*, edited by Shireen T. Hunter and Huma Malik, 48–69. Washington, D.C.: Center for Strategic and International Studies Press, 2005.

Seymour, Charles. *Intimate Papers of Colonel House*. Vol. 3. New York: Houghton Mifflin, 1928.

Sluglett, Peter. "The Mandates: Some Reflections on the Nature of the British Presence in Iraq (1914–1932) and the French Presence in Syria (1918–1946)." In *The British and French Mandates in Comparative Perspectives/Les mandats français et anglais dans une perspective comparative*, edited by Nadine Méouchy and Peter Sluglett, 103–27. Leiden: Brill, 2004.

Stein, Leonard. *The Balfour Declaration*. New York: Simon and Schuster, 1961.

Stevens, Richard P. "The Vatican, the Catholic Church, and Jerusalem." *Journal of Palestine Studies* 10 (Spring 1981): 100–10.

Storrs, Ronald. *Orientations*. London: Nicholson and Watson, 1945.

Tanenbaum, Jan Karl. "France and the Arab Middle East, 1914–1920." *Transactions of the American Philosophical Society* 68 (1978): 1–50.

Tauber, Eliezer. *The Formation of Modern Syria and Iraq*. London: Frank Cass, 1995.

Tavard, George. "Editorial." *Journal of Ecumenical Studies* 1 (1964): 99.

———. *Ecumenism: Two Centuries of Ecumenism*. Notre Dame, Ind.: Fides Press, 1978.

Thompson, Elizabeth. "Neither Conspiracy Nor Hypocrisy: The Jesuits and the French Mandate in Syria and Lebanon." In *Altruism and Imperialism: Western Cultural and Religious Missions in the Middle East*, edited by Eleanor H. Tejirian and Reeva Spector Simon, 66–87. New York: Middle East Institute, Columbia University Press, 2002.

Tibawi, A. L. *A Modern History of Syria, including Lebanon and Palestine.* London: Macmillan, 1969.

Times [London], *The History of the Times: The 150th Anniversary and Beyond, 1912–1947.* London: Times Printing House Square, 1952.

Trimbur, Dominique. "Une appropriation française du Levant: La mission en Orient du cardinal Dubois, 1919–1920." In *Une France en Méditerranée: écoles, langue et culture française, XIXe–XXe siècles*, edited by Patrick Cabanel, 109–28. Paris: Créaphis, 2006.

Tumulty, Joseph P. *Woodrow Wilson as I Know Him.* Garden City, N.J.: Doubleday, 1921.

Ulrichsen, Kristian Coates. *The First World War in the Middle East.* London: Hurst, 2014.

Vallier, Ivan. "The Roman Catholic Church: A Transnational Actor." In *Transnational Relations*, edited by Robert O. Keohane and Joseph S. Nye, 129–52. Cambridge, Mass.: Harvard University Press, 1972.

Valognes, Jean-Pierre. *Vie et mort des chrétiens d'Orient.* Paris: Fayard, 1994.

Venzon, Anne Cipriano, ed. *The United States in the First World War: An Encyclopedia.* New York: Garland, 1999.

Viroli, Maurizio. *For Love of Country: An Essay on Patriotism and Nationalism.* Oxford: Oxford University Press, 1995.

Wagstaff, J. M. "A Note on Some Nineteenth-Century Population Statistics for Lebanon." *British Society for Middle Eastern Studies* 13 (1986): 27–35.

Warman, Roberta. "The Erosion of Foreign Office Influence in the Making of Foreign Policy, 1916–1918." *Historical Journal* 15 (Mar. 1972): 133–59.

Wasserstein, Bernard. *The British in Palestine: The Mandatory Government and Arab-Jewish Conflict, 1917–1929.* London: Royal Historical Society, 1978.

Weizmann, Chaim. *Trial and Error: The Autobiography of Chaim Weizmann.* Philadelphia: Jewish Publication Society of America, 1949.

Winter, Jay. *Sites of Memory, Sites of Mourning: The Great War in European Cultural History.* Cambridge: Cambridge University Press, 1996.

Ye'Or, Bat. *Islam and Dhimmitude: Where Civilizations Collide.* Madison, N.J.: Fairleigh Dickinson University Press, 2002.

Young, Ernest P. *Ecclesiastical Colony: China's Catholic Church and the French Religious Protectorate*. Oxford: Oxford University Press, 2013.

Zamir, Meir. *Lebanon's Quest: The Road to Statehood, 1926–1939*. London: I. B. Tauris, 2000.

Zeine, Zeine N. *Arab-Turkish Relations and the Emergence of Arab Nationalism*. Beirut: Khayat's, 1958.

INDEX

Abdul-Hamidd II (sultan), 41n16, 50
Academy of Noble Ecclesiastics,
    16, 19
Agliardi, Antonio, 233, 235
Alacoque, Margaret Marie, 170
Alawite state, 213
Al Bechir, 162
Aleppo: Arab kingdom and,
    194; Catholic churches in, 111;
    convents in, 119; state of, 212
Alexander III (tsar), 52. *See also*
    Russia
Alexandretta, sanjak of, 213
Al-Khuri, Abdallah. *See* Khuri, al–
Allenby, General Edmund: and
    American Red Cross, 159;
    capture of Jerusalem, 8, 66–67,
    158, 225, 231, 247; capture of
    Palestine,108; as commander of
    Egyptian Expeditionary Force,
    152; entrance into Syria, 194; and
    Gaza victory, 152
Allies. *See* Entente Powers
American Committee for Armenian
    and Syrian Relief. *See* Near East
    Relief
American Jewish Committee, 144,
    154–55; *Jews in the Eastern War
    Zone*, 154; *10th Annual Report*, 154
American Red Cross. *See* U.S.
    humanitarian assistance
American University of Beirut, 201,
    218

Amette, Cardinal Léo Adolf, 87,
    145–46, 231–32
anti-Catholicism, 201, 219, 243,
    257
anticlericalism, 21, 28, 31, 34, 47,
    49, 169–70. *See also* France
anti-Semitism, 155, 243, 246
anti-Zionism, 10, 155, 234, 236–37,
    239, 241–45, 248, 255
Antonius, George: *The Arab
    Awakening*, 182, 219
apostolic delegate in
    Constantinople. *See* Dolci, Msgr.
    Angelo
apostolic delegate in Syria. *See*
    Giannini, Msgr. Frediano
Arab kingdom, 193–97, 199–208,
    227
Arab nationalism, 47n29, 199,
    205, 221; Benedict XV and, 198;
    extremism in, 203; Faisal and, 9,
    193; France and, 207, 212; lack
    of organization, 200; and Louis
    Massignon, 206; and zionism,
    227
Arab revolt, 147n21, 194
Armenian massacre, 140–42, 158,
    163
Asquith, Herbert, 68
Atran, Scott: *Surrogate Colonization
    of Palestine, The*, 239
Aubert, Roger, 248
Australia, 35

Austria, 22, 79, 111, 124–27, 167, 259; as Catholic bastion, 2, 26, 32, 69; as Central Power, 1n2, 69; clergy from, 107, 129; collapse of empire, 3, 26, 98, 169–70; and Constantinople, 70; diplomatic representation at Vatican, 32; granting of capitulations to, 44; and Holy See, 79, 109–10, 121, 131; and Josephinism, 71; and Ottoman law on Church property, 135; peace negotiation with Russia, 83, 86; transfer of French protectorate to, 69–71
Austro-Hungarian empire. *See* Austria

Balfour, Arthur James, 152, 231, 238, 240, 243, 248, 250
Balfour Declaration, 235, 238–43, 246
Ballobar, Count de, 69, 162, 252. *See also* Spain
Bargeton, Paul, 207
Barlassina, Luigi, 242, 244, 252–53, 255
Barrère, Camille, 47
Barton, James L., 158–59; *Story of Near East Relief*, 142
Batiffol, Pierre: *Pope Benedict and the Restoration of Unity*, 102
Baudrillart, Cardinal Alfred, 21, 70n5, 87; *Les carnets du Cardinal Baudrillart*, 22
Bavaria, 32, 171, 264
Bekaa Valley, 131, 213
Bekir, Sami Bey, 113
Belgium, 58n57, 109, 123, 251; and First World War, 25, 27; and Holy See, 31, 76, 169; humanitarian assistance to, 159; transfer of protectorate to, 247–48

Bell, Gertrude, 185
Benedict XIV (pope), 18; *Allatae Sunt*, 93n68
Benedict XV (pope): 16, 19–20, 22; and anti-Zionism, 10, 234, 237, 239, 243; and conclave, 17–18, 32; death, 4, 6, 8, 15, 143, 184, 245, 249, 256, 258; election, 20; and new world order, 4, 5, 8, 11–12, 136, 167, 261; moral authority, 8, 11, 20–24, 29, 33, 108, 137, 143, 147, 149, 153, 157, 172–74, 179, 197, 259, 261, 263; political prestige, 8, 11, 15, 23, 27, 168–69, 172–73, 179, 231, 245, 259, 261, 263; pontificate, 3, 10–11, 15, 21–22, 30, 36, 91, 152, 171, 177, 237, 262–64; pope of peace, 6, 15, 36; pope of the East, 4, 36, 90–91, 98, 105; and pro-German tendencies, 21–22, 32, 48, 144; statue of, 4, 143, 156–57, 259; and Zionist ambitions, 10, 233, 235–38, 241–43, 245, 263–64. *See also* papacy
Benedict XV, Church documents: *Ad Beatissimi*, 24, 35, 171; *Al Tremendo Conflitto*, 81n40, 169; *Annus Iam Plenus*, 173; *Cum Catholicae Ecclesiae*, 96; *Dei Providentis*, 98; *Dès le début*, 24, 26–27, 153, 168, 175–77, 259; *Inclytum Fratrum Minorum Conditorem*, 255; *Maximum Illud*, 10, 185, 187–91, 198, 208, 210, 254, 262; *Orientis Catholici*, 101; *Pacem Dei Munus*, 171, 178; *Principi Apostolorum Petro*, 105, 220; *Romanorum Pontificum*, 96, 189; *To the Belligerent Peoples and Their Rulers*, 25
Benedict XV, eastern diplomacy, 6, 67–69, 91, 106; and British

mandate in Palestine, 10, 229–32, 235, 263; and conflict with apostolic delegates, 74, 76, 199, 202, 262; in Constantinople, 80, 87, 89; emancipating from France, 195, 198, 203–4, 226, 247, 260, 261; and Faisal, 194–96, 198–99, 202; and France in Syria, 7, 23, 69, 186, 247; and Maronite Church, 216–17; and Ottoman government, 7–8, 69–72, 74–75, 78, 82–83, 261; and Protestant threat, 10, 231; and Zionism, 229, 231, 233, 235, 237, 243. *See also* Hagia Sophia; Holy See, eastern diplomacy

Benedict XV, Eastern ecclesiology: Catholic churches and, 90, 92, 106, 220, 237, 260, 262; and Catholic ecumenism, 92, 96, 102, 104–5, 250; Congregation for the Oriental Church in, 91, 98–100, 260, 262; Orthodox churches and, 6, 11, 67–68, 76, 82, 90–91, 96–97, 102–3, 106, 121, 220–21, 237, 258, 260, 262; Pontifical Oriental Institute in, 92, 101–3, 260; and Propaganda Fide, 100–101; unionism in, 5, 7, 10, 36, 68, 90–92, 96, 102–3, 105–6, 260

Benedict XV, general diplomacy: and decolonization, 4, 8, 185, 192, 198, 208, 261; emancipation from colonial powers, 9–10, 185–86, 190, 192, 194, 198, 203–4, 212, 226, 247, 261; and eurocentrism, 167, 185–86, 192, 261; with France, 7, 74–75, 81–83, 169–71, 211, 229, 247, 261; and impartiality during war, 21–24, 69, 137, 143–44, 147, 149, 163, 172–73, 226, 259; with Italy,

25, 35, 168, 171, 259; and just war theory, 20, 23; and League of Nations, 176, 178–80, 229; against nationalism, 9, 20, 24, 26, 30, 208; and new democratic states, 11, 81, 167–69, 171, 174, 259; and peacemaking efforts, 6, 15, 24–27, 36, 81, 168, 173; and peace negotiations, 27, 35, 168, 262; role of Church in new world order, 9, 11–12, 23, 81, 136–37, 167, 169, 172, 185–86, 192, 233, 235–36, 262, 264; with Russia, 83, 86–87, 89–90; and self-determination of minorities, 8, 176, 180, 192, 208, 237; and status quo ante bellum, 26, 179, 259; with United States, 174–76. *See also* Holy See, diplomacy; Roman question

Benedict XV, humanitarian assistance, 6, 23, 132, 145, 149, 173, 260, 262; and British government, 148, 151–53; Catholic missions in, 139–41; in English-language literature, 142, 146, 157, 159, 163; and exchange of prisoners, 140, 150; as philantropic act, 138, 147, 150; and relief of Jewish populations, 154–56; statue of Benedict XV, 4, 143, 156–57; and U.S. discrimination against Catholics, 157, 160; and U.S. government, 139, 150

Benedict XVI (pope), 36n69, 91, 263
Berchtold, Count Leopold, 70
Berlin, Treaty of, 64–65
Bethlehem, 223, 235
Bolshevik Revolution, 81, 83, 86, 90, 171–73, 224, 227
Bompard, Maurice, 47, 68
Bonzano, Giovanni, 145–46

Boppe, Auguste, 65
Bosphorus, 63, 84–86. *See also*
Constantinople
Boulad, Gabriel, 206
Bourne, Cardinal Francis, 209, 211, 232, 243, 245
Brazil, 76, 167, 169, 250
Brest-Litovsk, Treaty of, 83, 86
Briand, Aristide, 170
Britain: and anti-Catholic propaganda, 200–201; and Arab nationalism, 195, 203; and Benedict XV's humanitarian assistance, 148, 151–53; and capitulations to, 44; and colonial ambitions, 89, 181, 196; dominant position in Ottoman Empire, 40–41, 194; as Entente Power, 1n2; entry into war against Ottoman Empire, 68; interests in Palestine, 193, 224; and Protestantism, 31, 87, 230; rejection of Papal Peace Note, 26; strategic interest in Constantinople, 84–87, 89–90; and Zionism, 225, 230, 241
British mandate, 183, 187, 244, 246–47, 249, 258, 261; and Benedict XV, 10, 229–30, 232; as colonial device, 182, 184–85; over Palestine, 3, 8, 183, 227, 230, 261; and Protestant cause, 10, 230–31, 249, 251–52; and Zionist cause, 10, 230–31, 249, 251
British mission to the Holy See, 16, 19, 31–33, 152, 169
British protectorate, 200, 218, 225, 239
British Syria and Palestine Relief Fund, 159–60
Bronsart, General Friedrich, 132–33
Bulgaria, 1n2, 156
Bulletin de l'Asie francaise (Paris), 207

Cadi (Melkite patriarch), 197
Camassei, Filippo: and Arab kingdom, 197; arrest and deportation of, 108, 132–34; as Italian citizen, 129; and Jewish persecution, 155; liberation of, 133; persecution of, 129, 131–32; retirement of, 253; return to patriarchal seat of, 133
Cambon, Paul, 47
Canada, 35
capitulations, 43; abrogation of, 7, 49, 52–57, 64, 66, 68, 72, 260; abuse of, 54; Austria and, 70; as binding treaties, 54; end of protectorates and, 66, 71; extension to Russia, 50–51; as extraterritorial conventions, 44; France and, 6, 45–46, 49, 61–62, 116–17; French protectorate and, 7, 44–45, 49, 57, 65, 68, 116–17; and Holy See's interests, 55–56, 59, 72; Ottoman sovereignty and, 56, 66; status of Holy Places and, 65
Catholic Church, Latin, 78; diplomatic relations with Ottoman Empire, 75, 82; Djemal Pasha's threat against, 130; and ecumenical movement, 102; emancipation from colonial powers, 5, 185–86, 190–92, 204, 212; emancipation from Eurocentric model, 185, 192; France and, 121, 251; globalized identity, 11–12, 173, 235–36, 261; and Greek Orthodoxy, 88, 90, 92n67; as humanitarian world agency, 140, 157; and influence in Holy Places, 231; missionaries and, 262; Ottoman recognition of, 7; and persecution of clergy,

260; pope as head of, 195, 250, 261; representing Latin Catholic community, 78; role in new world order, 5, 9, 11, 23, 81, 136–37, 177, 185–86, 190, 234; St. Ephrem and, 221; as a transnational actor, 20n22, 23, 112, 173, 186, 192, 243; unity of, 96, 186; as universal institution, 11, 23, 78, 139, 173, 178–79, 185–86, 192, 242, 250; Zionist movement and, 234, 243

Catholic clergy: expulsion and deportation of Entente clergy, 107, 109–10, 121–26; mistreatment of, 123, 125; protection of, 8, 106–7, 126, 260; religious persecution of, 7, 107–8, 111, 120–22, 124–26, 129, 130–32, 134, 260; substitution of Austrian and German clegy, 107, 126–27, 129

Catholic communities: decrease under French mandate, 215; and *dhimmitude*, 37–39, 41, 56; French Catholic protectorate, 45, 225; independence under Faisal's government, 196–98, 200; legislation in Lebanon, 217; and *millet*, 37–39; and Orthodox communities, 121; postwar protection in Lebanon, 221; protection in Ottoman Empire, 5, 9, 11, 30, 36–37, 41, 67, 77, 82, 91, 106, 136, 260; Protestant discrimination against, 8, 157, 160–62; and Protestants in Palestine, 251, 255; religious persecution of, 56, 75, 77, 82, 111, 120–21, 145–46; restructuring of, 108, 136; as symbolic presence in Ottoman Empire, 42, 136;

vulnerability in Muslim world, 9, 36–39, 45, 77, 90, 136, 199–200, 203. *See also* Eastern Catholic communities; Latin Catholic communities

Catholic institutions. *See* Catholic property

Catholic interests: and abolition of French protectorate, 59; and abrogation of capitulations, 59; in new world order, 168, 180, 199; protection of, 2, 5, 7, 30, 36, 72, 74, 77, 87, 109, 127, 212; transfer to Spain, 69, 71

catholicism, 80–81, 87, 92, 133–34, 161, 186, 216, 218, 225, 231, 254, 256; associated with France, 211, 219–20, 261; future in Palestine, 226, 228

Catholic life, 139; disintegration, 118, 123–24, 134; maintenance of, 118, 120, 129; restoration, 110, 136

Catholic missions, 201; and Church in new world order, 186; emancipation from colonial powers, 9, 185, 188, 190, 192; and encyclical *Maximum Illud*, 10, 185, 187–88, 262; expulsion of Entente missionaries, 107–8, 110, 112, 122–23, 134, 139, 144; and globalized identity of Church, 12, 186; and humanitarian assistance, 139–40; and missionary nationalism, 188–90, 262; as property of Holy See, 113

Catholic Near East Welfare Association (CNEWA). *See* Near East Relief

Catholic property: closing of, 112, 118, 120–21, 134; confiscation of,

Catholic property *(cont.)*
7, 72, 107, 109–10, 114, 118–19,
121; as French property, 72, 107,
113–14; Ottoman law on Church
property, 134–36; as property of
Holy See, 108, 113–15, 117–20;
protection of, 8, 106–7, 260; sale
of, 108, 114–15
Central Powers, 1n2, 21–22, 31–32,
35–36, 53, 68, 83, 85–86
Cecil, Lord Robert, 21
Cerretti, Bonaventura, 168, 170, 229
Chibli (Maronite archbishop), 108,
129–31
Chile, 169
China, 79, 82, 187
Churchill, Winston, 240
Civiltà Cattolica, La (Rome), 237
Claudel, Paul, 228
Clemenceau, Georges, 47, 196,
204–5, 212, 232
Clement VI (pope): *Gratias Agimus*,
60
Clement XIV (pope): *Dominus ac
Redemptor*, 218
colonialism, 46, 167, 176, 180–82,
184–87, 189, 198–99, 205, 208,
212, 222, 224–26, 241, 261
colonialism, French: mandate and
protectorate as devices for, 9, 47,
182; and *mission civilisatrice*, 46,
189; postwar ambitions, 181, 196,
225; Robert de Caix as advocate
of, 9
Comite d'action française en Syrie,
146
Concert of Europe, 29
Congregation for Extraordinary
Ecclesiastical Affairs, 168, 190,
264
Congregation for the Oriental
Church, 91, 101, 260; archives of,
5, 15, 143; and Benedict XV, 91,
98–100; genesis of, 98–99; and
Propaganda Fide, 100–101; and
strengthening Eastern Catholic
churches, 10, 98, 257
Congregation for the Oriental
Churches. *See* Congregation for
the Oriental Church
Congregatio pro Ecclesia Orientali.
See Congregation for Oriental
Church
Congress of Paris (*1856*), 29, 64–65
Constantinople, 4; Benedict
XV's statue in, 143, 156; British
policy in, 89; as center of
Orthodox Christianity, 84–85;
ecumenical patriarchate of, 51,
85; French presence, 89; German
occupation, 89; and Holy See,
84; international status, 88;
and Russia, 83–87, 89–90. *See
also* Bosphorus; Dardanelles;
Ottoman government
Crimean War, 29n49, 40, 63–65
Croce, Giuseppe: *Alle origini della
Congregaione Orientale e del
Pontificio Istituto Orientale*, 99
Curzon, Lord George, 227
Custody of the Holy Land, 48,
59–60, 63, 111–12, 115–19, 128,
149, 252, 254–56. *See also* Catholic
property
Czechoslovakia, 169

de Caix, Robert, 9, 195n4, 198n11,
203–9, 215–16
decolonization, 4, 8, 184–85, 192,
198, 208, 261
Deedes, Wyndham, 147
Delcassé, Théophile, 34
Della Chiesa, Giacomo, 6, 16–17.
See also Benedict XV

Delpuche, Fr., 99–102
de Piedpape, Colonel, 211
d'Erp, Maximilian, 31
de Salis, Count John, 19, 21, 33, 71,
    89, 132, 231
dhimmitude, 37–39, 41–42, 44, 56,
    60, 226
Diotallevi, Ferdinando, 256–57
Djemal Pasha, 41n16, 53; and
    Custody of Holy Land, 116; as
    military governor of Syria, 75,
    119, 123, 145; and persecution of
    Catholic hierarchy, 130–34, 217,
    260; and persecution of Catholic
    population in Syria, 75; and
    persecution of Maronites, 145;
    and Young Turks, 109
Dolci, Msgr. Angelo, 80, 119, 122,
    126–27, 134–36, 147–48, 150,
    155–56, 161, 262; and conflict
    with papal vision, 74–76, 79, 262;
    correspondence with Holy See, 7,
    72–73, 75, 109; excommunication
    of Latin Catholic community
    by, 78–79; and humanitarian
    assistance, 140, 142–43, 149,
    153, 159, 163; independence
    from French tutelage, 58; as
    Italian citizen, 127; negotiation
    of diplomatic relations with
    Ottoman government, 71–77,
    79; and Ottoman religious
    persecution, 108. See also Holy
    See, eastern diplomacy
Dorotheos (archbishop), 104
Doulcet, Jean, 170
Drumont, Edouard, 155
Druses, 201, 213–14, 216
Dubois, Cardinal Louis, 209–12

Eastern Catholic churches: and
    Congregation for Oriental
Church, 98; ecclesial structure
    of, 5, 91–92, 97–98; French
    Catholic protectorate over, 94,
    225; Latinization of, 52, 92–93,
    95, 99–100; life in millets, 38,
    40, 45; and Orthodox churches,
    76, 92, 97, 103, 257; Orthodox
    proselytizing in, 52, 96; Pius
    IX and, 91; in postwar world
    order, 190, 257–58; Protestant
    proselytizing in, 52; relation
    with Propaganda Fide, 97–98.
    See also Benedict XV, Eastern
    ecclesiology
Eastern Catholic communities:
    as dhimmis, 6, 37–39; French
    Catholic protectorate over, 6,
    43, 45; as minorities in Muslim
    world, 10, 38–39, 42–43, 74, 77,
    101; as minorities in Orthodox
    Christianity, 40; protection of,
    67, 91, 206
Egypt, 62–63, 82n41, 89, 143, 156,
    209, 211, 213, 224, 240
Elkus, Abram I., 148, 155
Entente Powers, 144; Catholics in, 2,
    31; diplomatic representation at
    Vatican, 31, 34; Italy's entry into
    war as, 34; Ottoman Empire's
    entry into war against, 6, 85;
    and Papal Peace Note, 26; and
    revolt in Syria, 147; and Treaty
    of London, 34–35; United States
    allied with, 8, 159, 175; victory
    of, 3, 26, 70, 81, 85, 237; and war
    against Central Powers, 1n2
Enver Pasha, 41n16, 53, 149
Ephrem (saint), 105–6, 220–21
Etudes (Paris), 222
eurocentrism, 8, 167, 185–86, 192,
    261
European Powers. See Great Powers

Faisal (prince), 9, 193–208, 215, 227
Faith and Order Movement, 104
Fellinger, François, 133
Ferrata, Cardinal Domenico, 18
firman, 60–63, 116–17, 121
Fisher, Eugene: *Vatican and the State of Israel, The*, 234
fourteen points, 175–76, 181, 237. *See also* Woodrow Wilson
France: and anticlericalism, 21, 28, 31, 34, 47, 49, 89, 169–70; and Catholicism, 69, 81, 211, 219–20, 261; as colonial power, 46, 82, 207, 209, 212; as Entente Power, 1n2; entry into war against Ottoman Empire, 68, 72, 117; and Holy See, 10, 31, 34, 44, 47–48, 57–58, 74–77, 79, 82, 169–71, 198, 212, 228–29, 247, 260–61; *mission civilisatrice*, 46, 110, 144; and Papal Peace Note, 27; prestige in Ottoman Empire, 6, 40–41, 44, 46, 49, 69, 130, 194; and Russia, 62, 72, 85–87, 89
France, eastern diplomacy, 76, 94; and British mandate, 250; expulsion of French missionaries, 72, 110, 112; and Faisal, 196, 201, 204–5; and Greater Lebanon, 214–15; in Greater Syria, 9, 47, 49, 193, 196, 205, 207, 224; and Holy See, 45, 73; and prestige in Syria and Lebanon, 206–7, 209, 220; protection of interests in Ottoman Empire, 69, 211–12; and strategic interest in Constantinople, 84. *See also* de Caix, Robert; Massignon, Louis
Franciscan order, 60–61, 63, 128, 256
French Catholic protectorate, 61; abrogation of capitulations and,

7, 55, 68, 71; capitulations and, 44–45, 116–17; over Catholic communities, 6, 43, 136; in China, 82, 187; as colonial device, 47, 80, 110; over Custody of the Holy Land, 48, 59, 117; deconfessionalization of, 49; over Hagia Sophia, 87; over Holy Places, 62, 225; and Holy See, 49, 57, 74, 80–81, 107, 170, 186, 247; over Latin patriarchate, 48, 59, 63, 114; legitimacy of, 47, 49, 57, 68; and Leo XIII, 46, 72, 94; and Muslim populations, 47–48; and Orthodox communities, 47; in Ottoman Empire, 5, 6, 43, 45, 48, 79–80, 108, 170, 214; in postwar Palestine, 212, 227, 247; in Syria, 193, 199–201, 203; and Syriac Catholic Church, 121; transfer of, 57, 69–71, 112
French Catholic protectorate, abrogation of, 5, 53, 66, 68, 80, 107, 232, 260–61; and collapse of Ottoman Empire, 81; in Holy Land, 79, 225; and Holy See's interests, 59, 69, 114, 144; and Ottoman government, 45; restoration of, 70, 80
French mandate, 183, 187, 261; Benedict XV and, 232; as colonial device, 9, 184–85, 207; decline of Christian communities, 215; growth of Muslim population, 215; Jesuit lobbying for, 219; over Lebanon, 204, 219, 264; and principle of self-determination, 184; over Syria, 3, 8, 183, 193, 204–5, 207, 219, 264
Friedman, Isaiah: *The Question of Palestine*, 238

Fromkin, David: *Peace to End All Peace, A*, 2
Frühwirth, Cardinal Andreas, 127
Fundamental Agreement, 233. *See also* Israel

Gaisford, Hugh, 152
Gallarati Scotti, Duke Tommaso, 228–32
Garrels, Arthur, 156
Gasquet, Cardinal Aidan, 32–33, 168, 191n69
Gaudium et Spes (Vatican II), 11, 264–65
Georges-Picot, Francois, 225
Germany: ambassador and Holy See, 79, 109, 111, 119, 121–22, 124, 126–27, 129; Benedict XV and, 21, 26; Catholic propaganda in Ottoman Empire, 127–28; Catholics in, 2; as Central Power, 1n2; and exclusion from League of Nations, 179; against French protectorate of, 48; and German Catholic clergy, 48, 107, 122, 126–29; grand design of, 127; and Holy See, 26–27, 32, 71–72, 126–28, 133; occupation of Constantinople, 89; and Ottoman Empire, 3, 53–54, 71–72, 85, 127–28; and Ottoman law on Church property, 135; peace negotiation with Russia, 83, 86, 89; Protestantism and, 26, 251–52. *See also* Von Waggenheim, Baron
Giannini, Msgr. Frediano, 108, 110, 116–17, 134, 142, 211, 219; and anti-Zionism, 239–41; and Arab kingdom, 195, 197, 200; and Bishop al-Khuri, 217; and British mandate in Lebanon, 201; about

Catholic interests and property, 72, 113; conflict with Benedict XV's vision, 74, 199, 202, 262; and French protectorate in Syria, 199–201; and future of Holy Places, 65; and humanitarian assistance, 140, 149, 159, 163; as Italian citizen, 111, 123–24; about Protestant proselytyzing, 161–62, 200; and return to prewar model, 212, 217, 262
Gibbons, Cardinal James, 174; and Benedict XV, 17; and humanitarian assistance, 142, 148, 152, 159; as member of Near East Relief, 159–60
Giustini, Cardinal Filippo, 209
Glazebrook, Otis, 154
Gotti, Cardinal Girolamo, 76, 109, 112
Gouraud, General Henri, 203, 212, 217, 219
Great Britain. *See* Britain
Greater Lebanon, 9, 212–18, 220. *See also* Lebanon
Greater Syria, 7, 40, 49, 129, 215; as cradle of Christianity, 37; and France, 47, 51; France and Britain in, 86, 182; Holy See's humanitarian assistance in, 138, 140; protection of Catholicism in, 77, 127; symbolic presence of Christians in, 42, 43; Westernization of, 43
Greece, 258
Greek Orthodox churches. *See* Orthodox Churches
Gregory, J. D., 16, 21, 33
Grey, Sir Edward, 33
Griffith, Sidney, 39; *The Church in the Shadow of the Mosque*, 37; *Faith Adoring the Mystery*, 220

Hagia Sophia, 84, 87–88, 90
Hague peace conferences, 29
Haifa, 223
Hankey, Maurice, 250
Hanoteaux, Gabriel, 80
Hatt-i-Humayun, 41
Herzl, Theodor, 233, 235–36
Hitti, Philip K.: *History of Syria*, 182
Holy City. *See* Jerusalem
Holy Land, 60, 64, 114, 159, 228,
  230, 237–38, 247–48; abrogation
  of capitulations in, 7, 59; Arab
  aspirations, 227; Britain interest
  in, 224; British wartime promise,
  227; Catholic interests in, 56,
  71–72, 119, 246; Christianity
  in, 43; France's interest in, 224;
  Franciscan Custody, 48, 61, 256;
  French Protectorate in, 7, 59, 79,
  225; Italian protectorate in, 59;
  persecution of Catholic clergy
  in, 122; protestant offensive in,
  231–33, 251; Russian interest in,
  224; Russian interference in, 51;
  Zionist aspirations, 221, 225, 227,
  233–34. *See also* Palestine
Holy Places, 29n49, 48, 59, 225,
  230, 233, 238, 249; Belgian
  protectorate over, 247–48; British
  mandate, 231, 248; capitulations
  and, 65; Catholic rights in, 235;
  and collapse of Ottoman Empire,
  63; and Crimean War, 62–64;
  firmans about, 60–63; French
  protectorate over, 10, 62, 64–65,
  226–27, 232; and Holy See, 59,
  61–62, 136, 226, 228, 237, 246–
  47, 258; and Jewish state, 235,
  239; ownership of, 247, 60–
  63; Protestant offensive in, 231;
  Russian Orthodox protectorate
  over, 62, 64, 226–27; transfer

of Catholic interests to Spain,
  69, 71
Holy See: and Christian cultural
  heritage, 172; and international
  legal status, 28–29; and
  international prestige, 27, 29, 172,
  179, 197, 231, 233; loss of Papal
  States, 2, 28; loss of temporal
  sovereignty, 2, 23, 28–29; and
  postwar world order, 167, 168,
  172–73, 186; spiritual sovereignty
  of, 28–29, 172
Holy See, diplomacy, 30–31, 67;
  break of relations with France,
  47–48, 57–58, 74, 228; with
  Central Powers, 36; with Entente
  Powers, 34; exclusion from
  League of Nations, 174, 177;
  with Italy, 34–36; and peace
  negotiations, 27, 35, 168, 173;
  restoration of relations with
  France, 74–77, 80, 169–71, 212,
  229, 198. *See also* Benedict XV,
  European diplomacy; Roman
  Question
Holy See, eastern diplomacy; and
  abolition of capitulations, 53, 55,
  64; British control of Palestine
  and, 10; and Constantinople,
  84; emancipation from France,
  10, 189, 226; and French
  protectorate, 48, 53, 57, 74, 80–81,
  107; and Holy Places, 10, 59, 61,
  225, 227; interests and rights
  in Palestine of, 61, 71, 225; and
  Ottoman government, 7, 44–45,
  49, 58, 69–77, 79–82, 107–8, 111,
  119, 126, 198; and preservation
  of Catholic interests, 30, 36, 74,
  77, 193–94; and protection of
  Catholic communities, 36, 43–45,
  77, 193–94; and Protestantism,

250; and Russian Orthodoxy, 50, 52, 83; and Zionism, 233–36, 250. *See also* Benedict XV, eastern diplomacy

Holy Sepulchre, Church of the, 51, 60–62

Holy Spirit, Cathedral of the, 4, 157, 259

House, Colonel Edward, 27

Howard, Sir Henry, 33

Huby, Joseph, 222

Hungary, 171

Hussein, bin Ali, 147, 193

Hussein-McMahon Correspondence, 194, 196

Huyaek, Elias P., 108, 129–31, 197, 202, 215–17. *See also* Maronite Church

imperialism, French, 64, 185; and British, 199; and Catholic Church's emancipation, 11; and mandate system, 180, 184, 240; in Ottoman Empire, 63; in Syria, 9, 47

Imperial Orthodox Palestine Society, 52

International Red Cross, international, 140–42, 144, 163

Irani, George E., 234

Islam, 37, 199, 205, 223; Christianity and Islam, 59, 208, 218, 223, 241; Islamic conquest, 214; Islamic law, 37–38, 45; Islamic world, 39–40, 199; Islamism, 202, 212. *See also* Muslim world

Israel. *See* Fundamental Agreement

Istanbul. *See* Constantinople

Italy,181: and Benedict XV's peacemaking efforts, 25, 27; and British mandate, 250; and Catholic protectorate, 48, 59;

and diplomacy with Vatican, 15, 31, 34–36, 133, 170–71, 174, 177, 250, 262; as Entente Power, 1n2, 73, 117, 181, 224; entry into war, 25, 31, 34–35, 107, 111, 117, 123; influence at Propaganda Fide, 48; interests in Ottoman Empire, 87; and Libyan War (*1911*), 123; maintaining neutrality, 25, 259; missionaries expelled, 112, 126, 139; persecution of Italian clerics, 128–29; and Treaty of London, 34, 168, 174. *See also* Roman Question

Jacobites. *See* Syriac Orthodox Church

Jaffa, 156, 223, 241

Japan, 1n2, 167, 196n5

Jaricot, Pauline, 189

Jerusalem, 52, 59, 122, 129, 162, 225, 242–43, 251–52; Anglo-Prussian bishopric, 63, 158; capture of, 6, 8, 66–67, 133–34, 152–53, 158, 182, 226, 231, 238, 247; Catholic institutions in, 115; and Jewish state, 235; Orthodox patriarchate, 51, 60. *See also* Latin patriarchate of Jerusalem

Jesuits, 218–19

Jewish national homeland, 242, 244–46, 263–64; and Catholic Church rights in Holy Places, 235; establishment of, 10, 235, 237, 240–41, 247; Franco-Bristish tension about, 10; and Jewish nationalism, 221; as Jewish state, 243; and surrogate colonization, 239. *See also* Balfour declaration

Joan of Arc, 170

John XXIII (pope), 265; *Pacem in*

John XXIII (pope) *(cont.)*
  Terris, 11–12; apostolic delegate in
  Istanbul, 82n41
Jonnart, Charles, 170
Journal de Genève, Le, 20–21, 175
just war theory, 20, 24, 30

Kelbe, John, 251
Khoury, Gérard: *Robert de Caix et
  Louis Massignon*, 9n19; *Une tutelle
  coloniale*, 9n18, 198n11
Khuri, Abdallah al-, 217
Kreutz, Andrej: *Vatican Policy on the
  Palestinian-Israeli Conflict*, 233
Kudashev, Prince N. A., 88–89
Kutchuk-Kainardji, Peace Treaty
  of, 50

Libre parole, La (Paris), 155
Lammens, Henri, 222
Langénieux, Cardinal Benoit-Marie,
  46, 97, 99
Lateran Treaties, 28n46. *See also*
  Roman Question
Latin Catholic communities, 53, 60;
  and Congregation for Oriental
  Church, 100; French Catholic
  protectorate over, 6, 43, 45; as
  members of missions, 41; as
  minorities, 10; protection in
  Ottoman Empire of, 67; status in
  Ottoman Empire, 6, 41, 78–79
Latin Chancellery, 78
Latin patriarchate of Jerusalem,
  108, 129, 131, 134, 155; and
  Custody of the Holy Land, 63,
  254–55; expulsion of Catholic
  clergy from, 122–23; and French
  Catholic protectorate, 48, 59, 63,
  114; and Orthodox expansion, 72;
  revival of, 63
L'Atti (Constantinople), 157

Lausanne, Treaty of, 54
Lawrence, T. E., 194
League of Nations, 104, 167, 174,
  176–80, 182–84, 186–87, 229,
  248–50, 261
Lebanon: American Protestantism
  in, 218, 220; autonomy of, 201,
  204; Cardinal Dubois's visit,
  209–11; Catholic identity,
  202; Christian population in,
  42–43; emigration from, 213;
  and France, 203, 214–15; French
  mandate in, 219; and Greater
  Syria, 6, 9, 131–32, 145–46, 183,
  196, 204, 213, 216; and Huyaek,
  202; Maronites, 40–43, 201–2,
  214; Muslim population in, 221;
  and nationalism, 214; sherifian
  kingdom, 202. *See also* Greater
  Lebanon
Lebbe, Vincent, 187
Legrand, Hervé, 102
Lenin, Vladimir Ilyich, 83
Leo XIII (pope): and Benedict XV,
  18–19, 91; and Eastern Catholic
  churches, 64, 92, 94–97; and
  French Catholic protectorate, 46,
  94, 72; and Great Design, 64, 92;
  against Latinization of Eastern
  rites, 95; Ottoman government,
  71–72, 94; and unionism, 7, 68,
  91–93, 260
Life and Work Movement, 104
liturgical honors, 50, 58
Lloyd George, David, 68n2, 152,
  232, 240, 243
Lobry, François-Xavier, 211
Loiseau, Charles, 34
London, Treaty of, 34–35, 168, 174
London Society for the Union of
  Christendom, 104
Lorenzelli, Cardinal Benedetto, 76

Lugano, Switzerland, 35
Lvov, Prince G. E., 86

MacNutt, Francis: *A Papal Chamberlain*, 16n4
Malines Conversations, 250–51
Mar-Elias, Monastery of, 120–21. *See also* Syriac Catholic Church
Marini, Cardinal Nicolò, 161, 196–97, 202. *See also* Congregation for the Oriental Church
Maronite Church, 214–15, 218; and Archbishop Chibli, 108, 129; autonomy of, 40; and Druses, 201, 214; Ephrem and, 220–21; and Huyaek, 105, 108, 129–31, 215–17; and religious orders, 125; rite, 106; and Rome, 214, 216–17
Maronites: and France, 130–31, 214–15; history of, 214; and Lebanon, 40, 43, 131, 145, 201, 212–14, 215–16; and *millet*, 44; vulnerability in Muslim world, 202–3, 213
Marshall, Louis, 154–55
Massignon, Louis, 9, 204–8
Maysalun, Battle of, 205
McInnis, Rennie, 158, 252
Mercier, Cardinal Désiré, 248
Merry del Val, Cardinal Rafael, 17, 76, 169, 191n69
Messinger (rabbi), 155. *See also* Swiss Zionist Society
Metternich, Count Paul Wolff, 119
Millerand, Alexandre, 169, 204, 232
millet system, 37– 42, 44–45, 197, 218, 226
Minerbi, Sergio: and administration of Palestine, 230; and Benedict XV, 237–39; Cardinal Bourne and, 232; and Catholic Church's

anti-Zionism, 234, 245; *The Vatican and Zionism*, 10, 234
Monti, Baron Carlo, 19, 36, 88, 128, 257; *Diario del barone Carlo Monti*, 87
Morgenthau, Henry, 109–10, 141, 154, 157, 158n55; *A Personal Account of the Armenian Genocide*, 142
Mornet, Admiral Charles, 219
Mount Lebanon, 196, 213–14. *See also* Lebanon
Mudros, Armistice of, 136
Muslim-Christian Association, 241
Muslim world, 211, 223; anti-Catholic propaganda of, 200; Catholic minorities in, 9, 32, 37n1, 38, 42; Christian symbolic presence in, 42–43; and crusades, 59; and Eastern Catholics, 74, 197; harassment of Christians in, 5, 47, 56, 77, 82, 88, 195, 200, 212, 242, 261; and French Catholic protectorate, 47–48; and French mandate, 214; and Louis Massignon, 206; Muslim migrations in, 43, 213, 215; Muslim population in, 38, 41, 43, 47–49, 74, 122, 147, 211, 215, 218, 221, 223, 241; Ottoman Empire as part of, 32, 37, 42, 44–45, 74, 82, 136, 199, 222
Mussolini, Benito, 25, 28n46
Mustafa Kemal, 55, 79, 90n61
mutasarrifiyyah, 213
Mytilene, Treaty of, 56, 113

Nahum, Haim, 156
nationalism, 187; Arab, 9, 193, 200, 206–7, 212; and France, 189; Holy See and, 24, 26, 30, 91; Lebanon and, 214; of missionaries, 95,

nationalism *(cont.)*
187–88, 190; and patriotism, 188, 210
Nativity, Church of the, 62
Nazareth, 133, 223, 225n11, 235
Near East Relief, 158; American Catholic support of, 158–60; and American Red Cross, 159; and Cardinal Gibbons, 159–60; and Catholic Near East Welfare Association, 160; discrimination against Catholics by, 139, 157, 159–62; and James L. Barton, 142, 158–59; in Ottoman Empire, 139, 144, 148; proselitizing among Catholics by, 161–62; Walter George Smith and, 160–61. *See also* U.S. humanitarian assistance
Neidhart, General Alexis, 51
Nelidov, Dimitri, 31
Newman, John Henry Cardinal, 251
New Republic, The, 91
new world order, 176; collapse of empires and, 167, 169–70; colonial impulse of, 209; and emergence of new political players in, 167, 169; and Eurocentrism, 167, 185–86, 192; *Gaudium et Spes,* 11; and Holy See, 11, 167, 169, 176, 185, 190, 192, 198, 209, 236; and League of Nations, 167, 179, 186; mandates' rule in, 108; and Paris Peace Conference, 168; prestige of papacy in, 168–69; role of Church, 5, 8, 9, 11, 23, 108, 167, 186. *See also* Bolshevik Revolution
New York Times: on abolition of capitulations, 55; and Benedict XV's death, 4, 15; on mistreatment of Jewish populations in Palestine, 154, 156; on persecution of clergy, 122; on U.S. humanitarian assistance, 144–45, 148; on war as suicide of Europe, 81n40
Nitti, Francesco, 232

Orthodox churches, 40, 44, 61–64, 67, 86, 88–89, 95, 101, 104, 112, 224, 237, 251, 257–58; and Eastern Catholic churches, 6, 11, 76, 82, 90–92, 94, 98, 102–3, 106, 260, 258; expansionism of, 72; and French Catholic protectorate, 47; independence of, 135; ownership of Holy Places, 60; Russian protectorate over, 6, 50–51, 90, 227; weakening of, 5, 99, 103, 224, 227
Orthodox Christianity, 85, 87, 89, 94–95, 224, 227, 237; and Anglicans, 104, 257–58; and Catholic Church, 76, 88, 92, 98, 121, 200; Constantinople as center of, 84–85; Russia as guardian of, 84–86, 90
Osservatore Romano, L' (Rome), 132, 189, 237
Ottoman Empire: Britain and France in, 40–41, 46, 63, 72; collapse of, 2–4, 11, 50, 63, 68, 74, 79, 81, 83, 85–86, 98–99, 106, 169, 180, 182, 237; Eastern Catholic communities in, 6, 96; entry into war against Entente Powers, 1n2, 6, 53, 66, 72, 85, 109; and Germany, 1n2, 3, 53–54, 85, 127–28; Latin Catholic communities in, 6, 78; law on Church property, 134–35; *millet* system, 37–39; as Muslim Empire, 74; Tanzimat period, 39

Ottoman government, diplomacy, 6, 71, 78; and capitulations, 7, 44–45, 54–55, 66, 70–71, 260; and Catholic communities in, 37, 56, 77, 82, 90, 121, 126; and Catholic rights and interests in, 2, 72, 74, 87; confiscation of Catholic property, 7, 107; denunciation of protectorates, 54, 71, 73, 78; and French Catholic protectorate, 44–45, 107; and Holy See, 7–8, 44–45, 49, 58, 69–82, 107, 111, 117, 119, 126, 133, 198, 261; persecution of Catholic clergy, 7, 107–8, 125; and Russia, 50, 53, 62, 68, 72, 85; and United States, 8, 144, 147, 149

Pacelli, Eugenio, 55, 264. *See also* Pius XII
Palestine, 9, 79; Arab population in, 223, 237; British capture of, 108, 162, 190; British mandate over, 3, 8, 183, 187, 227–28, 244–45, 247; British protectorate over, 10, 193, 227, 239; Cardinal Bourne's visit, 211, 232; and Catholicism in, 111, 113, 134, 190, 221, 226, 228, 237; Christian population in, 42, 51, 223, 244; and Egypt, 62, 89, 240; French protectorate and, 225, 228; Holy See and, 61, 225–26, 228–30, 235; humanitarian assistance in, 8, 144, 149, 236; as Jewish home, 10, 221, 237, 242, 246–47; Jewish population in, 153, 155, 223, 240; Muslim population in, 223, 241; Protestant discrimination against Catholics in, 157, 160, 251; Protestantism in, 10, 162, 252. *See also* Holy Land

Palestine Weekly, The (Jerusalem), 245
Palestinian question, 222, 224–25
Palmerston, Lord Henry John, 240
papacy; moral authority, 11, 15, 29, 108, 168; moral failure, 21; political prestige, 11, 15, 168. *See also* Benedict XV
Papal States, 2, 28, 172. *See also* Roman Question
Paris Peace Conference: Faisal at, 195; Holy See excluded from, 35, 168, 174, 262; Huyaek's travel to, 202, 215; Jesuit lobbying, 219; League of Nations's covenant, 176; opening, 174, 195, 226, 242, 244
Paris Peace Treaty (*1856*), 64–65
patriarchate of Constantinople, ecumenical, 51, 85
patriotism, 30, 105, 188, 210, 216
Paul VI (pope), 11, 265. *See also* Second Vatican Council
Peace Note of August *1, 1917. See* Benedict XV, Church documents
Peters, Walter, 19; *The Life of Benedict XV*, 17n9
Piccardo, Msgr. Luigi, 132–33
Piffl, Cardinal Gustav, 18
Pius IX (pope), 115; Anglo-Prussian bishopric, 63; Latinization of Eastern rites, 52, 93; *Nulla Celebrior*, 63; Oriental policy, 91, 93; Roman question and, 27n45, 28, 29
Pius X (pope), 16, 18–19, 22–23, 91, 172; and anti-Zionism, 234, 236; death of, 17; and eastern policy, 91; election of, 17, 103
Pius XI (pope), 90, 105, 245–46, 249; and Benedict XV's initiatives, 11, 258, 265;

Pius XI (pope) *(cont.)*
  foundation of CNEWA, 160; and
  Lateran Treaties, 28
Pius XII (pope), 264, 265
Poggi, Vincenzo, 98; *Per la storia del
  Pontificio Istituto Orientale*, 99
Poincaré, Raymond, 87
Poland, 31, 159, 169, 179n37, 240,
  250
Pollard, John, 18, 263; *The Unknown
  Pope*, 3
Pompilj, Cardinal Basilio, 68–69
Pontifical Oriental Institute, 92,
  101–3, 257, 260. *See also* Benedict
  XV, Eastern ecclesiology
postwar world order. *See* new world
  order
Propaganda Fide, 43, 46, 93–95,
  108, 122, 189, 252; archives
  of, 5, 7, 15; Congregation for
  the Oriental Church detached
  from, 91, 99–101; and Eastern
  Catholic churches, 97–98; and
  humanitarian assistance, 143;
  Italian influence at, 48; and
  missionary nationalism, 190; and
  restoration of Catholic network,
  136; and secretariat of state,
  255–56
protectorates, 6, 43–44, 50–51, 53–
  54, 66, 71, 73, 78, 119, 212, 227,
  224
Protestantism, American, 218–19,
  253
Provisional Zionist Committee, 144
Prussia, 32, 63, 251

Ragonesi, Francesco, 35
Rahmani, Ignatius Ephrem II, 105,
  120. *See also* Syrian Catholic
  Church
Rakib Sahyoun (Palestine), 244

Rampolla del Tindaro, Cardinal
  Mariano, 16–19
Randall, Sir Alec: *Vatican
  Assignment*, 229
Ratti, Cardinal Achille, 169n3, 245–
  46. *See also* Pius XI
Ratzinger, Cardinal Josef (Benedict
  XVI), 263
rayas. See *dhimmis*
Red Cross. *See* International Red
  Cross
*Relazione sulle missioni e scuole
  cattoliche* (Straubinger), 128
Robinson, Paschal, 254–55
Rodd, Rennell, 19
Rolland, Romain, 140, 175n23
Roman Question, 27, 31, 34–35,
  168, 171, 262. *See also* Benedict
  XV, European diplomacy; Papal
  States
Russia, 84; and Britain, 85–86, 90,
  224; and capitulations, 50–51;
  Constantinople and, 83–86,
  89–90; and Crimean War, 29n49,
  40, 63; as Entente Power, 1n2, 31,
  84–85, 87, 89, 251; entry into war
  against Ottoman Empire, 6; fall
  of empire, 5, 11, 90, 99, 167, 224;
  and France, 29n49, 62, 64, 72, 85–
  87, 224; and Holy Land, 51, 224;
  and Ottoman Empire, 6, 43, 51,
  53, 63–64, 85; peace negotiation
  with Central Powers, 83, 86, 89;
  war aim, 85, 89; withdrawal from
  world politics, 88, 227. *See also*
  Bolshevik Revolution
Russian Orthodoxy, 84, 86, 89;
  Austria and, 26; and Catholicism,
  87; and Eastern Catholic
  churches, 50, 52, 83, 96, 98; and
  Holy See, 31, 34, 50–51, 64, 83,
  87, 90; and Imperial Orthodox

Palestine Society, 52; Moscow as third Rome, 51, 85; and patriarchate of Constantinople, 51; and patriarchate of Jerusalem, 51; and permanent ecclesiastic mission, 52, 63; protectorate over Orthodox churches, 6, 29n49, 50–52, 62–63, 84–86, 90, 224, 227, 251; weakening of, 90, 224

Sacred Congregation for the Propagation of the Faith. See Propaganda Fide
Samuel, Sir Herbert, 246, 248
San Remo, Conference of, 183, 187, 203, 232, 244, 247
Santa Croce, Church of, 226
Sardi, Msgr. Vincenzo, 55–59, 74
Scapinelli, Msgr. Rafaele, 70, 121, 124–25, 127, 191n69
Schönburg-Hartenstein, Prince Johann, 32
Scotta, Antonio: Diario del barone Carlo Monti, 19n15
Secolo, Il (Rome), 245–46
Second Vatican Council, 265; Gaudium et Spes, 11, 264–65
Second World War, 2, 264
secret consistory (1919 and 1921), 228, 230, 232–33, 243–45
Serafini, Cardinal Domenico, 131–32, 156
Serbia, 1n2, 70, 169
sherifian kingdom. See Arab kingdom
Sidon, 213
Smith, Walter George. See Near East Relief
Society for the Propagation of the Faith, 133, 189
Söderblom (Lutheran archbishop), 104

Sokolow, Nahum, 237–38
Sonnino, Sidney, 34
Spain, 61, 116, 156; Benedict XV's assignment in, 17; and British mandate, 250; and humanitarian assistance, 150; transfer of Catholic interests to, 69, 71–72
St. Joseph University, 162, 218–19
Stoddard, Lothrop, 186
Storrs, Colonel Ronald, 225, 244; Orientations, 225n12
Sublime Porte, The. See Ottoman government
Suez Canal, 62, 224n8, 240
Supreme Committee of the Arab Societies in Palestine, 242
Swiss Zionist Society, 155
Sykes-Picot Agreement, 196, 238
Syria, 37, 79; Christianity in, 42–43, 206; confiscation of property in, 109, 111; and Djemal Pasha, 75, 109, 119, 123, 130, 132, 134, 145; famine in, 145–46, 148; French and, 9, 51, 127 203; French Catholic protectorate over, 47, 49, 193, 203; French imperialism in, 9, 47; French mandate over, 3, 8, 9, 187, 193, 204, 207, 219; and Holy See's interests, 49, 77, 113, 134; humanitarian assistance in, 8, 144, 146, 148–49, 151, 153, 236; and mandate system, 183, 212; persecution of Catholic clergy in, 122, 124, 126, 130, 134; persecution of Catholic population in, 75, 111, 122, 126, 145–46; Protestant discrimination against Catholics in, 157, 160. See also Benedict XV, eastern diplomacy; Holy See, eastern diplomacy; Arab kingdom; Arab nationalism

Syria-Lebanon. *See* Syria

Syriac Catholic Church, 38, 105, 120–21, 214–15. *See also* Eastern Catholic churches

Syriac Orthodox Church, 120–21, 220

Syrian kingdom. *See* Arab kingdom

Syrian National Party, 200

Syrian Protestant College in Beirut. *See* American University of Beirut

Talat, Mehmed, 41n16, 53

Tanzimat period, 39

Thomas, Joseph Emmanuel, 105

Times (London), 33, 64, 230n26

Tonizza, Fr. Giacinto, 117

Tripoli, 213

Trubetskoy, Prince Evgeni, 84

Turkey, 4n12, 55, 64, 79, 82n41, 85, 90, 169

Tyre, 213

Ubaid (Maronite abbot), 197

uniatism, 92n67

unionism. *See* Benedict XV, Eastern ecclesiology

United States, 122, 167; apostolic delegate in, 145; as Entente Power, 1n2, 8, 147, 159, 175; entry into war, 1n2, 8, 31, 175; Henry Morgenthau as ambassador, 109–10, 157; and Holy See, 35, 79; and humanitarian assistance, 146, 157, 160, 236; and League of Nations, 177; and mandates, 181, 201, 227; and Ottoman Empire, 144, 147, 149; Ottoman expulsion of U.S. citizens, 8; as Protestant country, 5; rise of, 31, 99; transfer of French interests in Ottoman Empire to, 69. *See also* Wilson, Woodrow

Urban II (pope), 59

U.S. humanitarian assistance: American Red Cross, 139, 142, 144, 148, 159, 161, 253; and Cardinal Gibbons, 142, 148, 152; Catholic support for, 141–42, 157–58, 160, 220; discrimination against Catholics, 8, 150, 157, 160–62, 220; in English-language literature, 142–43; and Holy See, 146–48, 150, 157; and papal humanitarian assistance, 148, 152; as political tool, 141, 147; and U.S. government, 139, 141, 143, 146–49, 151; U.S. public opinion and, 141, 157, 163. *See also* Benedict XV, humanitarian assistance; Morgenthau, Henry; Near East Relief

Vannutelli, Cardinal Vincenzo, 76

Van Rossum, Cardinal Willem, 242, 256

Vatican, 4, 8, 34, 49, 55, 73, 78, 174, 190, 237; Belgium and, 248; Cardinal Amette's visit to, 231; City State, 28n46; diplomatic representations at, 3, 31, 36, 168–69; and humanitarian assistance, 151, 154; new states' diplomatic relations with, 3, 169; *Osservatore Romano* as official organ of, 189; and Pius X's diplomacy, 172; Roman question and, 15, 28, 36, 52; secret archives, 5, 7, 15, 132, 143, 205, 234; spiritual kingdom, 172; and Zionism, 235, 245, 264. *See also* Holy See

Vatican diplomacy. *See* Holy See's diplomacy

Versailles, Treaty of, 2, 176–77

Vico, Cardinal Antonio, 76–77, 191
Viroli, Maurizio: *For Love of Country*,
   188, 210
Viviani, René, 65
Von Bismarck, Otto, 252
Von Hartmann, Cardinal Felix, 18,
   127–28
Von Mühlberg, Otto, 32
Von Ritter, Baron Otto, 32
Von Wangenheim, Baron (German
   ambassador), 79, 109, 111, 119,
   121–22, 124, 126–27, 129, 133, 156

Weber, Max, 188
Weizmann, Chaim, 227, 239–40
Wilhelm II (emperor), 53
Wilson, Woodrow: Benedict XV
   and, 174–76; and colonialism,
   181, 184; fourteen points,
   176, 237; and humanitarian
   assistance, 152; and League of
   Nations, 178, 180; prestige and
   source of morality of, 22, 142–43,
147, 175; response to Papal Peace
   Note, 26–27
Wingate, Sir Reginald, 132, 133n78

Young Turks, 109; modernization
   efforts, 56, 66; policy, 53, 227;
   reform by, 42; revolution, 41, 107

Zimmermann, Enrico, 128
Zionism, 264; ambitions in Holy
   Land, 5, 225, 227, 231, 233, 235,
   238–39, 243–45, 249–250;
   Benedict XV's appreciation of,
   10, 233–35, 237, 239, 241–42,
   245, 263; Britain and future of,
   10, 225, 229, 231, 238, 240, 245,
   249; Catholic clergy and, 241–45,
   248, 255; Holy See's historical
   relations with, 233–37; Minerbi
   on Vatican and, 10, 234, 237,
   245. *See also* Provisional Zionist
   Committee; Swiss Zionist
   Society

The Holy See and the Emergence of the Modern Middle East: Benedict XV's Diplomacy in Greater Syria (1914–1922) was designed and typeset in Palatino nova Pro with Michelangelo display by Kachergis Book Design of Pittsboro, North Carolina. It was printed on 60-pound House Natural Smooth, and bound by Sheridan Books of Chelsea, Michigan.